Penguin Handbooks
Lloyds Bank Small Business Guide

C000319145

Before starting her own businesses, S
Andersen (chartered accountants) ar. ⸻ ⸻ ⸻ ⸻ (merchant
bank). She lectured in accounting and finance for a period and
established herself as a financial journalist. For a number of years she
wrote for *Money Which?* and has contributed many articles on
personal finance to national newspapers and magazines. In 1984 she
was co-founder of VAMP Ltd, a medical software and data
company. She also runs her own business, Tudor Myles & Co., which
specializes in advising on consumer affairs and producing communication materials for the financial sector. She is the co-author of
*Lloyds Bank Tax Guide 1987/8* (Penguin). Her forthcoming books
are *Go for Growth: The Hidden Entrepreneur* (Viking) and *Unit
Trusts*.

SARA WILLIAMS

# LLOYDS BANK SMALL BUSINESS GUIDE

PENGUIN BOOKS

Penguin Books Ltd, 27 Wrights Lane, London W8 5TZ (Publishing and Editorial)
*and* Harmondsworth, Middlesex, England (Distribution and Warehouse)
Viking Penguin Inc., 40 West 23rd Street, New York, New York 10010, USA
Penguin Books Australia Ltd, Ringwood, Victoria, Australia
Penguin Books Canada Ltd, 2801 John Street, Markham, Ontario, Canada L3R 1B4
Penguin Books (NZ) Ltd, 182–190 Wairau Road, Auckland 10, New Zealand

First published by Penguin Books 1987

Phototypeset in 10/12 Linotron Times by
Wyvern Typesetting Ltd, Bristol
Made and printed in Great Britain by
Hazell Watson & Viney, Member of BPCC Group
Aylesbury, Bucks

# CONTENTS

6 · CONTENTS

20. Your rights and duties as an employer   234
21. Insurance   257

SECTION V   FINANCIAL PREPARATION AND
CONTROL

22. Forecasting   264
23. Raising the money   282
24. Staying afloat   298
25. How to increase profits   317
26. Not waving but drowning   326
27. Keeping the record straight   331

SECTION VI   TAX

28. Tax and the sole trader   343
29. Tax and the partnership   365
30. Tax and the limited company   370
31. Tax on spare-time earnings   379
32. VAT   384

SECTION VII   PLANNING FOR RETIREMENT

33. Retirement   396

Reference   402
Index   411

# ACKNOWLEDGEMENTS

With such a comprehensive and wide-ranging book, there are few people who could claim that their own expertise allows them to write confidently on every topic. I am no exception; I have asked numerous people to give freely of their time and energy in helping me improve the quality and content of the guide.

Brigid Avison, my agent, approached Penguin with the idea of a small business guide. A significant part of the original plan for the book was hers; I am most grateful to her for the head start this gave me.

In the Penguin Group, Andrew Franklin has provided me with the encouragement to concentrate my efforts and energies on producing this guide. Mary Omond has polished the final text to a very high standard. I am also grateful to the sales and marketing departments at Penguin for all they have done.

I am delighted with the very constructive working arrangement with Lloyds Bank. In particular, I would like to thank Peter Barker, Bob Steadman and Keith Davis, for their very helpful and positive suggestions for improvement in the text. Working with them has been a pleasure. Stuart Ransom, Peter Bowen, Allan Kirtley and many others at Lloyds Bank have also lent their expert support to this book. It has benefited from all of them.

On specific chapters, the following individuals have commented and made suggestions: Ian Collins on marketing, Robert Ashby on finance, Richard Goat on selling, Chris Gulliver on buying a business, Peter Jelf on staff recruitment, Peter Forbes on retirement, John Bowers on rights and duties as an employer and John Kimmer on tax. The following organizations have also read and suggested improvements on various draft chapters or have been helpful in producing the guide: the Industrial Society, Arthur Andersen, Business in the Community, Wandsworth Business Resource Service, Department of Employment, the Patent Office, British Franchise Association, British Insurance Brokers Association, the staff at Alvering Library and Bowring Scholfields. I would like to extend my thanks to all the individuals and organizations concerned.

More than a few of the ideas and tips in the guide have been passed on by my husband, Peter Williams, who acquired the entrepreneurial habit some years ago. I hope you will benefit from his experience and the lessons he has learned. Finally, I must apologize to my eldest son, Charles, who was ignored for most of one summer school holidays so that many thousands of words could be typed into my computer. I hope he will think the final result worthwhile.

# FOREWORD

No one sets up a new business without a keen sense of excitement and anticipation. To be one's own boss can be highly rewarding, financially and psychologically, if one does well. And many small businesses do succeed. Some meet an untapped demand, some fill a niche in the market, and others provide a distinctive service that cannot be matched by larger organizations.

The importance of encouraging small businesses has been increasingly recognized in recent years, particularly since unemployment rose so sharply. Many new organizations designed to help small businesses have appeared. Some of these are government-backed; others are supported by grants from industry and commerce, including the banks. They all share a common aim – to help businesses to be successful.

At a time when more people than ever before are starting their own business, there is an obvious need for impartial advice and guidance. That is the purpose of this guide. It describes the various sources of help and advice, highlights what is important to success, and tackles some of the pitfalls and traumas of running a small business. It is designed primarily as a source of reference so that the small business owner can use it when faced with specific problems or challenges. Nevertheless, Sara Williams's style and clear layout make the guide a good read from cover to cover.

This is, I believe, an objective study which will prove valuable to the business proprietor, at whatever stage a business may be. For the potential entrepreneur, it brings out the many conflicting pressures to be considered, so that he or she will be better informed when deciding whether to take the plunge. For the recently established entrepreneur, it details a range of management techniques which should help to improve efficiency and increase profitability. And for all who run their own business, it offers clearly presented information about legal, financial and organizational matters.

I am very pleased that Lloyds Bank is involved in the production of this small business guide which will make a valuable contribution to the range of advice available to the self-employed. I am happy to commend it as a comprehensive source of information and as essential reading for anyone starting or running a small business.

Sir Jeremy Morse                                                  April 1987

# WHAT IS IN THIS GUIDE?

*Lloyds Bank Small Business Guide* will help your business get off to a cracking start. It plots the decisions you need to take, whether you are going to be self-employed, in partnership or forming a company. But it will not only help you start your business, the guide will be an invaluable reference once you are up and running. It is packed with ideas for increasing your profits, controlling your cash, improving your image and getting your message across – to name just a few of the topics covered to help you run your business. The guide will stay with you until you are no longer 'small'.

THE CHAPTERS IN OUTLINE:

## Section I: Before Taking the Plunge

1. *You and your ideas* (p. 15)
You: Who are you? What do you want? What will it be like? Why will you succeed? Why will you fail? How big a business? Your ideas: What are your skills? Which is the best market? No ideas at all? Defining your ideas.

2. *Who will buy?* (p. 28)
Who will buy?: What makes a useful market grouping? A step-by-step analysis to identifying market groupings. What do you know about your likely customers? Why will they buy? How much will they buy?: Market structure. Market share. Market trends. Investment needed in sales. How to do the research: Desk research. Interviews. Test trials.

3. *A spot of coaching* (p. 41)
Training courses. Checklist: How to choose a course. Counselling. The experience of others. Trade associations. Information from the media, books and exhibitions. Special help for the young, ethnic minorities and women. Enterprise agencies.

4. *Your business identity* (p. 51)
Sole trader *v.* a partnership *v.* a limited company. Quiz: Sole trader, partnership or limited company? How to set up as a sole trader. How to set up as a partnership. How to set up as a limited company. What directors must do. Forming a cooperative.

5. *Are you sure?* (p. 65)
Four checklists to help you make your decision: You. Your family. Your skills. Your idea.

6. *The business plan* (p. 76)
The objectives of the plan. How many plans? Who should do the plan? What should be in the plan?

7. *Timing the jump* (p. 83)
A step-by-step guide with four sections: Initial preparation. Getting into greater detail. Setting up. Ready to trade.

## Section II: Getting a Head Start

8. *Toe-dipping* (p. 89)
Testing the water. Permanent toe-dipping. Toe-dipping: What you need to know.

9. *Off-the-peg* (p. 94)
How to search for a business, a step-by-step guide. The business profile you want. Finding a business for sale. Investigation. How will your ownership change the business? Setting a price. Tips on negotiation. Brief guide to management buy-outs.

10. *Franchises* (p. 115)
A brief guide to franchises. The pluses and minuses for a franchisee. A step-by-step guide to choosing a franchise. How a franchise works in detail. The contract. Setting up as a franchisor.

## Section III: How to Sell Your Product

11. *The right name* (p. 134)
Choosing a name. Building your reputation.

12. *Beating the pirates* (p. 142)
What to do with an invention. A step-by-step guide to obtaining a patent. What to do with a design. A step-by-step guide to registration of a design. What to do with a trade or service mark. A step-by-step guide to registering a trade or service mark. Getting help and advice.

13. *Getting the message across* (p. 150)
The message: who, what, how. What can you expect advertising to do for you?: Brochures and leaflets. Public relations. Mail shots (with a step-by-step guide). Advertisements. Directories. Deciding the advertising strategy.

14. *Selling* (p. 162)
How to increase sales. How do you sell?: You. Sales representative. Agent. Distributor. Mail order. Over-the-counter. Personal selling skills.

15. *How to set a price* (p. 175)
The price range. The highest price. The lowest price. A step-by-step guide to setting prices. Price near the top end of the range. Price near the bottom end of the range. Pricing with more than one product.

## Section IV: The Working Environment

16. *Choosing your workplace* (p. 187)
Where is your business to be located? What sort of premises do you need? Searching for premises. Investigating and negotiating.

17. *Getting equipped* (p. 198)
What to consider when choosing equipment. Tips on how to protect yourself against the computer wolves. How to pay for equipment.

18. *Professional back-up* (p. 205)
The advice available, how to choose, cost for these advisers: accountant, bank, solicitor, surveyor/estate agent, designer/design shop/design consultant, corporate finance adviser.

19. *Getting the right staff* (p. 214)
The cost. The job that needs doing. The employee you want. Getting the right person to apply for the job. Interviewing. The effect of staff overhead on cost and break-even point.

20. *Your rights and duties as an employer* (p. 234)
Bird's eye view of your rights and duties. Legal life-cycle of an employee. Taking on an employee: a step-by-step guide. Pay. A safe and healthy working environment. Discrimination: what to watch out for. Maternity. Saying goodbye to an employee: a step-by-step guide. Part-time staff.

21. *Insurance* (p. 257)
Buying the insurance. Insurance you must have. Other insurance you can get. Insurance for you and your family.

## Section V: Financial Preparation and Control

22. *Forecasting* (p. 264)
Cash flow forecast. Profit and loss forecast. Balance sheet forecast. Example.

23. *Raising the money* (p. 282)
The money: how much? what is it for? what type do you want? Lenders and investors: you and your family, government, local authorities, charities, banks, private investors (including Business Expansion Scheme), venture capital funds. The presentation: how to do it (a step-by-step guide).

24. *Staying afloat* (p. 298)
Break-even point. The business plan to control the business. Cash. Your

customers. How to chase money you are owed: a step-by-step guide. Your suppliers.

25. *How to increase profits* (p. 317)
Cutting costs. Increasing prices. Selling more. Doing all three. Improving profits through your employees.

26. *Not waving but drowning* (p. 326)
The warning signs of failure. The final process: limited company, sole trader, partnership. What happens afterwards?

27. *Keeping the record straight* (p. 331)
Why you need records. Which records? A very simple system. When the business is more complicated. Using ready-made systems.

## Section VI: Tax

28. *Tax and the sole trader* (p. 343)
When you pay income tax. Working out your income tax bill. Business expenses. Capital allowances. What happens if you make losses. National insurance contributions. Capital gains tax. You and your tax inspector.

29. *Tax and the partnership* (p. 365)
How your partnership tax bill is worked out. What happens when the partnership changes? What happens if the partnership makes a loss?

30. *Tax and the limited company* (p. 370)
How taxable profits are worked out. What happens to losses. The tax you pay. Close companies. Paying yourself.

31. *Tax on spare-time earnings* (p. 379)
What you must do when you get spare-time earnings. If you count as self-employed. If your income counts as casual. If your business is to do with property. The black economy.

32. *VAT* (p. 384)
How the VAT system works. Who has to register? What rate of tax? Applying to register when you do not have to. How is the tax worked out? The records you need. Paying the tax.

## Section VII: Planning for Retirement

33. *Retirement* (p. 396)
Building up a pension. Capital gains tax when you retire.

*Reference* (p. 402)
A list of useful reading, names and addresses.

# 1. YOU AND YOUR IDEAS

As a way of earning a living, running your own business has two distinctive features. The first is that you do not submit yourself to a selection process; there is not, as there is with a job as an employee, a sifting carried out of possible applicants for a vacancy. There is no personnel manager wielding a battery of psychological tests or cunning interview questions to test your suitability for the job or the level of skills you have acquired.

You are the sole arbiter of your fitness to start and run your own business. This puts a very heavy responsibility on your self-knowledge, because without a doubt not everyone is suited to being an entrepreneur or self-employed. The only external check, which may be carried out on your fitness to found a business, occurs if you need to raise money; in this case, a bank manager or other lender or investor judges you. But by the time you reach this stage, you may already have committed time and money to your project.

The answer to the dilemma of this self-selection process is self-analysis: know thyself. Additional insight can be provided by the opinion of colleagues, friends or family. But this can be fraught with emotional problems. Those you ask for an opinion may feel under pressure to give a favourable view for fear of offending. If an unbiased view cannot be expected, do not seek an opinion at all. Later in this book (p. 65), there is a checklist which you (and others) can use to carry out an assessment of your character and abilities. This should provide some assistance in answering the question 'Am I the right sort of person to succeed in my own business?'

In this chapter, there is a description of the type of person who makes the break. Some people talk over a number of years of running their own show, but never take the ultimate step. Why do some people break the mould while others only dream of it?

The second unusual characteristic of starting your own business to create your own income is that you decide what type of business it is and what market you will be selling to. While you can select a salaried job in a firm of a particular size or selling to a particular market, you are restricted by the vacancies that are available.

When it comes to establishing a business, in theory, the world is your oyster. A well-run business should succeed in any market. In practice, however, you can make success more likely by choosing your product and market carefully.

## WHAT IS IN THIS CHAPTER?

The first section YOU answers these questions:

- Who are you? (see below)
- What do you want? (p. 18)
- What will it be like? (p. 19)
- Why will you succeed? (p. 21)
- Why will you fail? (p. 22)
- How big a business? (p. 23).

YOUR IDEAS looks at two ways to select a business idea:

- What are your skills? (p. 24)
- Which is the best market? (p. 24).

There is also help for those tyros who do not know where to begin:

- No ideas at all? (p. 25).

Finally, once you have two or three ideas for consideration, read:

- Defining your ideas (p. 25).

## YOU

The greatest determinant of the success of your business is you, your character and skills. This you *must* believe if your business is to have any chance of prospering. The type of person who blames external factors for failure and believes that their own decisions have little impact on the course of future events is not suited to building a business.

### WHO ARE YOU?

How frequently do you overhear, or partake in, conversations which run along the following lines?: 'In a couple of years I would like to start off on my own if I can. . .', 'I would love to have my own business but my financial commitments mean that I can't take the risk' or some other variant. Quite a number of people dream of running their own show, but relatively few take the plunge.

In some ways, it is not surprising that so few take the final step. Lying ahead of them, maybe for a number of years, is the unknown: financial insecurity, long working hours, long-term financial obligations and, at the end of it all, possible, or even probable, failure. What is different about those who jump and those who only talk?

The conventional image of an entrepreneur is of a strong-minded, positive risk-taker with a sense of destiny, seizing the ever-present opportunities. Well, this may be a reasonably close approximation of some successful entrepreneurs and you may be that sort of person, but this still does not explain why you are starting your own business and why now. There are many people like this who stay employees for the rest of their lives. No, the most plausible explanation for why some do and some do not is that those who go solo often have received a rude shock to their lives. Their previously cosy existence has been disrupted.

At the extreme, it is noticeable that refugees frequently start their own business. But more common examples today are:

- being sacked

- being made redundant

- not achieving the promotion you confidently expect

- having your plans/proposals/ideas rejected by your boss

- having a new boss foisted upon you

- being transferred to a different job or location

- finding the business you work for is to be sold

- reaching a particular age and feeling no sense of achievement, for example, coming up to forty

- seeing a friend, who is in very similar domestic or work circumstances to you, founding a business.

If you have experienced one of these shocks, the comfortable niche in life which you have created for yourself may suddenly feel restrictive and unsatisfactory. Your response may be to try to seize control of your own life by creating your own job.

Obviously, this shock theory does not explain everyone's decision.

There are those for whom starting on their own is a positive, not a negative, move. Some have mapped out their lives to include starting their own business. There are others for whom being an entrepreneur seems commonplace, because most of their family are. But there is no doubt that the proverbial kick up the backside is the starting point for many a new venture.

The conclusions that can be reached from this are that:

• not all the people starting a business have the necessary ingredients for success, and

• there may be many people who live out their working lives as employees who possess the vital skills and characteristics in full, but fail to take advantage of them.

## WHAT DO YOU WANT?

An important part of your self-analysis should include what it is you hope to achieve by starting a business. Motives may range from achieving monetary gain to enhancing status to establishing a comfortable working environment. You could have a combination of business and personal objectives. It may be a helpful exercise to sit down and note what your objectives are under the following headings which are not exhaustive:

• *money:* how much? when? in what form? as much as possible? enough to live on?

• *working hours:* number of hours? amount of holiday? flexibility?

• *risks:* like a gamble? only low risk acceptable? prefer calculated risks?

• *stress:* looking for lower levels of stress? can cope with stress?

• *type of work:* want to be able to do the work you like? want to choose which work to do and which work to leave for others? want to concentrate on what you are good at? feel your skills are being wasted? want to achieve your full potential?

• *independence:* fed up with being told what to do? no longer wish to explain your actions to your superiors? think you can do better than your boss?

• *achievement:* want to have the feeling of satisfaction that building your own business can bring? like to set yourself standards to achieve? to see if you can do it where others fail?

YOU · 19

- *power:* looking for the sense of power which being the boss can give? want to enhance your reputation or status? want to do better than someone else?

- *personal relations:* want to get away from the problems of having to coexist amicably with others? prefer the feeling of isolation? happier on your own, away from irritating workmates?

- *any other objectives?*

Once you have drawn up a list of motives which you hope to achieve from being your own boss, you need to assess how realistic these are. A number you will find fit ideally with the notion of being self-employed; others will be quite contradictory. Part of your self-analysis should be to see how good or how bad a match your objectives are to the reality. In the next section, you can derive some idea of what life on your own may really be like.

## WHAT WILL IT BE LIKE?

Most probably the answer is much worse than you can imagine. There are a few people who start out and find the whole operation flows smoothly from the beginning; there are others who pretend everything is going well, while the reality is quite different; and there are others who openly admit how hard it is. One of the more dispiriting aspects is that while you may expect hard work for one or two years, it could continue for several.

Statistics about the proportion of businesses which succeed and which fail are hard to come by for the UK. The best estimate is that a third of new businesses fail within two years of start-up. But commonly quoted figures for the US are that 60–80 per cent of new businesses fail in the first five years. It is believed that by the end of the first year about one-third have failed, within two years over half, within three years nearly two-thirds and finally, by the time the first five-year period is over, only around 20 per cent of those set up are surviving.

However, it is likely that a much higher proportion survives of those who raise venture capital, which is money provided by investors for new or developing businesses. This will be for two reasons. First, it is possible that venture capitalists can pick winners (and what they look for is strong management and a good market). Second, these businesses are properly funded and are less likely to run short of cash.

If you manage to survive, life will not always be easy. Your business life may follow this pattern:

- *money:* your income can prove to be a problem. At the outset, if not later on, you may find you cannot draw as much income from your business as you would like. Initially, you will need extra funds to fall back on; it can be very helpful if your husband or wife is earning so that your requirement can be fairly low

- *working hours:* while, in theory, you can choose your working hours and be flexible, in practice you may find that you work all the hours possible. If your business is not going well, you will need dedication, drive and energy to overcome problems; even if the business starts off well, you may still find you cannot turn your back on it, because you want to make as much money as possible in case things start going wrong! You cannot win. Whichever way it is, until your business is well-established you will need to work long hours

- *risks:* a gamble is unlikely to form the basis of a successful business; and if you only want to pursue low-risk ventures, you may be short of ideas to follow up. You stand the best chance of success if you are prepared to take calculated risks which allow you to make a sound estimate of the chances of success

- *stress:* come what may, running your own business is a very stressful experience. You need to be able to cope with it or to seek advice on ways of overcoming it (there are a number of alternative medicine organizations which advertise that they can help you overcome stress without resorting to tranquillizers). Stress is not only caused by business problems, but it may also occur in your domestic life as a result of allowing the business to overwhelm you. Your husband or wife and close members of your family need to be very supportive and to be prepared for what is to come

- *type of work:* you need to be a jack of all trades. Unless you are forming a partnership or hope to raise sufficient funds to allow you to employ someone who can complement your own skills, you will find you act as salesman, technical expert, accountant, administrator or whatever. The wider the range of skills you possess, the greater your chance of success. Be honest about what you can do well and what you do badly. If there are gaps, consider being trained in the area of inadequacy (see Chapter 3. 'A spot of coaching' (p. 41)) or try to make sure you can afford expert assistance

- *independence:* you remain totally independent in your business decisions only if you never borrow or raise money. Once you have done that, you may find that you have to explain your actions, although obviously not on a day-to-day basis

● *achievement:* founding and controlling a successful business can yield a tremendous sense of achievement, but what happens if there are failures? What would be your reaction? To be a successful business manager, you need to be able to deal with failure. You must be able to accept failure without finding the effect devastating and yet to draw all the lessons possible from it, so that in future you will not make a similar mistake and your performance will be improved

● *power:* power can be a destructive influence in a business. There is no problem if you are a sole trader, but once you begin employing staff, you are trying to operate your business through others. Should the desire for power lead you to try to control employees in a way which is counter-productive to their work performance, your power will be a negative influence on the success of your business. Managing people properly is more important

● *personal relations:* one of the advantages of running your own show is that you select the people who work for you and if you do not like them you do not need to employ them. But if you find it difficult to associate in a friendly manner with most people, you are unlikely to be a successful owner-manager. You need to be able to establish good relations with suppliers and customers, as well as with those you employ.

## WHY WILL YOU SUCCEED?
The conventional view is that your business is more likely to be successful if it fulfils three criteria:

● the people involved realistically assess their strengths and weaknesses and try to overcome shortcomings. This could apply to you alone if your business is as a sole trader. Or, if it is on a larger scale, it means you as the leading figure plus the rest of your management team should be balanced and with no obvious lack of skills. This is the most important criterion

● the idea and the market for it has the necessary growth potential

● financing is sufficient to cover the shortfall of working capital (p. 284), especially in the early days.

If you cannot fulfil these criteria at the moment, do not accept defeat; you may be able to in the future. Most of the processes can be learned and acquired if your personality allows for realistic self-assessment. At this stage in the chapter you should already have some self-knowledge about your strengths and weaknesses as an owner-manager. In Chapter 5. 'Are you sure?' the information is drawn together in a checklist (p. 70), which you can use as a quick test of where you stand.

## WHY WILL YOU FAIL?

You will fail if your operation does not match up well to the three criteria mentioned above. But some more specific examples of likely causes of failure are:

- overestimating sales and underestimating how long it takes to achieve them

- underestimating costs

- failing to control costs ruthlessly

- losing control over cash, that is, carrying too much stock, allowing customers too long to pay, paying suppliers too promptly

- failing to identify your market because of inadequate market research

- failing to adapt your product to meet customer needs and wants

- lacking sufficient skills in one of the following areas – selling and marketing, financial, production, technical

- failing to build a team which is compatible and complementary, if your business is on a larger scale

- taking unnecessary risks

- underpricing.

Many of these causes of failure are a result of lack of skills. Running your own business does not mean you have to be an expert at everything; but you do have to appreciate the importance of all these aspects so that you can control your business properly. Try to acquire an appreciation of the crucial factors to watch out for by seeking training or advice from others in those areas in which you are weak. Use this book as a starting point. If more help is needed, there are training courses to attend and advice agencies to consult (pp. 42, 44, 49).

HOW BIG A BUSINESS?

One factor to consider at an early stage is which track are you in – the fast-growth, medium-growth or slow-growth lane? You may know, from the assessment of your skills and character, that the most you aspire to is being a one-person business, pottering along steadily. Or your analysis may convince you that, with the right funds and the right management team, you have the potential to look for swift growth to a substantial size. Your plans about raising money are determined by this consideration.

## YOUR IDEAS

Frequently, the reason given for failing to take the step and start on your own is that you lack an idea of what you can produce and sell. This may be because there is a misconception about what is needed for a business to be successful. Your idea does not have to be novel, original or revolutionary. If it is, it may be helpful; but equally, it could be a hindrance. Trying to sell a product or service which has not been available previously can be an uphill struggle. Being first is not always best. The first to offer such a product has to educate a market and possibly establish a distribution structure. The second or third into a market can capitalize on all the effort and investment made by their predecessors. The moral is that you should not veer away from an idea because it is not original.

However, it does not follow that you can offer something identical to another business. If you do, how can the potential customer choose? It could only be on the basis of price (p. 175), which suggests that you will struggle to make a profit, unless, of course, you can sell in volume. The ideal product or service to choose as a basis for your business is one which you can distinguish from the competition by including some additional feature or benefit which is not available in other products.

If you are starting from scratch, how do you come up with a business idea? The first stage is to draw up a shortlist of two, three or four ideas which you can define and research before selecting the one to run with.

There are two possible ways of choosing an idea:

● using an established skill, product or knowledge

● identifying a market which looks ripe for development by your business and acquiring the necessary technique and knowledge.

In reality, the approaches must be closely interlinked; your business will

not succeed if you have the skill or product but not the market, and vice
versa.

## WHAT ARE YOUR SKILLS?

The logical business idea for most people is to choose an area in which
they already have considerable expertise. Many self-employed people
are simply practising their own acquired knowledge, such as engineers,
solicitors, design consultants, for example. Your expertise may be
acquired as a result of your education or training on the job. If you have
been employed as a manager of a supermarket, one obvious idea is to do
the same but on your own. Or you may have worked in some position in
the computer industry and so possess considerable knowledge about
products, the market and distribution.

Many people also opt to begin a business using a skill which they have
acquired in their spare time as a hobby. Obvious examples are the craft-
type business, such as jewellery-making and pottery. The disadvantage
with these is that you have not acquired any of the business knowledge
needed to turn hobbies into a living. You will not know the suppliers or
the distribution network, for example. However, given determination,
this disadvantage should not be insuperable. A more serious problem
may emerge later: you may have decided to base your business on a
pastime because you found it enjoyable; but a few months of struggling to
keep your head above water can soon turn a pleasure into a chore.

## WHICH IS THE BEST MARKET?

An alternative to choosing an idea based upon your existing skills and
knowledge would be to research some markets in which you believe there
are profitable opportunities. The ideal market to base your business in is
one which:

- is growing or is large

- is supplied by businesses which are not efficient or are outdated

- has a niche or sector (p. 29) which you can exploit

- is not heavily dependent on price to help consumers select one product
rather than another

- is not already supplied by products which are heavily branded, that is,
there is not considerable customer loyalty to products from one or more
businesses

- is not dominated by two or three very large suppliers, but instead has a number of smaller would-be competitors.

In practice, there is only a remote chance of finding such a market; and if you did, so would many other businesses, which would make it very competitive. But it would be unwise to base your business in a market which does not come up with some of these positive indicators. The moral is, do not be afraid of competitors; they prove that there is business there to get.

It is, of course, difficult to enter a market if you have none of the technical skills or industry knowledge necessary. In particular, if you need to raise money, the decision-makers will want to see some, if not considerable, knowledge and experience in that market. If you do not have it, you have to concentrate instead on demonstrating your all-round business skills and experience, the strength offered by your character and abilities, and the research you have undertaken into your chosen market.

### NO IDEAS AT ALL?

If you cannot come up with an idea on your own, do not despair. Try organizing what is called a brainstorming session. Ask two or three colleagues, friends or relations to join a discussion. Hold it as a proper meeting in peace and quiet, with paper and pencil in front of you. Spend a couple of minutes outlining the sort of idea you are after and what you have already considered but dismissed and why. Ask for their reactions and cross your fingers that some ideas will emerge. A brainstorming session need not last a long time. Probably a quarter or half an hour will be sufficient.

### DEFINING YOUR IDEAS

At this stage, you may not have focused on just one idea, but still be considering two or more. Whether it is only one or several, your next step is to draw up a pen portrait of each idea. Clearly, some of the aspects will be nothing more than wild guesses; you will need to carry out research before encapsulating your final choice in a detailed business plan with realistic forecasts.

The brief sketch should define the following points:

- a description of the product or service

- an indication of why it will sell

- a description of the intended market

- your estimate of the approximate price

- how you think it will be sold, for example, through shops, salespeople, distributors

- a first stab at the amount of sales you can make

- how it will be made, if it is a product

- its approximate cost.

Having drawn up these broad-brush definitions of a couple of the most promising ideas, you will find that during the detailed estimation and calculation stage, one idea will emerge as the favourite. You can concentrate on developing this one into your business plan.

## SUMMARY

1. An unusual aspect of starting your own business is that you make the decision yourself that you have the necessary qualities and abilities to make a success of it.

2. Analyse what you expect and hope to achieve from self-employment.

3. Do not underestimate the problems and difficulties which emerge for business owners.

4. Use the checklists in Chapter 5. 'Are you sure?' (pp. 65, 67, 69, 73) to identify your weaknesses and strengths.

5. Try to take advantage of the many training courses and advice agencies available to help improve those weaknesses listed in Chapter 3. 'A spot of coaching' (p. 41).

6. Do not be dissuaded from launching a business because you do not have an original idea. With the right management and a promising marketplace, a well-worn idea can be successful.

7. The market can be crucial in determining success or failure (rated second most important factor after management by providers of finance). Carry out detailed market research following the advice in Chapter 2. 'Who will buy?' (p. 28).

8. Develop brief descriptions of a couple of ideas before researching more thoroughly. Select the favourite and make up a detailed business plan before setting up the business.

OTHER CHAPTERS TO READ

# 2. WHO WILL BUY?

By now you have probably narrowed down your shortlist of ideas. You may know which market you want to enter; you may have got your eye on a product which you think has potential. What you must do next is to study your prospective marketplace in detail. Researching the marketplace comes before raising money, making profit and cash flow forecasts, finding premises or any of the other steps you have to take to form your business.

This is especially true if you need to raise money for your proposed business and have to produce a business plan. You will not obtain financial backing from anyone unless you can show with confidence that you understand the structure of your market and have a clear idea of where your product will be positioned compared to the competition. The crucial questions are – who will be your customers, why will they buy from you and how much can you sell.

Knowing the number of customers is not the only information yielded by studying the marketplace. Perhaps, more importantly, you should be able to obtain information about what your potential customer needs. This, in turn, should aid you to angle your product or service to satisfy the greatest demand. It is much easier to persuade people to purchase something they already want; educating a market to buy your product if the market has expressed no great desire for it can be a long haul.

## WHAT IS IN THIS CHAPTER?

This chapter is about market research and how you can proceed to find out about your particular market. But the first part of the chapter concentrates on what it is you need to know about the market, rather than how to carry out the research.

First, the chapter helps you to define the bit (or segment) of the market you are specifically going for, WHO WILL BUY? (p. 29): which are your customers and what are their common characteristics?

The next section, WHY WILL THEY BUY? (p. 32), helps you form your sales proposition to your target market. What are the main features and benefits which your potential customers are looking for? Can your product supply them? This process helps you to define your service or product specifically, and in relation to the competing products, so that your product is differentiated from the run-of-the-mill.

The third section, HOW MUCH WILL THEY BUY? (p. 34), leads into how you can utilize the information about market and potential customers to make realistic sales forecasts.

The final section, HOW TO DO THE RESEARCH (p. 37), looks at the nitty-gritty of carrying out the market research needed. How is it done? What sources do you use? Are some more important than others?

## WHO WILL BUY?

Knowing which market and which product is only the start of the work you need to do before you will be able to begin selling. First, you have to research the market. You are not simply looking for lots of statistics and information to blind potential backers with information. You need the details to help you plan your business strategy.

It would be a mistake to assume that you have an equal chance of selling to every customer in your market. If it *is* that sort of market, it implies that you are looking for volume sales. In turn, this suggests a market which is very sensitive to price levels and in which it is difficult to sort out one product from another. If this is the sort of business you are planning, think carefully. Few small businesses have the resources to make a success of this.

Basically, you should be looking for a niche in your proposed market which allows you to charge a reasonable price and so maintain reasonable profit margins. To achieve this, your product needs to be clearly distinguishable from the competition. In marketing jargon, this is called product differentiation.

The purpose of your research at this stage is to look for that niche. This process is called market segmentation. In everyday language, it means looking for a group of customers within your target market which has common characteristics, tastes and features. If you can find such a group, it allows you to tailor your product to meet their particular needs.

Once you have sorted out the groups, you must look at the competitive position. Are there already suppliers to that group of people? The existence of competition does not mean that you should not try to enter the market, but it does mean that you need to be able to offer customers some additional benefit in your service or product, and it must be a benefit they want.

For a small firm, a strong attraction of using this market segment approach to sales is that you may be able to achieve a dominant position in that segment. This could mean becoming the market leader with its attendant advantages of selling more at a higher price (p. 182).

If your business is on a smaller scale (perhaps only yourself or a couple of employees), it still makes sense to look for a niche to exploit, because of the advantages it offers in being able to keep your prices above rock-bottom level.

There are several different ways of grouping people. These include looking at potential customers by examining facts about their life, such as where they live or the kind of work they do. Or a more satisfactory way of grouping could be based on how they behave when they are deciding to buy a product, such as whether price makes a substantial difference to their buying decision. Use the step-by-step analysis (see below) to help you sort out groups or segments.

### WHAT MAKES A USEFUL MARKET GROUPING?

The fact that you can identify a group of people with similar tastes in your target market does not necessarily mean that you have unlocked a source of sales for your product. To be useful, a market grouping needs to have certain characteristics. In the first place, the segment needs to be big enough to give you the living you require. You must also be able to differentiate it from other groups, so that its size can be measured. Another necessary characteristic is that the segment must be easy to reach. There is no point in selecting a target group which is difficult to reach. If it is, you will experience problems getting your message across or supplying the product because of location. Finally, the group must have common features which actually lead to similar buying decisions.

### A STEP-BY-STEP ANALYSIS TO IDENTIFYING MARKET GROUPINGS

1. Is your target market a consumer market? Or is it an industrial or professional market? If it is a consumer one, go to 2.; if it is industrial or professional, go to 11.

2. Look at family and personal factors. Would age, sex, family size or marital status form the basis of different groups?

3. Is your product the sort which relies on supplying a local area? Location may be an important feature of a group.

4. Look at social class. Could this be important for your product?

**5.** Can you distinguish groups of potential customers on the basis of how much or how little they use or buy your product? Could your product be tailored or appeal to heavy or light users?

**6.** Are there psychological or social factors at work? Could the product appeal to those wishing to 'better themselves'? Are lifestyles important? Would prospective customers be likely to 'follow the crowd' or want to be seen as stylish?

**7.** Could there be snob or prestige appeal? Some customer like to think they are getting the best.

**8.** Price could be a feature which distinguishes one group from another. Is there an element of value for money in a target group's make-up? Some people go for the cheapest, no matter what. Most customers would say that they want good value for the money they spend.

**9.** How do the potential customers buy? Local shop, large supermarket or store? Mail order? Can you create a niche out of distribution methods?

**10.** Now go to **16**.

**11.** What type of industry will you be selling into? You could specialize in one industry or profession (called vertical marketing).

**12.** How big are the companies or business you are likely to sell to? Size can mean different procedures in buying and in frequency of purchasing. Can you create a distinguishing product benefit from the need to satisfy large, medium or small businesses?

**13.** Will one group of potential customers require quicker or more frequent deliveries than others?

**14.** Price could well create different market segments in industrial or professional users.

**15.** Will one group of customers be looking for a higher level of after-sales care or maintenance? Could this be your distinguishing product feature?

**16.** Consider what other categories might apply your market. Each market will have its own specialized characteristics apart from the general ones listed above.

17. Now look to see if there is a group with more than one of the characteristics listed above. This could define your target group or segment even more closely.

WHAT DO YOU KNOW ABOUT YOUR LIKELY CUSTOMERS?

To help you understand your potential customers, and to help you sell to them, you need to know a range of information about them. If it is a business you are selling to, you need to have information on the organization and buying policies. Investigate the other suppliers to your customers and acquire and analyse information on the services and products bought by them.

## WHY WILL THEY BUY?

Before you can answer this question, you have to find out what your customer wants. What are the benefits and features of a service or product which your target group rates most highly? Research is essential to establish this (p. 37).

Once you have the framework of your customer needs, you can begin to vary your service or product with the aim of meeting those customer wants and needs more successfully than any other supplier. There are a number of ways in which your sales package (that is, your product/service plus a range of other sales features of your business) can be altered to achieve the desired objective. These include:

● *appearance:* what material is the product made of? Does it look stylish? How about the colour? How is it packaged or presented? All these can be changed to match your target customer profile. If appearance is an important feature for your target group, it may be worth using a design consultant to help you achieve this (p. 210)

● *delivery time:* if speed of delivery is important to your potential customers, concentrate on how you can improve your delivery times

● *maintenance:* does your target market look for very prompt attention to faults? Or very frequent maintenance visits? Whatever it is, adjust your strategy to allow for this

● *performance:* identify the main requirement – for example, it may be speed, reliability or a low level of noise. This sort of consideration should be taken into account when you specify your product. If it is already past the specification stage, can it be altered?

• *quality:* this is rather an ethereal topic, as quality can be subjective, existing in the eye of the beholder. Or it can be objective, for example, the evenness of the stitching. You can create an impression of quality by building up the image or reputation of the product to suggest this (p. 134). The appearance of quality tends to depend on all the variables of a product: appearance, service, packaging, reliability, performance and so on.

By adjusting your service/product in this way to meet the wants and needs of your target market, you are trying to establish that you have at least one unique feature which your competitors don't have. You can use this as the basis of your selling message to persuade people to buy. Your target market will purchase the product if you convince them that it meets the need which they have, conscious or unconscious. Of course, if your competitors already meet these needs, it is difficult to see what additional benefit your product can offer, but usually there is something.

It would be a mistake to believe that buyers act in a rational way, comparing products and choosing their purchase on the basis of some organized assessment. Even in an industrial market, buyers are affected by a number of emotional factors, sometimes not openly admitted. These can include wanting to be like someone else, be considered stylish or a leader, or to be liked. Your potential customers may also want the best, a change, or to improve their personal standing. They may be trying to outdo the competition or to gain revenge on another person or business. So, if you do not believe your product can be differentiated in practical benefits, can it be distinguished in emotional ways?

One possible way you could think about your target market is to consider how they would match up to the range of cars available. The variety of cars available is very wide; each car model has tried to establish its own niche and it is possible to categorize buyers in your target market by the car you imagine they are most likely to buy. For example, if your market is likely to buy a Mini or Citroën 2CV, you can picture them as young, wanting something cheap and cheerful and not minding the lack of comfort. If it is a Rolls-Royce segment, your customers are looking for the ultimate in prestige, comfort and specification. A BMW is an executive car, indicating business success and achievement; the car is stylish and luxurious. A Volvo implies solid dependability. And so on.

Once you have a mental picture of what your target group is looking for in a car, you might be able to use this picture to adapt your service or product to meet those same needs.

## HOW MUCH WILL THEY BUY?

This is the third question which market research should help you answer. You cannot plan your business unless you have some estimate of how much you are going to sell and when that is likely to happen. You need this data to help you formulate your sales and cash forecasts.

The first step is knowing the market size. This could be either its monetary value or the number of units sold in the market. Beyond this you need an estimate of the market potential, which is unlikely to be the same figure as market size, because it is unlikely that everyone in the market will buy your, or an equivalent, product. Obviously, if you have the figure for the overall market, but have decided to concentrate your business resources on a particular market segment, your next step is to assess the size of the particular segment you are interested in. Even then, this may not give you your estimated market potential (the amount of sales you stand some chance of being able to make over a period of years).

The level of sales you can make over the years depends also on:

- the market structure

- the market share you can establish (and the competition you face)

- the market trends, that is, whether it is growing, static or declining

- the investment in time and money to sell your product. You need to be able to forecast how much you need to put in to get sales established and how long this will take. Many business failures occur because this is underestimated.

### MARKET STRUCTURE

This is the process by which the final product is sold to the end-consumer. In very simple markets, there will be only the business producing the goods and the final consumers buying directly from the manufacturer. But many markets are much more complex and there are several links in the selling chain before the final consumer is reached. As well as businesses selling direct, there could be a network of distributors, yet another layer of agents or dealers before reaching the retail outlets and the consumers.

You need to know how your particular market works to be able to estimate the value of sales. If you choose the direct route for sales (that is, you are selling to your end-users), once you have fixed the selling price and estimated the number of units you can sell, you know the value of the sales. Your forecast profit will depend obviously on the costs of the direct selling as well as all the other costs and overheads. Because direct selling can be an expensive burden, especially for a small business, many try to sell through other businesses. Or this may be the way that the market is already organized. In this case, your selling price to the distributor or network has to be low enough to allow the distributor to earn the required income and still sell to the consumer at the right price.

Any study of market structure can only apply at the time the study is made, because distribution networks are constantly evolving. The research should help you formulate your own sales plan. If there are many end-users with a ready-established distribution network, you may decide to sell via the distributors or agents and encourage sales to end-users by P R and advertising. However, if you are aiming at a few, large consumers, direct selling may be the answer.

MARKET SHARE

Unless you are supplying a completely new product or service, you are going to share the market with other businesses. To be in a dominant position (that is, the supplier of 25 per cent or more of the market) would be very rare for a small business.

To be able to forecast your sales you are going to need some idea of what share of the market your competitors have. You also need information about your competitors' business and products to enable you to position and price your own offering. Knowing the market shares gives you a measure of how successful the other businesses have been.

Monopolies are unusual, but there may be a duopoly (two businesses supplying 25 per cent or more of the market each) or an oligopoly (three, four or five businesses dominating it). However, many small businesses are likely to face a fragmented supply position, where there are lots of suppliers and one business is unlikely to achieve more than 5 per cent of the market. This is particularly true if it is a new industry or market.

Measuring market share is one thing, achieving it another. But there are some ways of influencing the share you can seize. On the whole, it is helpful to build a reputation for good, consistent quality. For this to be translated into market share, a second influence is maintaining a reasonable level of marketing activity: P R, advertising and sales activity. A third influence is if your product is recognized as being ahead of the competition in performance, design or whatever.

Look at your competitors in a detailed fashion. Some of the data it would be helpful to have includes:

- what are the competitive products and how much of each do they sell?
- how well have they done in the last few years?
- how is the company organized?
- how is their selling carried out?
- if they produce goods, how is it done and what are the facilities?
- who are the main customers?
- what is the pricing policy and what sort of delivery is offered?

## MARKET TRENDS

Market size, market structure and market shares do not remain the same. What happens today may be totally irrelevant to what is happening in one, two or three years' time. The usual method of deciding what is going to happen in the future is to look at what has happened in the past and project it forwards. This approach is fraught with dangers. At the very least, you need to adjust the figures for changes which may occur or are forecast to occur.

On a general level, anticipated changes in the economy can affect the buying patterns of individual markets. There may be changes forecast in tax or other laws which will influence purchasing decisions. New information or research may emerge on the effect of certain items (for example, health hazards).

On a more specific level, in your particular target market there may be new products or better products emerging. There may be specific changes caused by government or local authority policy. And so on. You need to look closely at your market to guess what changes will occur which might affect the market trends. In any conversations with people already operating in the market, remember to ask what likely changes they think are on the cards. You may be better able to take advantage of them as a new entrant with no constraints from existing products, methods of operating or overheads.

## INVESTMENT NEEDED IN SALES

This is really nothing more than your need to make realistic forecasts of how much you will sell, when you will be able to do it and what you need to spend on selling and promotion to achieve it. Inevitably, if you are starting your own business, you are optimistic, but do not let optimism blind you to the uncertainty of making sales.

If you are in any doubt, a rule of thumb might be to double the length of time you expect it will take you to achieve a certain level of sales. In this way, you will organize sufficient funds to keep the business going until you reach break-even. Of course, the danger of this rule of thumb is that your business may not seem sufficiently attractive to lenders and investors. Keep a balance.

It might be possible to obtain a more reliable estimate of sales by carrying out test trials (p. 40) on a limited basis, although this is difficult for a small business to do.

## HOW TO DO THE RESEARCH

There are a number of techniques for researching a market. The ways open to a small business are likely to be fewer than to a larger organization, simply because of money. In most cases, it will be you, the owner, who does the research.

The basic research methods for small businesses include:

- desk research, studying directories and other literature

- interviews with customers, suppliers, competitors, distributors, ex-employees of competitors

- test trials.

### DESK RESEARCH
The main sources of information are:

- directories

- government information

- information from within your own business, if already up and running

- trade associations

- the trade press and special features in the quality papers

- competitors' literature

- published statistics and reports

- former colleagues.

Your starting point for a lot of the information can be your local lending library or the reference library. You will need to organize your research in a systematic way, because the danger is that you may end up with too much information, a lot of it irrelevant, and with no way of being able to gain quick and easy access to the data that matters.

Some of the directories which may be useful include:

Kompass UK
Key British Enterprises
Kelly's
Directory of British Associations
Yellow Pages
Thomson Local Directories
Stubbs' Buyers Guide
The Retail Directory

UK Trade Names
Municipal Year Book
European Marketing Data and
  Statistics
A–Z of UK Marketing Data
Key Note
BRAD (to find trade magazines)

There will also be directories for the particular industry or market you are interested in. You must be wary, with all directories, of claims of comprehensive coverage. Entries often have to be paid for, so you can not assume that all the information is there.

The government also produce a range of statistics which are easily obtainable. However, they may not be very useful as they tend to be rather generalized. Read the booklet *Government statistics: a brief guide to sources* for some guidance.

Some of the more readily available government publications include:

Business Monitor
British Business
Economic Trends
Employment Gazette

Family Expenditure Survey
General Household Survey
Local Government Trends
Regional Trends

As well as these published sources of information, you should not neglect the information you have within the business if you are already established. Keep good sales records and encourage your employees to be on the look-out for market information.

There are also the trade sources of information. Find out which are the trade magazines and, if they are not free, take out subscriptions. Organize cuttings files. Contact the relevant trade association and obtain information about its members.

Use trade exhibitions as an opportunity to pick up literature about your competitors and talk to potential customers about the market, the suppliers, the products and the gaps.

INTERVIEWS

The term 'interview' can cover anything from a chat at an exhibition, to a brief telephone call, to a long face-to-face discussion in private. The main point is that you can pick up a lot of information simply by talking to people.

Whether you have started your business or not, good sources of information are customers, potential or actual. Perhaps you could carry out a telephone survey, limiting each interview to ten minutes, say. It would help you analyse the information if you had prepared a questionnaire sheet to fill in.

On the whole, you will find that most customers are usually ready to cooperate, as it may mean you develop a product more suited to their needs. Carry on the number of telephone interviews until you begin to feel that you are learning nothing new, because the same points are being repeated.

If you want detailed information, you will not find that the telephone is the best method of acquiring it. Instead, try to carry out a number of in-depth interviews.

If you are researching a consumer market, you should try to talk to the distributors and retailers as well as to the end-users. Most people are flattered to be asked their 'professional' opinion. Talking to the final consumers can be a bit of a problem because you may not know who these are. Perhaps a retailer will allow you to spend a day in the shop talking to customers? Asking people in the street outside the store is another possibility. If your product is likely to be exhibited at trade fairs for the consumer, spend some time there asking about the market and product. Use a brief questionnaire to ensure that you ask the same questions so that the information can be analysed.

Interviewing competitors may sound an odd idea, but there is no harm in it and it can help you understand what are common problems. If you come across any ex-employees of competitors, it is always worth a discussion, although you have to bear in mind that their view may not be entirely objective if they did not part on good terms with the business.

Before you start your business, you could carry out some discreet research into how the competition organizes their businesses by pretending to be a prospective customer. In this way you can gain some idea of the literature, prices, the way telephone queries are dealt with, selling methods or even how your potential competitors quote. It may seem unfair, but it is an unrivalled source of information and you may rest assured that once you are in business others will do it to you.

## TEST TRIALS

It would be a great help to you if you could test market your product, especially if you will be setting up production facilities or ordering very large quantities. If you can try out a few before you make the substantial investment needed, you would be able to refine the product, satisfy yourself that the demand does exist and define the likely sales cycle (the length of time from first contact to purchase). To test this, buyers of the trial product need to be followed up and interviewed.

## SUMMARY

1. Market research which is undirected is not very useful; it needs to concentrate on who will buy, why will they buy and how much will they buy.

2. It is much easier to sell a product which meets some already perceived need rather than to try to educate a market to buy a new, perhaps revolutionary, product or service.

3. Look for groups within your target market which you think you can sell to, either because no one is currently selling to them or because you can adapt your product to meet their needs.

4. Use the step-by-step guide (p. 30) to help you identify a suitable market group.

5. Rational and emotional factors affect your target group's willingness to buy. Research these and alter your product or sales approach to match.

6. Knowing how much customers will buy is crucial to your business planning. You need to research market size, market structure, market share, the competition and market trends.

7. Try to carry out your research in a systematic way so that it can be properly analysed. Use desk research, interviews and test trials, if possible.

### OTHER CHAPTERS TO READ
11. 'The right name' (p. 134)
15. 'How to set a price' (p. 175)

# 3. A SPOT OF COACHING

'I don't have the time' might be the instant reaction of a budding entrepreneur, if it is suggested that training or asking for advice would be beneficial. At the other end of the spectrum, there may be people who could make a success of self-employment, but feel 'I don't know how to start'.

Training, counselling and seeking advice can all improve your chances of success, so do not dismiss the idea. If you have not yet started on your own, try to fit in some sort of training before you do so. If you are already underway, look around to see what training or help is available to fit in with your schedule. One sad comment made by some of the organizations set up specifically to help embryo businesses is that people don't seek help until things are going wrong. Give yourself the greatest chance of success and consider it now.

There are an extraordinary number of organizations designed to help new or small businesses; indeed, giving advice to small businesses is probably one of the fastest growth industries in the UK. The format of the organizations varies widely. If you have nightmares about entering a formal educational environment, you can choose a one-to-one counselling session. If that idea makes you wary, a course may be the answer for you.

This chapter looks at the various sources of help and advice grouped into six categories. This is slightly artificial as many of the categories overlap; but it should help you to decide which direction to take to find the sort of advice which comes closest to meeting your needs.

The groups are:
1. Training courses
2. Counselling
3. Help and advice from other business people
4. Trade associations
5. Information from the media, books and exhibitions
6. Special help for the young, ethnic minorities and women.

The chapter also spotlights enterprise agencies and what they can do for you.

## TRAINING COURSES

The diversity of courses available makes it difficult to describe an 'average' course. On the other hand, this very diversity should ensure that you will find a course run somewhere which meets your needs and suits your personality, although obviously you do not want to travel too far.

### HOW LONG A COURSE?

The length of courses available varies from a one- or two-day taster, which would allow you to get the feel of whether self-employment is for you, up to a six-month course for those already committed to the idea. The courses can be full-time, for example, for three or six weeks; or the courses can be part-time. Part-time could mean either a series of weekends spent on the course, or it could be evenings, or it could be a period of a few weeks spread over a few months or a year.

### WHAT TOPICS ARE COVERED?

The content of most of the general self-employment or small business courses leans heavily on the finanical side. Topics such as cash flows, business plans and sources of finance, financial control and book-keeping are covered. There should also be a substantial content on selling and marketing. Apart from these key areas, other topics which may be covered include something on premises, micro-computers, employment law, recruiting, and other legal aspects of business and insurance.

As well as general small business courses, organizations run more specialized ones, for example, a two-day course concentrating on finance or marketing. If you feel fairly confident in general about your business expertise, this sort of course could help you to brush up your knowledge in your weakest area.

### WHAT SORT OF TRAINING?

Inevitably, with a fair number of courses, quite a lot of the information and training is given in a fairly traditional classroom format. However, in all courses there should be an informal atmosphere which allows for discussion and questions. The success of the course can depend as much on the quality and interest of the participants as on the teachers. Before you choose a course it might be worthwhile to try and find out a little bit about the other participants.

An increasing number of courses are trying to introduce a 'hands-on' approach. Your business plan will be presented to a small group and to the teachers for discussion, suggestion and improvement. In a few courses, there may be an opportunity to present your plan to a bank or other source of funds. This could simply be as a training exercise. However, if you present your case well, the bank may want to discuss your business idea in more detail.

## WHO TAKES THE COURSES?

Many of the courses are run by universities, polytechnics or colleges of further education or technology. So, not surprisingly, lecturers feature prominently among the teachers on these courses. They should be expert at articulating ideas and organizing information, but may be weak on practical business experience. A number of courses will include guest speakers, for example, from firms of chartered accountants or solicitors. This type of speaker will be nearer the coal-face than a lecturer, but they may not be so expert at teaching.

The ideal teacher for a self-employment or small business course is someone who owns a business and is also an expert teacher. The chances of staffing a training course with such people are fairly remote. Nevertheless, before you choose a course, look at the mix and backgrounds of the people running it.

## WHAT DO THEY COST?

The Manpower Services Commission funds a lot of the courses. This makes many of them free or relatively cheap.

## HOW TO FIND A COURSE

Try these sources to find the names and addresses of courses being run in your area:

- local Manpower Services Commission (see p. 402 for addresses and phone numbers)

- enterprise agency. Contact either your local one or the umbrella organization for agencies (p. 403). Also see below, *Enterprise agencies: What they can do for you*

- local college, polytechnic or university

- the small business pages in the *Guardian* and the *Financial Times*, which often give details of ad-hoc courses

- local newspapers

- one of the following organizations, which keep up-to-date on courses offered: British Institute of Management, Scottish Vocational Education Council (see p. 403 for addresses and phone numbers).

## CHECKLIST: HOW TO CHOOSE A COURSE

1. Decide whether you want a general or specialized course.

2. Try to find out about the teachers. Is there a good mix of practical business knowledge and teaching experience?

3. Seek information about participants on the course. If it is not possible to find out about the course you will be on, look for information about the typical mix of previous attenders.

4. Ask if the training is mainly classroom based. Go for courses with practical emphasis on business plans, especially if there can be a mock presentation for finance.

5. Check the cost – there may be training allowances available.

## COUNSELLING

Help and advice on a one-to-one basis is given by counsellors. You could approach an advice agency at any stage of starting a business. Initially, counsellors can help by discussing your business idea, bringing out its strengths and weaknesses and suggesting ways of carrying out market research.

At a later stage, advisers will help you to prepare a business plan, including cash flows; you may even find an adviser prepared to approach a bank manager with you. And counsellors will spend time with you if your business is hitting a sticky patch or if you feel you have a weakness in a particular area of your business and need fresh ideas or guidance.

Advice agencies very often will also provide an information service. So, if you need to know a particular business fact and do not have the information at your fingertips, try ringing your local advice agency.

### WHO PROVIDES COUNSELLING?

There are several sources:

- DTI's Small Firms Service (phone Freefone Enterprise for your nearest office)

- enterprise agencies (p. 49)

- other ad hoc agencies providing support for small businesses (p. 50)

- special schemes for the young (p. 47).

Many of the counsellors are executives from big business who have retired or are on secondment to the agency, so may have little experience of running their own small business. Inevitably this means that there must be areas where the advice will be weak. For example, it is likely that few of the counsellors will have had personal experience of debt collecting or keeping national insurance and PAYE records. Their strength may lie more in discussion of business ideas, knowing the network of people who can help and advise, finding out about markets, preparing plans and budgets, advising on finance or simply knowing their way around the business world.

## THE EXPERIENCE OF OTHERS

The business problem you are currently struggling with is unlikely to be unique; other businesses may have faced similar dilemmas. Picking someone else's brains can be a useful source of ideas and advice – if you can find the right brains, that is. There are formal schemes available to provide you with some additional management, or you can adopt a very informal way of benefiting from other people's experience.

The MSC runs a Management Extension Programme. This places redundant managers or executives in a small firm for a total of fifteen weeks. The cost of this extra pair of hands is nothing but your helper's out-of-pocket expenses. Contact your local MSC office for more details (p. 402).

A more informal way of meeting other business people is to find out if there is a small business club operating in your area. Try asking in your local library or local enterprise agency (some enterprise agencies run these). One such club which has been going for a number of years is the Durham Small Business Club Ltd. This is a fairly substantial organization and has ten full-time staff.

The aims of a club like this are to promote inter-trade between members, to promote the growth of small business in the area, to keep small businesses informed of relevant legislation, to provide a social situation in which business can be discussed and to act as a voice for small businesses both locally and nationally.

## TRADE ASSOCIATIONS

There are three well-known trade associations (see p. 404 for addresses).

### 1. ASSOCIATION OF INDEPENDENT BUSINESSES

This operates as a pressure group on government to help promote the development of small businesses. The membership fee depends on number of employees, but varies from £25 for a sole trader up to £400 for a firm with over two hundred employees.

### 2. THE NATIONAL FEDERATION OF SELF-EMPLOYED AND SMALL BUSINESSES

This association acts as a pressure group with government. It also offers a legal expenses insurance which covers you in certain areas up to certain limits – for example, up to £25,000 for an unfair dismissal claim and up to £10,000 for representation at a VAT appeal tribunal. The association has a 24-hour-telephone legal advisory service and there is a monthly newspaper. In the first year membership will cost you £34 (£40 for both husband and wife) and in subsequent years the fee is £24 (£30 for husband and wife).

### 3. THE SMALL BUSINESS BUREAU

This is a pressure group affiliated to the Conservative Party. It produces a monthly newspaper and various fact sheets, as well as providing an advisory service to members. The yearly subscription is £20.

## INFORMATION FROM THE MEDIA, BOOKS AND EXHIBITIONS

Some of the national newspapers devote a page each week to the small business sector. The *Financial Times* on Tuesday, the *Guardian* on Monday and *The Times* on Friday (days correct at the time of going to press) have pages which include business-to-business ads for businesses offering or wanting services, products or money, or businesses to buy and sell – but see p. 96 for how to find a business to buy. The pages also have some editorial. There may be an article on the experience of one small business, but there are also usually up-to-date bits of information, for example, about training courses, exhibitions, books and new finance packages.

There are quite a number of books written for small businesses. Some of them aim to be comprehensive, such as this one; others are more selective in particular areas. In 'Reference' (p. 402), there is a list of books which are particularly good and which complement this guide's information and advice. You could also contact your local library whose staff can be very helpful on suggesting sources of information.

At an early stage of your business planning, wandering around business exhibitions can give you some ideas and useful literature. These are also an opportunity to speak to potential customers and competitors. Ask your local enterprise agency if there is to be a local exhibition in the near future.

## SPECIAL HELP FOR THE YOUNG, ETHNIC MINORITIES AND WOMEN

### THE YOUNG

If you are under twenty-six and thinking of starting a business, or if you are unemployed with little prospect of obtaining employment, there are organizations set up to help you ease into self-employment. Some offer advice and guidance; others offer hard cash. The names and addresses of these organizations are given on p. 404 and are described below.

### 1. *Head Start*
Head Start aims to help young people who are at least seventeen but not more than twenty-five who have already developed some sort of skill, for example, a hobby, trade or interest.

First, you must attend a one-day workshop and a counselling session aimed at producing a rough business plan. If you still want to go ahead with self-employment after this, there is an eight-week part-time training course. The counsellors and trainers will be drawn from local companies and businesses and will be giving their time voluntarily. Counselling can continue after the initial training; you are provided with a 'business mate' for one year.

### 2. *Instant Muscle*
Instant Muscle operates in areas of high unemployment and concentrates on training and counselling, as well as getting support from the local business community in the form of premises or equipment. Young people are helped to identify their own skill and to look at the commercial possibilities of being self-employed.

On the whole, Instant Muscle is looking to support groups who operate as a limited company or cooperative rather than one person operating as a sole trader. However, if you are likely to be a sole trader who eventually will employ others, advice and counselling will be given. Instant Muscle advisers can also help you to approach bodies which may have funds available to get your business going and will help you find the facilities that you need to get started.

### 3. Livewire

This is a nationwide annual competition which has been running since 1984–5. There are cash prizes for the winners of the regional and national competitions, but the aim of the competition is to provide young people with the opportunity to get professional advice on business plans and ideas.

### 4. Project Fullemploy

Project Fullemploy has several enterprise centres in the UK, mainly in areas of high unemployment among young minority ethnic groups. The centres offer several courses: Business Enterprise Programme Courses, one-day seminars or workshops, part-time courses and crash courses. The enterprise centres also offer a drop-in information service.

### 5. The Prince's Youth Business Trust

The Royal Jubilee and Prince's Trusts provide grants of up to £1,000 for the young unemployed under the age of twenty-six. The grants can be used for tools and equipment, transport, fees, insurance, instruction and training, but not to provide working capital or to cover rent and rates, raw materials or stock. The Trust also provides loans. The loan is normally not more than £2,000, but it can go up to £5,000 if there are two or more people involved. The loan is for capital equipment or working capital, but it should not be used as money to live on (the enterprise allowance can be used for that, see p. 289). The loan is normally interest-free for the first year and a low rate of interest will be charged in years two and three. Repayment takes place during the second and third years.

#### ETHNIC MINORITIES

You may find that there is a local agency in your area specially to help members of ethnic minorities who start small businesses. Project Fullemploy (see above) is a national organization which specializes in helping young blacks. In Glasgow, there is the Ethnic Minority Small Business Centre, which offers consultancy, courses, computer services and information, mainly for the Indian, Pakistani and Chinese communities. A list of a few agencies is included on p. 404.

WOMEN

Although women face exactly the same business problems as men do, some agencies consider that they can overcome the problems better if they have had some assertiveness training. The addresses of a couple of organizations which may be able to help you are on p. 404.

## ENTERPRISE AGENCIES

WHAT CAN THEY DO FOR YOU

Describing an enterprise agency is a bit like squeezing a marshmallow. They are nebulous bodies, dissimilar in name, in size, in how they are funded and in what they can do for you. However, they all have a common aim. The shared objective of the enterprise agencies is to help and advise small businesses.

The umbrella organization for agencies, Business in the Community, said there were 250 agencies in May 1987; the Department of Employment gave the figure as 370 in March 1987! The size of the agency can vary significantly; the largest agency has over twenty staff, the smallest have two. The agencies are funded in different ways. Some agencies get funds from local authorities, but most get financial backing from large firms. This can be in the form of hard cash for running the agency or in seconding staff from the company to the agency to act as adviser.

The agencies offer a variety of services which could include:

- free business advice
- information
- counselling
- training courses
- advice on property
- advice on use of computers
- LINC (p. 293) helps to introduce people wanting to invest in small businesses to those wanting funds for their business.

If you have difficulty finding your local enterprise agency, contact the umbrella body, Business in the Community (see p. 403 for telephone number and address).

As well as the local agencies, there are also agencies which provide assistance and help on a regional or national level. These include:

- the Scottish Development Agency
- the Highlands and Islands Development Board
- the Welsh Development Agency
- the Local Enterprise Development Unit in Northern Ireland
- the Council for Small Industries in Rural Areas.

Addresses and telephone numbers for these organizations are given on pp. 403–4.

Finally, do not forget that local authorities are sometimes willing to help financially.

## SUMMARY

1. Choose your training course carefully. Check that it is a practical course with emphasis on your own business plans.

2. Counselling can be a useful source of advice, not just when you start but when you have been in business for some time.

3. Other business people can provide help and contacts – see if there is a small business club in your area.

4. You may be able to find special counselling help if you are young, black or female.

# 4. YOUR BUSINESS IDENTITY

An important decision to make early on is to decide what legal form your business will take. Whatever you decide is not irrevocable, but it will take time and money to undo mistakes.

You can choose between:

- sole trader
- partnership
- limited company
- cooperative.

If you want to work on your own, your choice is either sole trader or limited company. If you want to work with others, your choice is between partnership, limited company or cooperative (or you could be a sole trader if you intend to employ others, rather than work with them).

The form you choose can hinge on emotional factors, as well as objective ones. If you choose a cooperative as your form, this may be because of political, social or ethical reasons. If you choose a partnership, this may be because you have a close colleague with whom you work well. However, the choice between a sole trader or limited company will probably be made because of monetary reasons, such as which is best from the tax point of view.

### WHAT IS IN THIS CHAPTER?

This chapter compares the pros and cons of becoming a sole trader, a partnership or a limited company. And on p. 57, there is a quiz, which should help you make your decision. Next, the chapter shows you how to go about setting up each of these legal forms. Finally, it looks briefly at forming a cooperative.

## SOLE TRADER *v.* PARTNERSHIP *v.* LIMITED COMPANY

There are thirteen elements you have to look at so that you can weigh up the pros and cons of each legal form.

## 1. THE CREDIBILITY OF THE BUSINESS

There is probably very little to choose between a sole trader and a partnership when it comes to credibility. On the whole, it is thought that a limited company may give your business more credibility; but this may not work if a customer researches your company and finds, for example, that it has a paid-up capital of £100, which is the typical situation of a very small business.

*Summary*
On balance, if you are going to be selling to large companies, becoming a limited company will probably have the edge on credibility.

## 2. WHAT HAPPENS WITH MONEY YOU OWE

If you are a sole trader, you are liable for all the money your business owes (your liability is unlimited). Your own personal assets, such as your house, furniture and car, can be seized to pay your business debts; in the final breakdown, you can be made bankrupt.

This unlimited liability also applies to a partnership, with a further drawback: you are liable for your partner's share of the debts, and this may include an unpaid tax bill on partnership income.

By contrast, the concept of limited liability appears very attractive. Shareholders' liability for debt is, in most cases, limited to the amount they paid for their shares in the first place. The personal assets of directors can only be touched if that company has been trading fraudulently. But this protection for your personal assets may be illusory. When you are starting in business and still operating on a fairly small scale, it is common for you as a director to be asked for personal guarantees against the business debts. This includes bank overdrafts, leasing agreements for cars and equipment, rent for premises and could include money you owe suppliers.

*Summary*
If yours is the sort of business which buys materials or services from other businesses, needs a small overdraft or has to operate from rented premises, forming yourself as a limited company has the edge. You may be able to get away without guaranteeing all of these debts; it is certainly worth negotiating to avoid doing so.

## 3. WHAT YOU DO TO START UP

It is very easy to start up as a sole trader. You do not need to get a lawyer involved; simply tell your tax inspector and your local DHSS office.

In theory, it is equally simple to start a partnership, as you do not have to get a written partnership agreement. But, this would not be a sensible or businesslike approach. Partners argue; you should accept that this may be so, no matter how unlikely it appears when you start your business. You must get a solicitor to draw up a written agreement which covers things like profits split, work split, tax split and partner changes. See p. 61 for more on what should be in the partnership agreement.

You can start a limited company from scratch. Alternatively you can buy one 'off-the-peg', which costs between £100 and £140, and for a further £40, you can change its name. In either case, you need two people as shareholders: one to be a director and the other to be the company secretary. You have to register the company with the Companies Registration Office, which involves a number of formalities. You should get a solicitor to help with starting your business as a limited company.

*Summary*
Setting up as a sole trader involves the least work and fewest formalities.

### 4. YOUR ACCOUNTS

As a sole trader and a partner, your accounts need to show a true and fair picture. But the exact form of the accounts is not laid down by law. In practice, this means you do not have to produce a balance sheet. It would, however, be advisable to do so to impress your tax inspector (see p. 274 for what a balance sheet is).

In contrast, the form of accounts for a limited company is laid down by law. The accounts have to be filed at the Companies Registration Office: any member of the public can inspect them there.

*Summary*
The rules about your accounts are more onerous if you set up as a limited company.

### 5. GETTING YOUR ACCOUNTS AUDITED

As a sole trader or partnership, you do not have to get your accounts audited, if you do not want to. You may want to consider doing so, if the cost would not be too exorbitant, as it can help in dealings with your tax inspector. It may also help you if you need confirmation of income from your business – for example, to get a mortgage to buy a house.

If your business form is a limited company, you have to get your accounts audited by an accountant.

*Summary*
The rules about auditing of accounts only apply to a limited company.

## 6. PAYING NATIONAL INSURANCE

If you are a sole trader or a partner, you pay national insurance in two ways. If your earnings are above a certain amount, you pay what are known as Class 2 contributions. These are weekly flat-rate payments of £3.85. You may also have to pay Class 4 contributions, which is worked out as a percentage of your profits, but you can get some tax relief on these. Paying national insurance entitles you to most benefits; but you cannot receive unemployment benefit, invalidity pension, widow's benefit or the earnings-related portion of the retirement pension.

If you form a limited company, you will usually become a director and so, for legal purposes, an employee of the company. You will have to pay national insurance contributions as an employee and your company will have to pay contributions as your employer. These rates are much higher than those for a sole trader or partner. For example, for a salary of £20,000 the rate is £1,380 as an employee plus an employer's contribution of £2,090, but only £877 if that were the level of profits for a sole trader.

*Summary*
National insurance contributions will cost you more as a limited company, although you are entitled to more benefits.

## 7. THE RATES OF TAX ON YOUR PROFITS

If you operate as a sole trader, you will pay normal rates of income tax on your profits (including any salary you pay yourself). These rates can go up to 60 per cent.

The amount of tax charged on profits from a partnership depends on the income tax rates paid by individual partners on their income. But the tax which each of you pays will depend on what you put in your partnership agreement.

As a director of a limited company, you will pay tax on your salary at the normal rates of income tax – up to 60 per cent. You pay corporation tax on the profits which you leave in the business. If your profits are £100,000 or less, you will pay the small companies' rate of 27 per cent (correct at April 1987).

*Summary*
If you are paying higher rates of tax on the profits from your business as a

sole trader or partner, you could pay less tax if you form a limited company.

## 8. WHEN YOU PAY TAX

Once you have been going two or three years as a sole trader or partnership, you will normally pay tax on what's known as a *preceding year basis* (p. 345). The effect of this is that you could pay tax up to twenty months after you earned the profits. This is an advantage and helps your cash flow if your profits are rising each year.

The rules are stricter if you run a limited company. On your salary, you pay tax each month under the PAYE system. On the profits of the company, you pay tax nine months after the end of the accounting year.

*Summary*
There may be cash flow advantages if you pay tax as a sole trader or partnership, rather than as a limited company.

## 9. WHAT YOU CAN DO WITH LOSSES

If you are a sole trader or in a partnership, you can set off losses:

● against future profits of the same trade

● against other income in the year of the loss or the year after. This includes any personal income you or your wife or husband may have.

If you form a limited company, the relief is not so generous. You can set off losses:

● in one period against company profits of the previous period of the same length

● against future profits of the company

● against any capital gains the company makes.

*Summary*
If you are likely to make losses in the first year or so, you would be better organizing your business as a sole trader or partnership, if you have another source of income.

## 10. PROVIDING YOURSELF WITH A PENSION

The amount of contributions a company can make to a pension scheme free of tax is limitless. As well as the contributions your company can make on your behalf, you can also invest up to 15 per cent of your salary as a director and employee, and get tax relief on the full amount at your highest rate of tax.

In contrast, if you are a sole trader or in a partnership, you can get relief on up to $17\frac{1}{2}$ per cent of your taxable profits (strictly, net relevant earnings, see p. 398) to put into a pension scheme. Note that from April 1988 there are major changes in the provision of pensions (p. 397).

*Summary*
The advantages are heavily weighted towards a limited company.

## II. CAPITAL GAINS IN THE BUSINESS

As an individual, if you sell something and receive more for it than you paid, you have made a capital gain. You may also make a capital gain if you give away an asset or dispose of it, and its value at the time is higher than the original cost. A certain amount of net capital gains are free of tax each year. For example, in the 1987–8 tax year, you are allowed net gains of up to £6,600 free of tax. On gains over that amount, the rate of tax is 30 per cent. And there is even better news. You are allowed to index gains; this means gains which are solely the result of inflation are not so likely to be capital gains.

If you are a sole trader or partner, capital gains in your business are treated in the same way. As you can see, the tax treatment is relatively light.

But if you form a limited company, you face a double tax if you make a capital gain when you sell one of the assets of your business. There is no tax-free limit, so corporation tax is due on all gains. And if you want to get your hands on the proceeds, you can only do so in the form of salary or dividends; and this means income tax to be paid on top of tax already paid.

*Summary*
If you want to sell an asset of your business, you would be better off tax-wise if your business was in the form of sole trader or partnership, rather than limited company.

## 12. RAISING MONEY

If you need money for your business, the form of your business can dictate your choice.

As a sole trader, your options are fairly limited and basically depend upon your bank manager and getting an overdraft. As an outside possibility, you may find an individual who could lend you the money.

In a partnership, you may be able to find a new partner to bring in some extra capital.

But, if you form a limited company, the choice is wider. You may be able to raise venture capital from a fund; and you can only raise money under the Business Expansion scheme if you are a limited company. You may also be able to raise money from your bank secured with what is known as a floating charge on your assets. For more about these methods of raising money, see p. 282.

*Summary*
Your choices for raising money are wider if you form a limited company.

### 13. SELLING PART OF YOUR BUSINESS

This can be slightly tricky if you are a sole trader or in a partnership. One way of solving this could be to take on a partner (or a further partner), but this obviously means you must have trust in the person. If part of your business is easily separated, you might be able to sell it as a going concern on its own.

It should be somewhat easier to sell part of your business if it is in the form of a limited company. You could sell some of your shares. This may not be so easy if the company is unquoted; but it should be less of a problem if the company is quoted on the Unlisted Securities Market or the Third Market, for example.

*Summary*
Selling part of your business is easier if it is in the form of a limited company.

## QUIZ: SOLE TRADER, PARTNERSHIP OR LIMITED COMPANY?

Use this quiz only as a rule of thumb. It is essential to read the detailed comparisons on pp. 52–7. In this quiz, the scoring of each factor is equally weighted, that is, assumed to be of equal importance to you. You should put in your own weighting. For example, if raising money is crucial to your business, multiply the score by a number, such as 3, to give this sufficient weight in your decision.

Set up a piece of paper with three column headings: sole trader, partner, limited company. Answer each question and fill in the score for each form of business.

| | SOLE TRADER | PARTNER | LIMITED COMPANY |
|---|---|---|---|
| 1. Are you selling to large businesses?<br>If YES, score and go to 2<br>If NO, go to 2 | 0 | 0 | 2 |
| 2. Are you likely to be buying substantial supplies from other businesses on credit?<br>If YES, score and go to 3<br>If NO, go to 3 | 0 | 0 | 2 |
| 3. Do you have another person you want to start the business with?<br>If YES, score and go to 4<br>If NO, go to 5 | 0 | I | I |
| 4. Can you trust that person completely to make decisions on your behalf, to pay the tax bill and debts?<br>If Yes, go to 5<br>If NO, score and go to 5 | 0 | 0 | I |
| 5. Are you willing to meet the more onerous reporting requirements for a company?<br>If YES, go to 6<br>If NO, score and go to 6 | I | I | 0 |
| 6. Are you prepared to have your accounts audited each year?<br>If YES, go to 7<br>If NO, score and go to 7 | I | I | 0 |
| 7. For the effect of national insurance contributions<br>Score and go to 8 | 2 | 2 | 0 |
| 8. Do you expect to pay higher rate tax on your profits (that is, taxable profits of £17,900)?<br>If YES, score and go to 9<br>If NO, go to 9<br>If profits are likely to be over £50,000, multiply score by 2 | 0 | 0 | 2 |
| 9. Do you expect your profits to rise each year?<br>If YES, score and go to 10<br>If NO, go to 10 | I | I | 0 |
| 10. Do you expect to be making losses initially?<br>If YES, go to 11 | | | |

| | SOLE TRADER | PARTNER | LIMITED COMPANY |
|---|---|---|---|
| If NO, go to 12 | | | |
| 11. Do you have another income, for example, your husband's or wife's? | | | |
| If YES, score and go to 12 | 1 | 1 | 0 |
| If NO, go to 12 | | | |
| 12. Want to pay as much as possible into a personal pension scheme – for example, if you are forty or over, say? | | | |
| If YES, score and go to 13 | 0 | 0 | 1 |
| If NO, go to 13 | | | |
| 13. Is there some large asset in your business, on which you are likely to make a capital gain? | | | |
| If YES, score and go to 14 | 1 | 1 | 0 |
| If NO, go to 14 | | | |
| 14. Is raising money, other than by overdraft, an important consideration? | | | |
| If YES, score and go to 15 | 0 | 0 | 2 |
| 15. Might you want to sell part of your business at a later stage? | | | |
| If YES, score | 0 | 0 | 1 |

TO FIND YOUR SOLUTION

Tot up the scores in each of the three columns. The higher the score, the more suitable the business form. Overleaf, there is an example of a husband and wife using the quiz to decide on the legal form of the business.

## HOW TO SET UP AS A SOLE TRADER

It is really very easy and straightforward. You need to:

• tell your local tax inspector, if you are becoming self-employed. You will find the address in the telephone directory, under Inland Revenue. Ask for Form 41G

• tell your local DHSS office. You will find it listed in the telephone directory under Health and Social Security, Department of

• check with the Planning Officer that your place of work will be suitable (p. 196)

*Example*: Peter Jones is thirty and wants to start a business selling frozen Chinese food.

|  | SOLE TRADER | PARTNER | LIMITED COMPANY |
|---|---|---|---|
| 1. He will be trying to sell to large retail chains | 0 | 0 | 2 |
| 2. He is likely to be getting supplies from other businesses on credit | 0 | 0 | 2 |
| 3. He is going into business with his wife Laura | 0 | 1 | 1 |
| 4. He trusts her absolutely | – | – | – |
| 5. Neither he nor Laura find book-keeping easy | 1 | 1 | 0 |
| 6. He would prefer not to have his accounts audited | 1 | 1 | 0 |
| 7. National insurance contributions | 2 | 2 | 0 |
| 8. Peter's business plan shows taxable profits of over £30,000 after three years | 0 | 0 | 2 |
| 9. His business plan shows the profit picture improving each year | 1 | 1 | 0 |
| 10. Yes, in the first year he will make a loss | – | – | – |
| 11. Laura will still be earning as an employee | 1 | 1 | 0 |
| 12. Peter and Laura are not yet bothered about pensions (both aged thirty) | – | – | – |
| 13. No special asset | – | – | – |
| 14. Any money will be raised as an overdraft | – | – | – |
| 15. This doesn't seem a possibility | – | – | – |
| TOTAL | 6 | 9 | 7 |

The best business form for Peter and Laura is a partnership between the two of them.

● if you decide to trade under a name different from your own, remember to include your name as proprietor on your headed paper (p. 138)

● consider whether you have to or whether you should ask to register for VAT (p. 384).

## HOW TO SET UP AS A PARTNERSHIP

The fundamental drawback of a partnership is that each partner is jointly liable with the other partners for all the debts and obligations that each partner incurs. This financial responsibility can include all your own personal assets, which could be seized to pay partnership debts (which might not have happened as a result of your actions but of your partner's).

You must be able to trust your partners. Do not drift into an informal partnership. Make sure you and your partners have discussed difficult problems right at the start and come to some clear agreement.

### TYPES OF PARTNERS

There are several different sorts of partners; but only two are suitable for consideration in a business partnership:

- a full partner who will share in the profits and losses in an agreed proportion and will be part of the management
- a sleeping partner who will have no part in the management of the business, but will still be held responsible for the debts of the partnership.

### THE PARTNERSHIP AGREEMENT

This is a job for a solicitor. Briefly, an agreement should include among other points:

- the names of the partners, the name of the firm and its business

- the date the partnership starts and how long it will last

- the capital and the interest on it

- the profits split

- management and control of the business

- holidays

- what happens on retirement, on death and if one of the partners wants to leave.

## HOW TO SET UP AS A LIMITED COMPANY

This is also a job for a solicitor. If you form a company from scratch it can take several weeks. You will get a Certificate of Incorporation when you register the company with the Registrar of Companies. You will need a number of documents; the two main ones are the Memorandum and Articles of Association. There are also a number of forms to fill in; your solicitor will help.

The Memorandum should state the name of the company (this will need to be approved by the Registrar), the location of the registered office, the objects of the company, its limited liability, its share capital and details of the shares.

The Articles should have the detailed rules about internal management of the company.

Instead of forming a company, you can buy a ready-made one. This is a quicker process, but it may take three or more weeks to change its name to whatever you want to call your business.

There are certain rules about displaying information. For example, the Certificate of Incorporation and the registration date need to be displayed publicly and the registration number must appear on the company stationery.

## WHAT DIRECTORS MUST DO

There are quite a number of responsibilities and restraints. In the first place, directors have to attend board meetings and disclose their private interests and shareholdings. An additional responsibility is that they should not knowingly allow the company to trade when insolvent (p. 329). If they do, they may have to pay for the debts incurred by the company while insolvent. They may also be disqualified from being a director of any other company.

Second, there are limits placed on their power by the Articles of Association and by the fact that theirs is an elected position, so they can be removed.

Third, directors are subject to extra tax rules about expenses and fringe benefits (p. 377).

## FORMING A COOPERATIVE

### WHAT IS A COOPERATIVE ALL ABOUT?

There are four basic points:

1. The management, objectives and use of the assets of a cooperative must be controlled by its workforce. If the assets are not all owned by the workforce at the outset, it must be an aim of the cooperative to own them eventually.

2. You need to organize a voting system. An example would be one vote for each worker. Decisions would be made on a simple majority.

3. The only payment for providing money for a cooperative can be interest, not a share of the profits. The profits should be shared among the workforce.

4. You should agree at the outset that the cooperative can be disbanded only if its members agree. And the proceeds from selling the assets should not be distributed to the members.

## CHOOSING A LEGAL FORM

You will need to get legal registration or incorporation for the cooperative. There are four possible legal forms.

First, you could form a partnership. The disadvantage with this is that there is no limited liability. And the business could be sold for the benefit of its members; this is not in keeping with a fundamental principle of a cooperative (see above). On the other hand, you can form a partnership with only two people, whereas to form a cooperative society (see below), you need seven.

Second, you could form a limited company; but the aims of a company run counter to some of the basic principles of a cooperative, so it would be difficult to organize.

Third, you could seek registration as a cooperative society under the Industrial and Provident Societies (I & PS) Acts 1965–75. You will need seven founder members. You will find registration will be quicker if you apply through a 'promoting body', such as the Cooperative Union and the Industrial Common Ownership Movement. ICOM Model Rules can be used to form it.

Finally, you could organize the cooperative as a company limited by guarantee. This has the advantage that it needs only two people to form it.

## HOW IS A WORKERS' COOPERATIVE ORGANIZED?

A member of a cooperative is anyone who shares in its control. A member must be either a worker or a founder member. Not all workers need to be members; some cooperatives specify a lower age limit and others have a probationary period. But at least half the employees should be members.

## SUMMARY

1. A limited company has several advantages: limited liability, greater credibility, lower tax, better pension rules, more avenues for raising finance and easier disposal of part of your business.

2. Sole trader and partnership have less onerous rules about accounts and auditing, lower national insurance payments, better tax treatment of losses and capital gains and the tax rules help cash flow.

3. If you are forming a partnership, get a solicitor's help to draw up a written partnership agreement.

4. The simplest way of all to start a business is to begin as a sole trader.

OTHER CHAPTERS TO READ

# 5. ARE YOU SURE?

Every would-be entrepreneur should take stock before undertaking the final commitment; reassessments are a vital part of the decision process. Are you the right person? Have you got the necessary skills? Will you be able to earn enough to live on? Is your idea the best one? All of these aspects are crucial and deserve to be analysed and considered more than once.

WHAT IS IN THIS CHAPTER?

This chapter draws together all the key points made in the previous four chapters, presenting them in a series of four checklists. This should allow you to reconsider previous decisions to confirm that you are on the right road.

The checklists are:

- You (see below)

- Your family (p. 67)

- Your skills (p. 69)

- Your idea (p. 73).

## CHECKLIST: YOU

Underline the word in one of the four right-hand columns which best describes how you fit each question. You can also ask friends, colleagues or relatives to fill in the checklist about you, so that you can obtain an external view of your character and fitness for self-employment. Make sure they respond in a truthful and unbiased way.

| | 1. | 2. | 3. | 4. |
|---|---|---|---|---|
| 1. Can you work long hours? | always | sometimes | occasionally | never |
| 2. Do you have persistence and stamina? | all the time | most of the time | occasionally | rarely |
| 3. Is this business important, more than leisure or family, for example? | completely | much more | as important | less important |
| 4. If the business struggled for five years, would you keep going? | yes, easily | yes, fairly easily | yes, with difficulty | no |
| 5. Is financial success your main guide to what you have achieved? | completely | mainly | partially | not at all |
| 6. Are you thought of as a survivor? | always | usually | occasionally | never |
| 7. If you were in a tight corner, would you be able to come up with an original way out? | frequently | sometimes | rarely | never |
| 8. Do you keep going until a task is complete? | always | usually | sometimes | occasionally |
| 9. Are problems a challenge? | always | usually | sometimes | never |
| 10. Can you live with insecurity about job and income? | yes, easily | yes, fairly easily | yes, with difficulty | no |
| 11. Are you self-confident? | yes, always | yes, usually | sometimes lack confidence | no |
| 12. How do you view failure? | an opportunity to learn | disappointing | a setback | disaster |
| 13. Can you take criticism? | always listen; may reject | always accept | don't like it | always reject |
| 14. Do you ask for comments on your performance so that you can do something better the next time? | always | usually | sometimes | rarely |

| | 1. | 2. | 3. | 4. |
|---|---|---|---|---|
| 15. Do you believe your success will be dependent on outside factors? | strongly disagree | disagree | agree sometimes | agree always |
| 16. Do you like being the leader in situations where you can be assessed? | very much | quite a lot | not really | not at all |
| 17. Are you good at finding the right person or source to help you achieve what you want? | very good | quite good | not very good | poor |
| 18. Do you recognize when you need help? | always | usually | sometimes | no |
| 19. Do you set your own high standards to compete against? | always | usually | sometimes | rarely |
| 20. In the past, which sort of risks have you preferred taking? | calculated risks | high risks | low risks | seldom take risks |
| 21. Can you identify which decisions are important and which are not? | yes, always | yes, usually | yes, sometimes | no |
| 22. Can you delegate to others? | yes, when appropriate | yes, sometimes | with difficulty | no |
| 23. How is your health? | very good | good | quite good | poor |

When you have completed the checklist, look at the pattern of underlined words. The more underlined in columns 1. and 2., the greater your probable success as a business owner.

## CHECKLIST: YOUR FAMILY

If you are single, you may not need to consider this section. But if you have a husband or wife and children, involving them in the decision to go it alone is important. Starting a business is an all-embracing existence and your family life is unlikely to remain the same after taking the plunge. They will need to understand that the home atmosphere should be very supportive, particularly during the early business problems.

Your family may also turn out to be an important business resource.

They can provide extra input in all you do: clerical, manual, problem solving, for example. With a family, deciding to found an enterprise is likely to be more successful as a family decision. Having said that, many succeed without the support of their families; but, in this case, the strain on domestic relations can be severe. In the extreme, the choice may be business or marriage.

Cross out whichever is inapplicable:

1. Have you discussed your thoughts about starting a business with your family?                                                                *yes*   *no*

2. Are they willing to help out if necessary?                                                *yes*   *no*

3. Will they be able to live easily with job or financial insecurity?   *yes*   *no*

4. Have they accepted that there may be a permanent drop in living standards?                                                                        *yes*   *no*

5. If you need to raise money using your home as security, do they understand the full implications?                                   *yes*   *no*

6. Is your family self-sufficient, that is, can they manage without you to do the shopping, keep the garden tidy, do the decorating?   *yes*   *no*

7. Does one of the members of your family earn a living in another way, which can be used to tide the whole family over?   *yes*   *no*

8. Have you worked out a family budget to see how you will cope?                                                                                      *yes*   *no*

If you have not, this pro forma cash flow may help you. Remember to use conservative estimates of your likely income and allow for all the costs.

| Month: | 1. | 2. | — | 11. | 12. |
|---|---|---|---|---|---|
| Balance at bank at start of mth | ... | ... | — | ... | ... |
| *Income* | | | | | |
| Estimated from business | ... | ... | — | ... | ... |
| Other family | ... | ... | — | ... | ... |
| Total income | ... | ... | — | ... | ... |
| *Expenses* | | | | | |
| Mortgage/rent | ... | ... | — | ... | ... |
| Loan interest | ... | ... | — | ... | ... |
| Rates | ... | ... | — | ... | ... |
| Pension | ... | ... | — | ... | ... |
| Life insurance | ... | ... | — | ... | ... |
| Tax on business income | ... | ... | — | ... | ... |
| Electricity/gas/ phone/fuel | ... | ... | — | ... | ... |
| Travel/car | ... | ... | — | ... | ... |
| House: insurance/ repairs | ... | ... | — | ... | ... |
| Food | ... | ... | — | ... | ... |
| Clothes | ... | ... | — | ... | ... |
| Subscriptions/ newspapers/ magazines | ... | ... | — | ... | ... |
| Other: | | | | | |
| ... ... | ... | ... | — | ... | ... |
| ... ... | ... | ... | — | ... | ... |
| ... ... | ... | ... | — | ... | ... |
| Total expenses | ... | ... | — | ... | ... |
| Balance at bank at end of mth | ... | ... | — | ... | ... |

9. Have you talked to your bank manager about your intended business and showed him your cash flow to demonstrate how you hope to cope in domestic finance? *yes no*

When you have completed your family checklist, the more times you have answered 'yes' the better prepared you are for starting your business.

## CHECKLIST: YOUR SKILLS

This checklist should help you to look honestly at what you can do well and what you do badly. If there are skills you lack, this does not mean that you cannot go ahead. But you will have to compensate in one of three ways:

- be trained or seek advice from an enterprise agency

- fund the business so you can employ those skills which are lacking

- use professional advisers, if appropriate.

As you answer each question, underline the appropriate word or words:

## FINANCIAL

| | |
|---|---|
| 1. Have you kept accounting books, for example, sales and purchases daybooks, cash books (see p. 333)? | *many times*<br>*on a few occasions*<br>*not at all* |
| 2. Have you had to chase debts owed by your customers (p. 310)? | *yes, frequently*<br>*yes, sometimes*<br>*no, not at all* |
| 3. Have you ever installed a system of credit control (p. 308)? | *yes*<br>*no* |
| 4. Have you ever negotiated credit terms with a supplier (p. 313)? | *yes*<br>*no* |
| 5. What is your experience of drawing up cash flows (p. 265)? | *extensive*<br>*a little*<br>*none at all* |
| 6. Do you understand the importance of controlling cash (p. 304)? | *yes*<br>*no* |
| 7. What is your experience of drawing up budgets (p. 302)? | *extensive*<br>*a little*<br>*none at all* |
| 8. Is break-even analysis a technique you have used before (p. 299)? | *yes, frequently*<br>*yes, sometimes*<br>*no, not at all* |

9. Do you know when and how you would use:

- an overdraft (p. 285)                                 *yes   no*
- leasing (p. 203)                                      *yes   no*
- factoring (p. 312)                                    *yes   no*

10. What is your experience of estimating and           *extensive*
raising long-term financial needs (p. 282)?             *a little*
                                                        *none at all*

11. Do you know what are the sources of                 *yes*
long-term funds, for example, venture capital           *no*
(p. 294)?

12. What is your experience of drawing up               *extensive*
business plans (p. 76)?                                 *a little*
                                                        *none at all*

13. What is your experience of presenting your
plan to financiers (p. 295)?                            *extensive*
                                                        *a little*
                                                        *none at all*

## MARKETING

14. Do you understand the different ways you can        *yes*
establish prices (p. 175)?                              *no*

15. What is your selling experience (p. 162)?           *extensive*
                                                        *a little*
                                                        *none at all*

16. Do you know how to analyse market sectors           *yes*
(p. 30)?                                                *no*

17. What is your experience of identifying product      *extensive*
benefits (p. 32)?                                       *a little*
                                                        *none at all*

18. What is your experience of:

- advertising (p. 157)                                  *extensive*
                                                        *a little*
                                                        *none at all*
- public relations (p. 154)                             *extensive*
                                                        *a little*
                                                        *none at all*

● product distribution (p. 165)                                        *extensive*
                                                                        *a little*
                                                                   *none at all*

19. Have you drawn up terms and conditions of                               *yes*
sale on previous occasions?                                                  *no*

## OPERATIONAL

20. Do you know how to introduce a stock                                    *yes*
control system?                                                              *no*

21. Do you understand all the ins and outs of                      *yes, very well*
your product; that is, how it works, what it                       *yes, somewhat*
does?                                                            *no, not very well*

22. Do you understand the effect that control of                   *yes, very well*
costs can have on profits (p. 318)?                                *yes, somewhat*
                                                                    *no, not really*

23. Do you understand the manufacturing process                    *yes, very well*
of your product (if applicable)?                                   *yes, somewhat*
                                                                    *no, not really*

## GENERAL MANAGEMENT

24. What is your experience of staff recruitment                        *extensive*
(p. 214)?                                                                 *a little*
                                                                     *none at all*

25. What is your understanding of employment                            *extensive*
law (p. 234)?                                                             *a little*
                                                                     *none at all*

26. Do you know how to set goals and objectives                             *yes*
for employees?                                                               *no*

27. Have you introduced reporting systems for                               *yes*
staff on a previous occasion?                                               *no*

28. What is your experience of project                                  *extensive*
management?                                                               *a little*
                                                                     *none at all*

| 29. Have you previously built a management team? | | *yes* |
| :-- | --- | --: |
| | | *no* |

Once you have finished assessing your skills and abilities, you will have some indication of what improvements you should make. A first step is reading the relevant chapters of this book.

## CHECKLIST: YOUR IDEA

This is an opportunity to have a final check on your idea before you start becoming involved in the actual formalities and expense of forming your business. Note that where the word 'product' is used, this could also be 'service' or 'skill'.

Tick the appropriate column:

| | YES | NO | DOES NOT APPLY |
| :-- | :-: | :-: | :-: |
| 1. Have you defined your product ideas? | . . . | . . . | . . . |
| 2. Have you carried out market research into your idea? | . . . | . . . | . . . |
| 3. Have you discerned a market sector or niche which you will sell to? | . . . | . . . | . . . |
| 4. Is that segment big enough for you to build a business on it? | . . . | . . . | . . . |
| 5. Have you researched the characteristics of your likely customers? | . . . | . . . | . . . |
| 6. Have you identified what are the benefits and advantages not yet available to that segment? | . . . | . . . | . . . |
| 7. Will you be able to supply a product which meets those needs? | . . . | . . . | . . . |
| 8. Do you know how your product will be different from the competitors? | . . . | . . . | . . . |
| 9. Have you estimated how much your likely customers will buy and when that will be? | . . . | . . . | . . . |

| | YES | NO | DOES NOT APPLY |
|---|---|---|---|
| 10. Have out found out how the product will be sold, for example, direct selling, retail, distributors etc.? | . . . | . . . | . . . |
| 11. Have you made a realistic forecast of the market share you can attain? | . . . | . . . | . . . |
| 12. Is the market likely to grow in the next few years? | . . . | . . . | . . . |
| 13. Have you talked to potential customers and do they like your product? | . . . | . . . | . . . |
| 14. Have you carried out any test selling and has it confirmed your estimates of sales? | . . . | . . . | . . . |
| 15. Will the product live up to the reputation you intend to project? | . . . | . . . | . . . |
| 16. Have you estimated a price you can sell for? | . . . | . . . | . . . |
| 17. Do you know how the product will be made? | . . . | . . . | . . . |
| 18. Can you work out an approximate cost? | . . . | . . . | . . . |
| 19. Do you have an initial idea of overheads for the business, for example, rent, telephone, heating and lighting, etc.? | . . . | . . . | . . . |
| 20. Have you made an approximate guess at the profits and when they will be earned? | . . . | . . . | . . . |
| 21. Will this give you an income you can live on? | . . . | . . . | . . . |
| 22. Will you need to raise money and is this a realistic amount? | . . . | . . . | . . . |
| 23. Have you thought carefully about what the principal risks are to your business? | . . . | . . . | . . . |
| 24. Can you put an estimate on the likelihood of these risks occurring? | . . . | . . . | . . . |

Now you have completed this checklist; the more times you answered 'yes', the better prepared you are and the greater the chance of success.

# WHAT NEXT?

If you have worked carefully through these four checklists, you are now faced with one of three options:

- give up because you are not the right person to be self-employed or the idea is not suitable

- carry out further research or training or seek a better idea

- proceed.

To proceed, you need to make several decisions and carry out actions. These include choosing advisers, formulating a detailed business plan, deciding the form of your business, working on what your business or product will be called. Chapter 7. 'Timing the jump' (p. 83) should guide you through the maze.

OTHER CHAPTERS TO READ

1. 'You and your ideas' (p. 15)
2. 'Who will buy?' (p. 28)
6. 'The business plan' (p. 76)

# 6. THE BUSINESS PLAN

Life can be very chaotic when you are starting or running a small business. The telephone calls to make, the letters to write, the decisions to take – all the day-to-day emergencies can push aside the sort of long-term strategic planning which is essential to keep your enterprise on the right track. Do not let short-term problems divert you from your longer-term objectives.

Writing a business plan is merely encapsulating your longer-term objectives, estimates and forecasts on paper. Once you have put down your plan, do not necessarily accept that it is set in concrete. Forecasts and objectives change as new bits of information and your better experience emerge. The important point is to incorporate your best estimate, given your current state of information. There is nothing like writing something down to help clarify your mind and reveal your uncertainties and weaknesses.

WHAT IS IN THIS CHAPTER?

- The objectives of the plan (see below)

- How many plans? (p. 77)

- Who should do the plan? (p. 78)

- What should be in the plan? (p. 78)

## THE OBJECTIVES OF THE PLAN

The two most important reasons for producing a written plan are:

- to show to outsiders to help raise money

- to use within the business to keep yourself on your planned course or to alert you to things which are not going according to your strategy. This use is discussed in more detail in Chapter 24, 'Staying afloat' (p. 298).

To persuade someone to lend or invest enough money in your business enabling you to achieve your strategy, you will need to:

- show that the lender or investor stands a good chance of being paid back or getting a good return on their investment

- instil confidence about your abilities to manage the business and, if applicable, show that you already have the beginnings of an experienced management team

- demonstrate that there is a good market for your product or service.

To achieve these objectives you must bring out what is exciting about the prospects of your business, combined with a thoroughly prepared presentation of the back-up figures and research.

Beware of filling your plan with nothing but a turgid series of facts and figures; you must allow the reader of your plan to be able to identify instantly what is so interesting about your business. You need to do this to persuade your reader that it is worthwhile studying the detailed forecasts, which can be very time-consuming. Lenders and investors can be presented with so many plans for consideration that unless yours grabs the reader's attention it could be consigned to the bin before your carefully prepared figures are looked at.

## HOW MANY PLANS?

As there are two reasons for having a written plan, will one plan suffice? The answer to this depends on who is advising you. A bank manager, or other person who may be providing finance, may say there should be only one plan, as they would like to know the absolute truth about what is happening in your business. But some small businesses adopt a different strategy and have two plans. One plan is for outsiders; this plan must be one *which will not fail* and so it will be fairly conservative about projected sales and costs. The reason for adopting a conservative approach with outsiders is that you must not be seen to fail as this can erode confidence in you and your judgement. This could make it difficult to keep the support of your bank manager when you need it later. Of course, if your plan is being used to raise money, your figures must achieve a balance between optimism and realism if you are to persuade banks and others that your business will be successful and so worthy of a loan or an investment. You must always remain confident that the figures are really achievable; if you are misleading the lenders and investors, you are also misleading yourself.

The second plan is for your own use and will set higher targets, although you must believe you can do that level of business. If you pitch the figures too low, you might not achieve as much as is possible. The well-known fleas-in-the-box analogy applies to your plan; if you put a lid on the box, the fleas learn to jump to that height only, but, if there is no lid, they jump as high as they are capable of doing. Your business plan should set that lid higher.

## WHO SHOULD DO THE PLAN?

It is your job. You will know the product and the market better than anyone else. You have to be prepared to present the plan to banks or other sources of finance, so you need to be fully confident about all the statements and forecasts. You will have that confidence if you have provided the data.

However, as it is so important for your plan to look professional, you may consider seeking advice and help on its production. This is available from:

● enterprise agencies and training courses. Many of the counsellors will be prepared to help you put your plan together (see Chapter 3. 'A spot of coaching' (p. 41)). This help is often free

● accountants can help you prepare the figures. Some of the bigger firms of accountants will have specialist departments to do just this (see Chapter 18. 'Professional back-up' (p. 205) for more on this)

● corporate finance specialists. This is a relatively new profession and such people are mainly interested in helping you raise substantial sums of money from venture capital sources (see Chapter 18. 'Professional back-up' (p. 205)).

If your forecasts are likely to be fairly complicated and to need changing, you might consider using a computer program designed to enable you to produce forecasts and to examine the effect changes will have on the results.

## WHAT SHOULD BE IN THE PLAN?

SUGGESTED LENGTH

I. SUMMARY OF YOUR PLAN, highlighting the attractions of your business        one or two pages

     a)   what is the business?
     b)   what is the market?
     c)   potential for business
     d)   forecast profit figures

    e)  how much money is needed

    f)  prospects for the investor/lender

## 2. THE PAST

    a)  when business started

    b)  brief summary of past performance (put accounts for last three years in an Appendix)

    c)  indication of how relevant or not past performance is to future progress

*one page plus Appendix*

## 3. MANAGEMENT (this is a crucial section)

    a)  your past employment and business record – identify achievements, not just a chronological statement

    b)  the record of other people working with you

    c)  if there are obvious weaknesses in your management, how you propose to deal with them

*as many pages as needed*

## 4. THE PRODUCT OR SERVICE

    a)  a simple description of what it does (avoid technical words). If essential, technical description can go in an Appendix

    b)  why the product is unique or distinct

    c)  brief survey of competition

    d)  how the products will be developed, what new products are being considered, when replacement will be needed for existing product range, what competitive products may emerge

    e)  any patents applied for

*two pages plus Appendix*

## 5. MARKETING (also crucial)

The market:

    a)  its size, its past and future growth

    b)  analysis of market into sectors; identification of sector your business is aimed at

    c)  likely customers: who are they, type (that is, industrial or consumer, large or small), size, how they buy

*three or four pages (detailed market statistics in Appendix)*

   d)  your competitors: who are they, their size, their position in market, likely response to your challenge

Selling:

   a)  promotion, advertising (if any)

   b)  who will sell

   c)  some idea of your sales pitch (for example, the benefits of your product)

   d)  how you will price

## 6. OPERATIONAL DETAILS

   a)  where you will be based – location, premises

   b)  suppliers

   c)  manufacturing facilities

   d)  equipment needed

length depends on nature of business

## 7. FINANCIAL ANALYSIS

   a)  summary of the forecasts

   b)  monthly profit and loss forecast for two years

   c)  profit forecast for further three years (optional)

   d)  monthly cash flow forecast for two years

   e)  cash flow forecast for further three years (optional)

   f)  forecast balance sheet for two years

   g)  audited accounts for last three years (if available)

   h)  the assumptions behind your forecasts

   i)  what are the principal risks which could affect figures

two or three pages plus figures in Appendix

## 8. THE PROSPECTS

   a)  your objectives – short-term, long-term

   b)  the finance needed and what it is needed for

   c)  shareholdings suggested (if appropriate)

one or two pages

d) prospects for the investor or lender (if
appropriate, including possible value of business
if floated on the stockmarket, so investors will
be able to cash in their investment)

## THE LENGTH OF THE PLAN

In the outline above, suggested maximum lengths for each section are given. If your need for finance is small (£1,000 or £2,000) and your business simple, these would be too long. Probably all you will need for your bank manager is two or three pages plus the financial forecasts – a bit more if it is not your own bank manager. However, if you need a large sum of money, such as £100,000 plus, you may need to put rather more in than the above suggestions. But keep at the forefront of your mind that you need to get across to your reader what is interesting about your business.

One possible way around the conundrum of giving all the necessary information without boring a potential investor would be to include a note of what other figures and data are available, if requested.

## PRESENTING YOUR PLAN

Financiers will assume that if your presentation to them is unsatisfactory, your presentation to customers is equally unsatisfactory. So while it may seem obvious, your plan will look better if it is neatly typed and presented in a smart folder. The information will also be more understandable if you do not try to cram too much on one page. How you should present your plan and who you should approach for money is covered in Chapter 23. 'Raising the money' (p. 282).

## SUMMARY

1. If you want to raise money for your business you will need to have a well-presented, carefully researched business plan to support your request.

2. Producing a business plan also helps you to keep control of your business by allowing you to look at how your actual performance differs from your forecast performance – and forcing you to explain the differences.

3. Preparing the plan can help you clarify your thoughts about the success or failure of your business venture. It can also help highlight in your mind the important steps which need to be taken.

4. Consider whether one plan will suffice for outsiders and inside use, or if two plans will be more helpful to you.

5. Your plan must get across to readers what is interesting about your business. Stress your management ability and demonstrate carefully the market for your product.

6. An ideal format for your plan for outside use is to have between three and ten pages of text which draw out the important points, plus a series of financial figures. Excessive detail should be confined to Appendices.

7. You can get help to produce the plan from an advice agency, an accountant or a corporate finance specialist. It is crucial to try out your plan on someone independent before you try it out on the lenders and investors.

8. Use the checklist on p. 78 to help you decide what should be in your business plan.

9. Your plan should be typed and neatly presented in a folder.

10. Include cash flow forecasts, profit forecasts, and possibly a balance sheet forecast. The more money you wish to raise the more detail your forecasts need to have and the greater period they should cover.

OTHER CHAPTERS TO READ
22. 'Forecasting' (p. 264)
23. 'Raising the money' (p. 282)

# 7. TIMING THE JUMP

Starting a business can be a confusing operation: so many decisions to take, so many actions to carry out. It can be important to keep to the right path. If you fail to take one step when it is necessary, this can delay your start. For example, failing to appreciate the right moment to give up work or to claim the Enterprise Allowance can mean less money and, as a result, you may find the early days more of a financial struggle than they need to be.

## WHAT IS IN THIS CHAPTER?

This chapter should help you keep to the critical path. It is based on fifty-eight steps which need to be taken. Not all of them will apply to every business; you should judge which are crucial for your business and which you will not need to do. Nor is the order sacrosanct in every case. You may find it more convenient to combine two steps and carry them out at the same time, even though one of them does not need critically to be carried out until later. However, the steps should be taken in the approximate order given.

The step-by-step guide has four sections:

- Initial preparation (see below)
- Getting into greater detail (p. 85)
- Setting up (p. 86)
- Ready to trade (p. 87).

## INITIAL PREPARATION

**1.** Carry on in your job, if you are in paid employment; carry on drawing unemployment or supplementary benefit, if unemployed. You can undertake the initial preparation while still doing this (p. 89).

**2.** Analyse your character and abilities. Are you the right person to start on your own? (p. 16).

**3.** Discuss with your family the possibility of starting a business. Are they aware of what it will mean to family life? Will they be committed to it? (p. 67).

**4.** Come up with a shortlist of ideas for a business. Do you have the necessary skills? Does the market look promising, at least initially? (p. 24).

**5.** Briefly define product ideas (p. 25).

**6.** Brush up inadequate skills. Apart from reading the relevant sections of this book, consider training courses and advice agencies (pp. 42, 49).

**7.** Consider whether you should start the business with someone who has complementary skills, that is, who is strong in those skills in which you are weak. Negotiate who gets what share.

**8.** Decide how big a business you want. Will it be large- or small-scale? How much growth potential do your busines ideas have? Do you have the essential management skills to opt for a fast-growth route?

**9.** Did your self-analysis suggest that you needed on-going help? Or have you been unable to come up with a sound business idea? Examine the possibility of buying a franchise. This is only realistic if you have at least 30 per cent of the purchase price (p. 115).

**10.** Investigate the possibilities of buying a business if you have the necessary funds (p. 94).

**11.** Carry out detailed market research into a shortlist of ideas (p.37). Do this whether you are starting from scratch, buying a franchise or buying a business.

**12.** Identify a market sector (p. 29). Establish what will be different about your product (p. 32). Estimate market size, market share, market structure, market trends (p. 34). Investigate competition and their products (p. 35). Forecast amount of sales and timing of sales (p. 36).

**13.** During steps 11 and 12, narrow down possible business ideas to leading prospect.

**14.** Review yourself, your skills, your family, your idea (p. 65). Take decision to proceed, do further work or abandon. It is better to drop the idea now than carry on with doubts.

# GETTING INTO GREATER DETAIL

**15.** Draw up an initial business plan. Forecast sales, costs, cash flows. At this stage, figures will be very approximate (p. 264).

**16.** Make a preliminary decision about your need to raise money. Roughly, how much will you need? Who is the likeliest lender? (p. 287).

**17.** Discuss with your family what you will be able to invest. Consider what security you can offer (p. 287).

**18.** Seek out and employ the professional advisers you need. This could include solicitor, accountant, bank, design consultant, corporate finance adviser (p. 205).

**19.** Decide how much you will spend setting up, but remember to keep a margin of safety. Tailor the amount to how much you are willing to risk yourself, as the funds you can raise will be a multiple of what you can invest.

**20.** If you are currently employed, are you able to give the necessary effort to get the business going? Or do you need the extra income? Consider giving up work.

**21.** Test your product to confirm its performance. Test market your product or service, if possible (p. 40).

**22.** Apply for a patent to protect the product or register the design or trade mark, if applicable (p. 142).

**23.** What form will your business take: sole trader, partnership, cooperative or limited company (p. 51)? If you choose a limited company, decide whether to buy a ready-made company or to form one from scratch.

**24.** Name your product and business (p. 134). Keep in mind what sector of the market you are selling to and what the benefits of the product are. The name is part of your selling effort.

**25.** Register the company name, or change the name of the ready-made company you are buying (p. 61). First, research that there is no other company with that name (p. 138). Sole traders and partnerships need take no action.

**26.** Draw up a partnership agreement, if applicable (p. 61).

**27.** Come up with some initial ideas about letterheads or consider those put forward by design consultant (p. 210).

**28.** Develop ideas about how to sell your product or service. Identify the product benefits and advantages. What means will you use to get your message across: leaflets, brochures etc.? (p. 150).

**29.** Identify possible suppliers. Begin your negotiations.

**30.** Develop a pricing strategy (p. 175).

**31.** Refine a business plan (p. 76). Be pessimistic about sales and costs.

**32.** Ask an adviser or colleague to go through the plan with you, challenging all the assumptions and figures. Are you confident you have identified the principal risks?

**33.** Review the plan yet again. Does the business look viable? Will you go ahead, research further or abandon? Never be afraid of appearing weak by deciding not to go ahead. All the momentum is to push forward because of all the work and commitment put in so far. But, if the idea does not hold water, the right decision is not to proceed but to research something else.

## SETTING UP

**34.** It is now that you need to consider what equipment your business will need. Investigate how to pay for it: cash, hire purchase or leasing (p. 202).

**35.** Establish guidelines on what credit to offer, what credit to take from suppliers, how you will control cash (p. 304).

**36.** Find out what insurance you will need for your business (p. 257).

**37.** Estimate the amount of initial stock and the amount of production run (if applicable).

**38.** Make first approaches about raising money.

**39.** Decide if you will start trading before you raise the money or if you will wait until you have finalized. Remember with complicated finance, it can take several months.

**40.** Register for V A T if you are forced to and, if not, consider whether it would be beneficial (p. 384).

**41.** Set up a simple accounting record system (p. 331).

**42.** Consider what accounting period will be most advantageous from a tax point of view (p. 345), although you do not need to take a decision yet.

**43.** Start the search for premises, if you are not trading from home.

**44.** Finalize your decision about letterheads and order stationery, once you have completed your search for premises and know your business address.

**45.** If you will need staff when you start trading, start the search now.

**46.** Carry on developing your ideas about image (p. 135), how to sell (p. 169) and how to get your message across (p. 150).

**47.** Draw up terms and conditions of sale, if applicable. Set up the sales records (p. 164).

**48.** If you will be selling direct yourself, develop a sales dialogue. Carry out training sessions in the form of a role-play with your husband or wife or a colleague (p. 169).

**49.** Set up a financial control system, that is, how you will compare actual performance with budgeted performance as drawn from business plan.

**50.** Finalize your decision about brochures or literature.

**51.** Draw up contracts of employment for any staff you will be employing.

**READY TO TRADE**

**52.** Finalize premises, fitting out, employing staff, sales methods.

**53.** If you are still employed, hand in your notice. If you are unemployed, claim the Enterprise Allowance from the start of trading.

**54.** Inform the Inland Revenue if you are going to be a sole trader or partner (p. 60).

**55.** Inform the DHSS of your decision to start your own business.

**56.** If you are forming a company, ask the Inland Revenue for information on how to operate the PAYE tax system (p. 244).

**57.** Set up a reporting system for your staff, if you will be employing several.

**58.** Plan the opening.

## SUMMARY

1. Use this step-by-step guide to help you start your business in the right way.

2. The guide is in approximate order; in particular, actions may vary depending on whether you decide to postpone trading until you have raised the money you need.

# 8.  TOE-DIPPING

Toe-dipping might apply to two sorts of people. First, you might have some sort of business idea but be uncertain whether you want to give up your present paid employment to commit yourself to surviving on your idea. It may strike you as a good idea to test the water a little bit in your spare time or to find out more about the idea before you commit yourself further (see below, TESTING THE WATER). The second sort of person who could be interested in toe-dipping might be someone who has to stay at home, for example to look after dependants, children or elderly parents (see p. 90, PERMANENT TOE-DIPPING). If this is the case, the amount of time you can devote to your enterprise could be fairly limited. So, you need to be realistic and select a suitable type of business (p. 90).

## TESTING THE WATER

There are quite a few drawbacks to trying out your business idea without devoting all your time to developing it. If you are in full-time employment, you will be trying to carry out your business in the evenings or weekends, when you are tired. You will need an awful lot of energy to keep going. The result may be that you give up simply because you are too weary.

The second drawback is closely linked. Because you do not have the time your business idea needs, you will not carry it out successfully; you will assess it a failure because it has not achieved what you hoped. The real reason may be that you have not stoked the fire enough.

The third drawback is that there are not very many businesses which you can start only in the evenings and weekends, because they are not natural business hours for anyone else. Telephone answering machines do not always provide the solution. The best you can do is to have the phone manned as much as possible.

The big advantage of toe-dipping is that you carry on earning money from your job while you are starting up. This may be essential if you have no other income coming in, as your business is unlikely to provide you with an income for some time.

The model way of testing the water is not necessarily to start full trading while still employed elsewhere, but to use your spare time to carry out all your market research and prepare your business plan during this period. When the initial preparation is completed, you should be able to assess whether your business idea will work and have some idea of when you should be generating an income to live on. Now would be the time to cease full-time employment. One possibility at that point is to try to raise some money to fund the business, but obviously this is not a step to be taken lightly.

## PERMANENT TOE-DIPPING

Your motivation may be quite different; you may not be attempting to start a full-time business at all. You may simply want to earn more money on the side. You may be in full-time employment or you may have domestic responsibilities. In either case the number of hours available for business is limited. And that is the way it is going to stay, at least in the foreseeable future.

You will need a very special sort of business idea. The ideal trade should allow you to fit the work into odd or irregular hours and should not need a permanent presence. Some suitable ideas include:

• *fashion and beauty:* hairdressing, beauty, therapy, dressmaking, fashion design, knitting, invisible mending and alterations

• *office services:* book-keeping, typing, word processing, duplicating, addressing and stuffing envelopes, data preparation, printing

• *writing:* books and articles, translating, copy-editing, proof-reading, indexing

• *arts and crafts:* drawing, illustrating, photography, picture framing, candlemaking, glass engraving, jewellery, pottery, soft toys and dolls, design work

• *home-based activities:* catering and cooking, upholstery, childminding, curtain making, garden produce, taking lodgers, rearing animals (goats, poultry, bees, rabbits), boarding animals

• *assembly work:* toys, lampshades, clothes, Christmas crackers, fire extinguishers, watch straps, jewellery and so on

• *miscellaneous:* teaching (music, exam coaching), repairing (bicycles, china, clocks), agents (mail order, party plan organizer, telephone selling), dealing, building, decorating, electrical repairs, car maintenance, light removals, odd jobs, physiotherapy.

## TOE-DIPPING: WHAT YOU NEED TO KNOW

### STARTING UP

You have to follow exactly the same steps as you would if you were starting in business in a big way. Read Chapter 7. 'Timing the jump' (p. 83). The key steps are:
Establishing your market: your customers and competitors (Chapter 2)
Defining what you are selling (Chapter 2)
Sorting out your suppliers (Chapter 24)
Deciding whether you are a company, sole trader or partnership (Chapter 4)
Planning where to work (Chapter 16)
Organizing your records (Chapter 27)
Preparing your business plan (Chapter 6)
Sorting out finance (Chapter 23).

### TAX

Tax on spare-time earnings is covered in Chapter 31. (p. 379). You will see there are some definite steps to take to present your business in the most advantageous way from a tax point of view.

One particular problem which is faced by people earning money at home is the peril of working for only one business. This may be the case with outworkers or homeworkers assembling things, or doing typing or knitting and so on. If you work mainly for one company, you may be classified as an employee and your tax treatment will be less favourable. On p. 380, there is a list of the sort of things your tax inspector will look for in deciding whether you are employed or self-employed.

### ORGANIZING YOUR WORKPLACE

Most toe-dippers work from home. This has several advantages:

- it is free
- it involves no travelling
- the work can be combined with any domestic tasks to be done
- there are no fares or lunches to be bought
- you can wear what you like

• it protects your house from burglars.

However, working from home involves an extraordinary amount of self-discipline. It is all too easy to find some domestic job that needs doing. It can also be frustrating to have your work interrupted by callers or other members of the family. And your work never goes away; you cannot leave it behind when you walk out of the office door. This can lead to extra worry.

Good organization is the key to being able to work successfully at home. Your work space needs to be separate from the rest of the house; a room is ideal, but a corner set aside for work is better than nothing.

You should also try to be strict about the time set aside for work. Try to start at a definite time each day, even if it means leaving the washing-up until later. Persuade friends that you are serious about your work and you will be hard at it between certain times, so that they restrict social calls to outside those hours.

Working from a home which you own may mean that some capital gains tax will be due, when you sell it. But you should be able to organize things so that this does not happen (p. 356).

FAMILY SUPPORT

It will be difficult to succeed in your business if you do not have the support of your household: your husband or wife and your children. Before you start, get their cooperation and help.

## SUMMARY

1. Trying to start a business while still in a job can lead to failure. Instead, use the time while you are employed to do the basic research about the market and your likely sales and costs. After this, decide whether to take the plunge or not.

2. If you know that you only want spare-time earnings, not a full-time business, choose your business idea carefully to allow you to fit it in with other commitments.

3. Follow Chapter 7. 'Timing the jump' (p. 83) to set up, even if it is to be only a spare-time business.

4. Working at home needs careful organization of your workspace and working hours.

OTHER CHAPTERS TO READ

# 9. OFF THE PEG

At some stage in thinking about your business ideas, it probably flickers across your mind that it would all be much simpler if you could buy a ready-made business. Your reasoning might be that this would get you off to a flying start and cut down the period of hard work needed to establish a business from scratch.

But would it? The truth is that there is no easy way to having your own business. Either you must accept that there is a hard slog ahead of you, building up your own business, or, if you decide to buy an established business, you must expect to pay for someone else's work in having built it up successfully. What is more, if you decide to buy, you might end up paying too much for a business which still needs you to work very long hours. If you want to buy a ready-made business because you think it will be easier, you should seriously examine your motives in wanting to take on the responsibility of your own business.

The real temptation to buy a business from someone else is that you might buy a bargain, perhaps because the owner is desperate to sell, or because the business has been run badly and you can see a few easily applied steps which could transform its profitability.

There are three main ways you can get yourself off to a flying start. You can do this by buying:

- a franchise (p. 115)

- into a partnership (p. 99)

- an established business.

This chapter looks closely at buying an established business or buying into a partnership. Franchises are dealt with separately in the next chapter.

WHAT IS IN THIS CHAPTER?

- How to search for a business, a step-by-step guide (p. 95)

- The business profile you want (what you are searching for) (p. 95)

- Finding a business for sale (p. 96)

- Investigation (pp. 98–106)

- How will your ownership change the business? (p. 106)
- Setting a price (p. 107)
- Tips on negotiation (p. 111)
- Management buy-outs (a brief guide) (p. 113)

## HOW TO SEARCH FOR A BUSINESS, A STEP-BY-STEP GUIDE

1. If you are already in business, pinpoint your overall objectives, the missing factors in your present business and what is holding back growth.

2. Develop a profile of the sort of business you are interested in acquiring – either all of it or a stake (see below).

3. Carry out the same market research as you would do if starting a business from scratch (p. 28).

4. Research the businesses available for sale and produce a shortlist of the likely contenders (p. 96).

5. Investigate the shortlist of businesses carefully (p. 98).

6. Consider what effect your purchase would have on the business (p. 106).

7. Establish a price for the business; or, better still, a price to open the negotiation and a maximum price you would consider paying (p. 107).

8. Plan the negotiation carefully (p. 111).

## THE BUSINESS PROFILE YOU WANT

You should try to avoid the random search for a business to buy or a good deal to make. If you were starting your own business, you would set out your thoughts and ideas. This is exactly what you should do when considering which sort of business you could run successfully if you were to buy one already set up.

To help clarify your thoughts, it is a good idea to write down in specific terms a profile of the ideal business. This should include the following, among other points:

- the ideal market (or even more specifically, the segment). This choice should follow from a review of your own skills (p. 69), coupled with some market research which should enable you to pinpoint a market providing you with the opportunities any successful business needs. See Chapter 2. 'Who will buy?' (p. 28)

- the products or services which fulfil this marketing strategy

- your view of the main factors in a business which could enable you to be successful

- the price of the business, the maximum you could pay and how that would be financed

- the ideal size of the business you are looking for

- where it would best be located (for business and personal reasons)

- whether the business needs to be successful already or whether you are looking for a company which your extra management skills could render profitable

- the minimum level of profitability you could accept and the minimum level of income you require from the business.

Once you have drawn up this profile, you should use it to judge the suitability and likelihood of success of all the prospective businesses you could buy. On the whole, do not be tempted to abandon the principles enshrined in your profile, because you see what you think will be a bargain. It is safer to adhere to the outline you elucidated in a calm, rational manner when you were not under any pressure to do a deal.

## FINDING A BUSINESS FOR SALE

There are two basic approaches which you can adopt; these are not mutually exclusive. You can:

- look at businesses which the owner is advertising for sale

- search out suitable businesses which the owner may not have decided to sell, but which fit your profile.

The advantage of the second method is that you may be more likely to find the business you want; the disadvantage is that you may not be able to persuade the owner to sell, certainly at a realistic price. If you carry out this research, be prepared for several false starts.

## WHERE ARE BUSINESSES ADVERTISED FOR SALE?

There are several sources:

● newspapers and magazines. The Small Business pages of the *Financial Times*, *The Times* and the *Guardian* include many businesses for sale. If you are looking locally, your local newspaper may have a section for this. Other possible sources include *Dalton's Weekly* and the *London Weekly Advertiser*.

The details given in the advertisements will be very brief; it may only include the market, the general location and some indication of the income from a business. Note that a number of the advertisers may be the receivers of the business, trying to sell it as a going concern. If the advertisement is by a liquidator, the aim will be to sell off the assets or bits of the business, as it will not be possible to sell as a going concern because there is no goodwill

● business transfer agents and estate agents will carry details of small businesses for sale; estate agents will be mainly concerned with retail businesses. You can find the names and addresses of agents in the area you are interested in by looking in Yellow Pages. These agents are not independent advisers but acting on behalf of the business being sold

● asking around in the area you want. Try accountants, solicitors and banks. These sometimes maintain a register of businesses for sale. You can also try someone already in the industry for ideas of who might be for sale. Advertise in the local newspaper or trade magazine for a business you want.

### CONDUCTING A SEARCH FOR A BUSINESS

Apart from following up all the sources listed above, is it possible to identify other possible businesses not yet put up for sale? Yes, by studying the market segment you want to enter. Carry out market research into that sector, identify the competitors and investigate the backgrounds. You may well find that the businesses already for sale are the worst buys. On the whole, go for what you want and not for what is available.

Some useful sources of information include:

- accountants
- the membership lists of relevant trade associations
- Yellow Pages
- Extel cards for unlisted companies
- trade exhibitions
- trade journals and magazines for articles on new products and services.

## INVESTIGATION

Once you have a shortlist of two or three businesses you could be interested in, the next step is to investigate thoroughly and then to investigate all over again. It is crucial to be absolutely confident that you know all the pitfalls, as well as the good points of the business you are buying. Do not be hurried into negotiation and acquisition for fear of losing that so-called bargain.

Investigation is largely a question of using your common sense and being very distrustful about what you are buying. Guidance in this section is very much of the 'Don't forget to do this or that' or 'Look out for. . .', but it cannot be an exhaustive list of what you must do. There are also specific investigations which need to be made for each business you look at; some of these will be exclusive to that business.

### WHAT HELP CAN YOU GET WITH AN INVESTIGATION?

It would be wise to employ an independent adviser to help you analyse a potential purchase. The most likely candidate for the role of adviser will be an accountant, as a considerable part of the investigation will be analysing existing accounts and assessing asset values.

However, accountants may be expert at the quantitative aspects of a business but miss the qualitative aspects, such as how crucial present employees are to the business. Help and advice from someone in the industry can be invaluable.

### WHY IS THE BUSINESS BEING SOLD?

This can be difficult to establish satisfactorily. For example, if it is being sold because the present owner doubts that it will prove to be profitable in the future, you are not likely to be told this. Your investigation of the business prospects must try to identify this sort of reason.

The most likely cause of a sale is that the owner wishes to retire. If this is the case, you need to keep your eyes open for signs that the business is running out of steam as the owner's retirement nears. It is also possible that the business and its equipment are now out of date.

Sometimes you may come across small businesses which are being sold by larger companies. The reason given may be that it does not fit with the strategy or pattern of the larger business. The real reason may be because the large company cannot make it profitable, so you need to look for the warning signs. Look carefully at the past history and what accounting policies have been used.

If the business is in the hands of a receiver, it will be advertised for sale as a going concern. You cannot take for granted that this is so. Investigation needs to pinpoint whether the assets are actually owned by the owner, whether any genuine goodwill exists and, obviously, the reasons for the financial difficulties.

A sale for any of these reasons may present opportunities for the right business person. The ability to turn round a run-down or unprofitable business is a management and business skill, which you may possess. The important point in acquisition is to know the real reason for the sale before you negotiate to buy. Then you can price the business correctly and assess the impact you could make, post-purchase.

WHAT IS BEING SOLD?

What you are buying depends on the legal form of the business. If you want to buy a business operated by a sole trader or partnership, you are strictly buying its assets, excluding what the previous owner owed and was owed. You could buy all or only some of the assets. If the business has traded under a different name, not the owner's personal name, you might consider buying the right to carry on using this. This is a wise decision only if there is some goodwill attached to the business name. Your agreement to buy should be very specific about the assets you buy and the price you pay.

On the other hand, if the business is a limited company it has a life of its own, separate from the shareholders. In this case, you could be buying only assets or you could be buying the company itself. If it is the latter, as the new owner you will acquire a business which has obligations and liabilities, such as contracts and debts, as well as assets.

PARTNERSHIPS

An added ingredient if you are buying a share in a partnership is the necessity to investigate the prospective partner (or partners). All the other business aspects – for example, track record, business prospects, assets – need careful study, but it is also essential to find out what you can about the partners. This is for two reasons.

First, as a partner you are jointly and severally liable for the debts of the partnership. In practice, what this means is that if there are bills to be paid and your partners do not pay up their share, either because they do not have the assets to cover the debts or because they refuse, you can be made to pay for the whole debt, not just your share of it. You must satisfy yourself that the new partners hold some assets which would cover the likely value of their share of any debts and find out their track record of paying bills. A history of unpaid bills or lack of assets of any value (for example, not owning a house) might raise question marks in your mind about their suitability as partners.

Second, the ability to co-exist amicably in a partnership is crucial. Personality conflicts can be crippling and may mean, whatever the economic sense of the proposed partnership, that the future of the business would be in a jeopardy.

If you are buying a share in a partnership in which there are already two or more partners, be prepared for the negotiation to take a long time. Two or more people have to agree; it is not just one person deciding, as would be the case if you were buying from a sole trader.

Use a solicitor to help you draw up a written partnership agreement or to vet the one offered to you by the partnership (see p. 61 for an idea of what needs to be covered). It might be wise to attach a note to the partnership agreement which would cover areas such as how the business is to be run, who has responsibility for what, what is the extent of the decision-making for each partner and so on. These are not strictly part of a written formal agreement, but it is crucial that each of you has a clear understanding of how the business will be run.

## THE ACCOUNTS

The past accounts of the business are written evidence of what has happened in the last few years. But how good is the evidence? The minimum you should insist on seeing is the accounts for the last three years; these should be handed over to your accountant for stringent analysis. However, there are some points you should bear in mind. If the business is a sole trader or partnership, accounts do not have to be audited. Indeed, the only reason that accounts need to be prepared is for tax purposes, and the accounts need only be a statement of sales and expenses; a balance sheet is not necessarily required. The evidence about the track record could be decidedly patchy and even inaccurate.

The fact that the accounts are prepared for tax purposes may suggest that the sales are understated; indeed, vendors may claim just that. But you should be wary of accepting that profits are really higher than stated in the accounts.

Once your accountant has examined the accounts thoroughly, you should begin questioning whether there are any specific reasons why, for example, the profits were high during the period reviewed. Was there no competition? If so, is there now? If the business is retail, has the pattern of shopping facilities altered to make the location less attractive now than formerly? Will there be a rent review, with a likely increase in rent, which will make a dent in future profits? And so on. Query anything which you think might have affected the results of the present owner, favourably or unfavourably.

## LAND AND BUILDINGS

With land and buildings you need to consider the following points:

• *position:* this is particularly important for shops. You need to study a shop's location very carefully. What are the other shops in the immediate area selling? Direct competition need not be a disadvantage, as customers sometimes like to have a choice and will go to a location with two or more shops selling similar products. The population of the shop's immediate catchment area could be crucial to the success of the business; you should not assume that you can persuade people to travel far to your particular store. What sort of population lives near by? Is there high unemployment? Are inhabitants likely to have high purchasing power?

The future plans for the area, if any, need to be discovered. Are there any redevelopments planned? Any road changes mooted? The effect of these needs to be considered.

An important consideration for many types of retail business is how many potential customers will pass the shop each day, for example, on the way to work, to do other shopping. Test this out for yourself by standing outside the shop on days which are likely to be busy for the business and on days likely to be quiet

• *tenure:* if the property is not freehold, what are the terms of the lease? For how much longer does the present lease run? When is the next rent review due and is there any indication of the likely increase? Who has the responsibility for maintaining the exterior of the building? Check that the seller has the right to transfer the lease. Would you be able to sell or sublet at some future date?

● *condition:* pay for a survey to be carried out to establish the extent of your likely bills for the property. Run your eye over the decoration and shop or office fittings. Are there any improvements you could make which would improve the potential of the property and what would these cost?

● *space:* what is the useful selling space? Is this sufficient to stock the quantity and range of goods you intend to carry? Will there be any surplus space? Could this be used profitably – by you or some other business?

● *insurance:* what insurance currently covers the property? Is this relatively expensive or cheap?

● *valuation:* take expert advice on the value of the property. You should also ask your solicitor to check the title, any covenants which apply and the likelihood of planning changes.

PLANT AND EQUIPMENT

With plant and equipment you need to cover the following points at least:

● *condition:* is the plant and equipment old or badly maintained? Is the technology outdated? What volume of business or production levels could the equipment deal with? Can it cope with periods of maximum demand?

● *value:* this can be a problem to establish to both vendor's and buyer's satisfaction. The vendor may well seek to be paid a value based on the cost of the equipment. As a potential buyer, you need to look closely at the market value, as this may well be less than cost. Indeed, if the equipment can be used in that business only, the market value may be very low, although the value to this business may well be higher than that. You will have to negotiate a price

● *future commitments:* if you are buying a company, you should investi-gate what capital expenditure has been contracted for which you would be responsible. This may also apply to any advertising expenditure to which the company is committed.

STOCK

Stock is likely to be the major area of disappointment after a purchase.

Opt for ruthless reductions in the value in the accounts or make an agreement to buy, subject to certain conditions being met, if you can. Check the following points at least:

● *how much:* first of all, establish that the amount of stock in the business agrees with the figure in the accounts (particularly if you are buying the business, not just selected assets). Once you have established how much stock there is, you need to analyse whether this is the right amount and the right sort for that business. Get guidance on the mix of stock from an expert in the industry.

Be wary of buying too much stock, even at apparent bargain prices. Keep an eye out for any outdated or damaged stock as well.

You should also check if the business has had a proper stock control system. If it has not, this should raise questions about quoted amounts. It can also be worthwhile to find out whether it is possible to return any stock items to suppliers

● *value:* as with plant and equipment, it is likely that the seller will hope to be paid the higher of cost or market value for the business stock. You, on the other hand, may only be willing to settle for the lower of cost or market value (and that may be a very low figure indeed). You should not deviate far from your value of the stock.

DEBTORS: THE CUSTOMERS WHO OWE YOU MONEY

Your investigation should cover:

● *how old?* your main query about debtors must be: 'Will they pay and when?' Ask the seller for what is known as an age analysis of debts. This should show how much is owed and how long it has been owing. Very old bills may suggest that they will not be paid; or may simply suggest that the owner is very dilatory about collecting money. Whichever it is, you need to know

● *credit rating:* the analysis of debtors should pinpoint which customers owe the larger sums. Assuming that you were to keep these customers if you purchased the business, it is worth checking the credit backgrounds of those businesses (p. 308). You do not want to buy a business which relies heavily on a few customers who are bad payers

● *credit collection:* investigate how the existing owner collected debts. An improvement in this could enhance the profitability of the business

● *value:* once you have made a careful analysis of unlikely payers and allowed for the cost of collecting the debts, you should be able to arrive at an estimate of the value of the debtors.

## OTHER ASSETS

There are a range of other assets which the business may hold:

- *cash:* confirm the level with the bank or wherever the cash is held

- *patents, trademarks, etc.:* investigate their status, for example, is the trademark registered? You should find out what would happen to these 'intangible assets' if the business should fail. They may prove to be unrealizable assets if the rights revert to their original owner, for example

- *investments:* if the business holds investments, perhaps in other companies, your accountant should ensure that an appropriate value is placed on them

- *goodwill:* the price you will eventually fix is unlikely to be the sum of the values you set on the individual assets. Negotiation may well result in a price above the asset value. The surplus is known as goodwill.

Goodwill can also be described as the reputation of the business and what you are paying to acquire that reputation. Valuing goodwill is a very uncertain process. Will the goodwill disappear once the present owner is no longer part of the business? Will customers and suppliers stay with the business on the same terms, assuming those to be satisfactory?

## LIABILITIES: WHAT THE BUSINESS OWES

The main liabilities to be investigated are:

- *loans, debentures and overdrafts:* establish the amount, the conditions, the period of the loans and the interest rate. This should be fairly easy to sort out

- *creditors:* an examination of an age analysis of creditors should give you some idea of the sort of credit periods suppliers have been extending to the business in the past. If the business has paid very slowly, it may suggest that its reputation with suppliers is fairly low.

## SALES

To achieve an estimate of the potential of the business, you will need to look carefully at the sales figures. Carry out a product or service analysis. Does one product account for the vast bulk of the sales? What is the profit margin on this product? Does your analysis suggest scope for stream-lining the product list?

Your study of the debtors will also have thrown up information about the customer structure. Does the business rely on one or a few customers? Do those customers account for the major portion of the profits as well as the sales? An over-reliance on a few can mean the business may be fairly risky and prone to sudden downturns should a customer cease using the product.

Crucial information about sales potential can be ascertained by talks with the major customers. These may throw light on the quality and reputation of the business and product. Further evidence can be obtained by a study of the level and nature of credit notes and a study of the per-centage of sub-standard goods produced.

Look for any special relationships which exist with major customers, such as an extended credit or returns arrangement.

Other aspects of the sales figure you should study include:

- the element of windfall sales, which are unlikely to be repeated

- the sales by territory or area

- the pricing and discount structure

- the distribution of the product

- competition

- the seasonality

- the existence of fixed price or fixed volume contracts, particularly if buying a company.

## THE PRODUCTS

If the business is the manufacture or distribution of a product, you will need to find out more about it. The areas you should concentrate on are:

- *cost:* ask yourself if there are any reasons why the costs should rise or fall in the near future. Have there been any changes in the prices of raw materials and are there seasonal variations? Is there a shortage of skilled labour to make the product? Are there any changes likely to the suppliers? Are there any key supplies which need careful management?

- *profit margin:* an examination should also be made of the cost of each individual product compared to its price. Do all the products cover direct

costs and make a contribution to overheads? Which gives the highest
contribution and which the lowest? What is the pricing policy? Have
discounts been offered? Turn to Chapter 25. 'How to increase profits'
(p. 317) for information about profit margins, contribution and overheads and Chapter 15. 'How to set a price' (p. 175) for pricing

● *orders:* if it is a company, what is the amount of advance orders? Will
these all be retained if ownership of the company changes hands?

### EMPLOYEES

If the present owner has staff, you will have to find out what your
obligations will be to them if you buy the business. If the owner is a sole
trader and you are buying some of the assets, there will probably be no
legal obligation to offer continued employment; but there may be if you
are carrying on the business. If the business is a company, you will most
likely have legal obligations to the employees. This is particularly
important if it is your intention to replace the staff or make them
redundant on change of ownership. You will need to ask your solicitor for
advice.

Even more crucial than the legal responsibilities for employees can be
the extent to which the business relies on key personnel. You need to
understand their calibre, attitudes and responsibilities – before the deal.
It is vital to sustain their enthusiasm and commitment through the period
of ownership change.

## HOW WILL YOUR OWNERSHIP CHANGE
## THE BUSINESS?

Finding out what has happened in the business in the last few years and
what changes are likely to occur as a result of external factors does not
give you a complete picture. It ignores the fact that you intend buying the
business and have some ideas of how it could be improved. You need to
consider what changes you would like to impose on the business, what
they might cost and what improvement in profits you estimate they would
make.

Realistically, you should also recognize that a change in ownership may
mean lower profits rather than higher. This might occur if the business is
heavily dependent on personal contacts. The previous owner may have
established an extensive network of relationships which means that, in a
shop, for example, a substantial proportion of the customers come

because of the owner's personality rather than because of its location, its prices or its range of goods. No matter how confident you are that you will handle customers courteously and cheerfully, you may not have that magic ingredient your predecessor possessed. Some customers may drift elsewhere, certainly initially at least.

On the other hand, you may estimate that, in a business where personality is important, the previous owner has not been ideally suited to the nature of the work and that you will be able to bring a change for the better because of your own character.

Other changes you may introduce are more tangible and you will be able to estimate the effect and cost of their introduction. The three main ways you can increase profits are by:

- cutting costs
- increasing prices
- selling more.

Chapter 25. 'How to increase profits' (p. 317) may give you some ideas.

Some changes may involve you in spending money, for example, redecorating or refitting a shop, reorganizing the production facilities, buying new equipment, restocking. Include the cost of these intended improvements in the initial cost of acquiring the business. This allows you to set a realistic price which you can pay for the business.

## SETTING A PRICE

The right price for any business does not exist as a theoretical calculation. The only price which is 'right' is the price which both the buyer will pay and the seller will accept. It is all down to negotiation. This may bear no relation to the prices calculated as a result of the value of the assets or the earnings potential which the business gives you. The first step is to jettison all notions about real value. The second step is to throw out of the window all notions that the price given in the agent's details, for example, is the price you will have to pay. Negotiation is everything.

However, you should enter any negotiation with two prices in mind. If you are the buyer, the lower price will be the price you use to open the negotiation; the higher price is the maximum you will be willing to pay. You should not start negotiating unless you have a clear idea of this maximum price. If you are the seller, the lower price is the minimum you will accept for the business and the higher price, the one you adopt initially.

Nevertheless, it is vital to have used a number of methods of arriving at a price. These can give you a benchmark for establishing lower and upper prices. You must have a base point to work from. The accountant who is advising you should carry out these calculations for you, but you should know the basis for the figures. The three commonest ways of setting a value are:

- asset value

- earnings multiple

- return on capital employed.

### ASSET VALUE

Your investigation (pp. 98, 106) will have helped you set values for individual assets. If you are buying the whole business or it is a company, the figure you are interested in is the net asset value, that is, value of the assets less the value of the liabilities. There is no rule on whether you should use the cost of the asset or its market value as a basis for your price estimate. It is a question of judgement, although you will be wise to choose the lower of the two.

The final value agreed upon between buyer and seller is unlikely to be a simple sum of the individual assets; any additional value is called goodwill (p. 104).

If property forms a major part of the business, you may automatically think that the price you pay is asset value. However, it is very important to look at what sort of profits those assets will be able earn for you. See the example in th box on the right.

### EARNINGS MULTIPLE

A second way of valuing a business is to apply some multiple to the earnings from the business, perhaps two or three times. Clearly, you will not take the present owner's figures for earnings at face value; apart from investigating whether they are a fair reflection of what has happened, you also need to take into account in your calculations what interest charges you would be paying after the purchase of the business. This should include loans for any improvements you intend making. See the example in the box on p. 110.

*Example*

George Gabriel is interested in buying a shop. He has seen one business, a health food store, in which he is particularly interested. The details he has been given are:

Price for the freehold of the shop plus the flat above   £55,000
Price for the stock   £6,500
Goodwill   £4,000

In total, he is being asked to pay £65,500.

George needs to carry out his own investigation. First, he looks at the shop. The size is reasonable (500 sq ft) for a specialized business and the location is excellent. However, the shop has been fitted in an idiosyncratic way, not especially suitably for the type of business. Although the condition of the fittings is good, George would want to replace them; in particular, he would like to include facilities for serving take-away food, including hot food, which the shop does not have at present. He estimates that the cost of these alterations will be around £8,000, of which £3,000 is for the additional food facilities.

When it comes to the living accommodation, this seems in reasonable condition. He asks a valuer to give some idea of what an alternative 3-bedroom flat would cost in the area and is given an estimate of £20,000 to £25,000.

A close examination of the stock reveals that some of it is damaged but, most importantly there are very big stocks of a few slow-moving items. George would place a value of only £2,000 on the stock acceptable to him. Nor is he convinced that there is that much goodwill associated with the business; the present owner's odd personality has militated against this.

George's value for the business based on asset values would be:

£55,000 less £5,000 fittings which need replacing
plus £2,000 for the stock.

This makes £52,000 for the business, rather than the £65,500 asked.

*Example*

George Gabriel (see the example on p. 109) now works out a value for the business based on an earnings multiple. He has been told that the present owner derived an income of £18,000 from the business. George estimates that, with the improvements he intends, he can increase this figure to £20,000 in the first year; he hopes to push it up to £25,000 subsequently.

George has £45,000 of his own; he intends to spend £2,500 on extra stock plus £8,000 on improvements. This leaves £34,500 towards the purchase of the business. He'll have to borrow the rest of the purchase price – an additional £17,500 if he buys the business for the valuation above. At an interest rate of 10 per cent, this means interest charges of £1,750 a year.

So George's earnings figure for the last year would be:

£18,000 – £1,750 = £16,250

And for the current year:

£20,000 – £1,750 = £18,250

And once the shop has reached its full potential:

£25,000 – £1,750 = £23,250

These figures give the following values of the business:

2 times multiple: £32,500, £36,500, £46,500
3 times multiple: £48,750, £54,750, £69,750

For negotiation, George should refer to the past year's earnings figure only and go for the two times multiple. This gives a much lower figure for valuation than the asset value basis does. In fact, the range of values he obtains suggests that, on the whole, the asset value basis will result in a figure which is too high for him to get the return he needs on his investment. From these figures, his negotiation should start at £32,500 and go no higher than £55,000, say.

There are a couple of other factors which might influence his decision; one increases the value he would be willing to pay, the other lowers it. These are:

• the savings he will obtain from living above the shop, for example, mortgage payments or rent

• the loss of interest his £45,000 was earning.

RETURN ON CAPITAL EMPLOYED

To assess value on this basis you need to decide in advance on a rate of return which you require on the money you invest. This should certainly be more than the rate of interest you could get from leaving your money in a building society account. Once you have decided, you work out what the income before interest and tax is as a percentage of the capital invested. If the figure you get as a result of this calculation is less than your required rate, you would decide not to buy or to lower the figure you were prepared to pay until the return equals your required return.

## TIPS ON NEGOTIATION

The negotiation is the key to future prosperity. This may well be the only time you are involved in negotiating to buy a business, so there is no opportunity to practice negotiating skills. But negotiation must be done if you are to buy the business at the right price for you.

Here are some negotiating tips:

1. An obvious point, but do not agree to the price first quoted.

2. Open the negotiation at the lowest price you can. This price must be one which you can back up with credible reasons, so a good deal of planning is needed before negotiation begins. A shock opening bid can lower the seller's expectations and undermine resolve.

3. Look carefully at apparent bargains. If the seller accepts your first low bid, perhaps given the seller's better knowledge, your opening price was too high. Think again.

4. During the negotiation you can undermine the opposition's confidence by asking a lot of 'what if' questions. Some examples, which may or may not be relevant to the business you are considering, include 'What if the next government is Conservative/Labour?' 'What if your major customer goes bankrupt?'

5. Do not fall into the trap of making a concession for the sake of the goodwill of the negotiation. The opposition will most likely strengthen his or her resolve to hold out for the highest price possible.

6. Do not answer questions of how much you can afford to pay, at least until you wish to use it as a negotiating tactic at an appropriate time. Answering the question at the timing of the seller's choice may lead you

into discussion of helping you foot the bill by loans or easy instalments. Later you can use what you can afford as a limit on price.

**7.** Sometimes, you will find that if you start out as a tough negotiator, the reaction from the other side is a soft response. A tough reply to a tough opener is more unusual.

**8.** Never be offensive and over-critical, it simply draws a defensive response.

**9.** Keep your reactions very low-key; never indicate whether the news is good or bad. Keep calm.

**10.** If the other side makes a concession, do not feel you must respond in kind. Stay tough. There is no law that if you make an agreement with the seller, the agreement should be mid-way between the two initial positions. On the contrary, the purpose of negotiation is to try and make sure the pendulum swings your way.

**11.** If you are probing for solutions which will allow you and the seller to agree, always begin your possible concessions with 'If'.

**12.** Planning your arguments and rehearsing them before the negotiation will give you confidence in the strength of your bargaining power.

**13.** Try role-playing before the negotiation occurs with a colleague or wife acting as an objectionable seller.

**14.** Whatever the treatment meted out by the seller, do not let it get to you and your confidence in your own bargaining position. Do not be affected by the other's apparent wealth, status, success or attitude.

**15.** The best way to counter any threat is to indicate that you are indifferent to it being carried out. Making threats yourself can be unproductive.

**16.** If it is possible to produce some outside authority who limits your bargaining position, do so. This could be your wife, your partner or the person lending you money.

**17.** Keep in mind whether the goodwill of the previous owner is needed after the change of ownership.

**18.** It is often useful to link part of the price to future performance. This reduces the risk of failure against forecast.

## BRIEF GUIDE TO MANAGEMENT BUY-OUTS

In recent years, there has been a growing number of management teams buying out and running the business in which they were previously employed. There are three main occasions when this occurs.

First, a large organization decides to sell or close down a subsidiary. This could be because:

• the business does not fit the strategy of the organization

• the business does not give the rate of return required by the organization, or it could even be unprofitable

• the parent company does not have the resources to provide the funds needed by the business or it simply needs to raise cash.

Second, a private company may want to sell out *in toto*. This may be for personal reasons, such as the family not wanting to run the business any longer or the need for cash.

Third, the company may have gone into receivership. There may be a part of the business which could be profitable if separated.

Raising money is likely to be the major problem for a management buy-out, as the management team is unlikely to be able to finance more than 10–20 per cent of the business. There is also a need to raise the money quickly before the opportunity slips. Lenders and investors will want to go through the same process as with any investment or lending decision (see Chapter 23. 'Raising the money' (p. 282)).

## SUMMARY

1. Do not be tempted into paying too much to buy a ready-made business because you want your business life to get off to a flying start.

2. Clarify your thoughts about the market you want to enter, the size of business you want to run, the type of product or service you want to offer and how much you want to pay *before* you start searching for a business to buy. Summarize it in a business profile.

3. Consider seeking out a business which fits your profile as well as investigating all those currently advertised for sale.

4. Use independent advisers to help you investigate a partnership or business.

5. Adopt a sceptical approach to investigation; query and question everything about the business.

6. Be realistic about the effect of a change in ownership; there could be changes for the worse as well as the better.

7. Set two prices before you go into negotiation; the lower one with which you start the bidding, a higher price beyond which you will not go.

8. Negotiation is everything. There are no rules; there is no right price for any business. It is up to you to summon your facts and marshal your arguments to keep the price as low as possible.

9. Use the negotiation tips listed above.

OTHER CHAPTERS TO READ

# 10. FRANCHISES

It would be lovely if there were a way you could start your own business with a much greater chance of survival than most people. And this is just what is claimed by the franchising industry. The statistics seem to back this up, although they are rather patchy. What information is available suggests that a franchised business has a much greater chance of surviving the first three years (the danger years) than other new businesses.

Clearly you don't get something for nothing. The price of choosing the franchised route can be high. It is up to you to weigh up the costs of buying a franchise and the risks of starting from scratch.

Some of the costs are obvious; you may have to pay a lump sum at the outset as well as paying an amount each year to the person selling the franchise. Less obvious is the cost if you buy a franchise in which you have to buy products from the seller's company at a price determined by it; in this way, you cannot benefit from shopping around to buy your supplies at the cheapest possible price.

One of the economic theories behind the success of franchising is that the franchised business can earn for the product as a whole, higher-than-normal profits. The intention of the seller of the franchise is to cream off the above-normal bit of the profits, for example, by charging a percentage of sales each year, leaving only the normal bit of the profit for the person who buys the franchise. These higher-than-normal profits can build up a brand image for the product or business by carefully positioning the product in the market and using advertising and PR to promote it. In this way, the end-user of the product, the consumer, will pay higher prices than for an equivalent product.

If you think you can create the right image for your own business, franchising could be expensive for you. You might do better trying to go it alone and not seeking the apparent safety net of a franchise.

### WHAT IS IN THIS CHAPTER?

This chapter looks mainly at what happens if you buy a franchise (become a franchisee) and only briefly touches on how to form a franchise to sell to others (become a franchisor). It concentrates on what is called *business format franchising*. This sort of franchising is where you buy a complete business system or way of trading. All the franchisees trade under a common name, appearing to be branches of one large firm, rather than a whole series of independent businesses.

The chapter includes:

- A brief guide to franchises (see below)
- The pluses and minuses for a franchisee (p. 117)
- Step-by-step guide to choosing a franchise (p. 119)
- How a franchise works in detail (pp. 121–9)
- The contract (p. 129)
- Setting up as a franchisor (p. 132).

## A BRIEF GUIDE TO FRANCHISES

This brief guide to a typical franchise describes what happens in the different stages of a well-organized and properly developed franchise; occasionally, there may be a franchise which is not developed in a model fashion and you should beware of buying one of these. Use the step-by-step guide on p. 119 to help you sort out the wheat from the chaff. In the first stage, a business is developed or set up. It could be based on a novel or revolutionary product, a comprehensive and well-organized business method, a particular marketing style and so on. The business (or pilot) will have run for a couple of years, so that all initial problems have been sorted out. Preferably there should be more than one pilot, which demonstrates that the business idea can be repeated.

Next, the owner of the business (the franchisor) decides to expand, not necessarily by creating more branches but by selling franchises to the business format already developed in the pilot operation. Note that the two forms of expansion, selling franchises and opening branches, can be carried on at the same time. The franchisor develops the franchise operation which should be a mirror of the successful pilot. The franchisor should produce an operating manual, which would show how each franchise should be set up and run.

Once the format has been developed, the franchisor will try to find suitable people to buy the franchise (a franchisee) for a particular territory. There will be careful investigation by the franchisor to make sure that the franchise is sold to a suitable person who will develop the particular territory successfully. A prospective buyer should investigate the franchise, the pilot operation, the contract, operations manual and so on to ensure that the franchise will be worth buying. Mutual suspicion should rule.

When the franchise is bought, the contract (p. 129) will be signed and the buyer will usually pay an initial fee to the franchisor. The initial fee will probably include a straight fee to the franchisor, as well as the money needed to set up the business, for example, premises, initial stock and so on. For this fee, the franchisor helps the franchisee set up the business: helps with finding premises, fitting them out, stocking the business, training, finance, the opening.

After the opening, the franchisor should continue to provide advice and should carry on advertising and marketing the product name. The franchisee will normally pay a fee each month, perhaps based on a percentage of sales or profits. The product will normally be purchased from the franchisor, which may be another way that the franchisor makes his or her profit instead of the percentage on sales. The franchisor has the right to make visits to the franchisee's business to examine the accounting records. At the end of the contract, which often lasts five years, the franchisee can usually renew, subject to the franchisor being satisfied with the franchisee's performance.

## THE PLUSES AND MINUSES FOR A FRANCHISEE

Your main consideration before buying any particular franchise is whether it will work as a business for you and provide you with the sort of living you require. Assuming that you have found such a franchise, there are some advantages and disadvantages of which you should be aware.

### THE PLUSES

1. It is your own business.

2. If the business format has been well worked out and tested in the pilot operation, many of the problems experienced in setting up a business can be side-stepped. This reduces your risk.

3. You receive on-going advice and support. This can be particularly important for someone who has had little business experience.

4. You hope you are buying a product with a recognized brand name. To create a brand image all by yourself can involve considerable resources. But in the case of a franchise, the franchisor should carry on promoting it,

using the management service fee (or royalties) or possibly an advertising levy (p. 123) which all the franchisees will pay. So the brand name of your business will be getting a bigger selling push than could be achieved by each franchisee's individual contribution.

5. In the case of many franchises, you need no knowledge of the industry before you start your business. The training given by the franchisor should be sufficient to overcome any ignorance.

6. Franchisors, because of size, have greater negotiating power with suppliers than you do on your own, although not all of them pass this benefit on to the franchisees.

## THE MINUSES

1. While it is your own business, you are expected to act in the best interests of other franchisees and the franchisor. You could find this irritating and restrictive.

2. As well as the initial fee, part of your profits will have to go each year in a payment to the franchisor. You might find this galling.

3. Often the continuing fee to the franchisor is based on your sales rather than profits. This could lead to problems if you are struggling to make profits, perhaps because the costs are too high. This will not be reflected in the level of the fee.

4. The franchisor has the right to demand that you send in sales statistics and other documents promptly, plus the right to come to your business premises and inspect your records. Again this might strike you as a loss of independence.

5. You have to adhere to the methods laid down in the franchisor's operating manual. This could be restrictive and allow little room for you to exercise your own initiative and enterprise.

6. You may have to purchase all your stocks from the franchisor. This allows little room for you to seek competitive alternatives. Again, you could find this stifling, if what you want to do is to run your own business.

7. Should the franchisor, despite all your preliminary research and investigations, fail to maintain the brand name by promotion or fail to meet commitments about training and the search for better products, frankly there is little you can do about it. If this is all buttoned down in the contract, however, you may be able to get somewhere.

8. If you want to sell the franchise before the end of your contract, the franchisor has to agree.

9. The franchise runs for a certain number of years. Normally, if your performance is satisfactory (whatever that means, see p. 130), you will be able to renew for another period; but you may have to commit to spending more money on refurbishment and more modern equipment. What happens about a second, third or fourth renewal is not always clear. You should assess the return on the money you invest over the first period of the franchise only. If, for some reason, you are not able to renew, you may have little to sell, because you cannot sell the name or the goodwill.

## A STEP-BY-STEP GUIDE TO CHOOSING A FRANCHISE

1. Keep a healthy dose of scepticism about franchises, franchisors and franchise specialists.

2. Make your own choice of advisers, do not use those suggested by the franchisor. The most unbiased advisers are likely to be a clearing bank – all of which have specialized franchise units giving independent advice – and the solicitor and accountant you employ to advise you.

3. Get your accountant to examine the forecasts given to you by the franchisor and to advise you on how realistic they are.

4. Ask your solicitor to go through any contract carefully to bring out clearly the restrictions and also the ways in which the franchisor will be making money.

5. Find out how many franchises have already been sold and how long they have been going.

6. Find out, visit and talk to existing franchisees. Do not allow yourself to be restricted only to the franchisor's choice as references. Ask whether a support group of franchisees has been formed.

7. Be particularly careful if the franchise you are interested in is one of the first to be sold. You will need to study the pilot operation with a fine-tooth comb. Does it mirror your likely business? Is the manager of the pilot an average sort of person with the same sort of

knowledge and skill as you? Are the premises and their location much the same? Is the stock identical?

**8.** Watch out if the initial fee is relatively large and the continuing fee relatively small. It is essential that it is in the franchisor's interests for the business to continue to be promoted and properly managed. The success of your business depends on how effective the franchisor is in marketing and purchasing.

**9.** Look carefully at the arrangements for purchasing equipment and stock. You do not want to be forced to buy new equipment if it is unnecessary, nor do you want an arrangement in which the franchisor can increase the mark-up on products sold to you.

**10.** Investigate the franchisor. The continued existence of the franchisor's business is important to you, because it carries out the marketing, purchasing and other centrally organized functions. Get references and credit ratings. Ask the franchisor to give you a copy of the latest accounts and ask your accountant to study them.

**11.** Be careful about buying a franchise from a franchisor who is not a member of the British Franchise Association (see p. 466 for address). Membership of the association does not guarantee the success of your business or the franchisor's business; indeed, one member got into difficulties in 1986. A number of quite reputable franchisors do not belong to the association. However, members agree to abide by a code of ethics. Ask a franchisor why it is not a member, if that is the case.

**12.** Check that you will have the exclusive right to sell within the territory to be allocated, or, at least, that your right to sell is protected. Exclusive rights are being phased out as a result of anticipated competition legislation.

**13.** Examine what will happen if you die, want to sell your franchise, disagree with your franchisor or want to renew at the end of the term of the franchise. These points are looked at in more detail on pp. 130, 131.

**14.** What sort of product is it? It must have a useful life of at least the length of the franchise which you are purchasing. There is very little point in buying a five-year franchise for a product with a life of only three years.

15. Carry out market research in exactly the same way as if you were setting up the business on your own. Chapter 2. 'Who will buy?' (p. 28) should help you to do this. Do not rely on market statistics or views passed on by the franchisor.

16. Check that the product has been patented or the name registered as a trademark, otherwise the franchise you buy could be worthless.

17. How will the advertising levels be maintained? Does the franchisor make a firm commitment in the contract to spend certain amounts on promoting the brand name?

18. What is the quality of the field force run by the franchisor? How often will they visit? Are they competent to give sound business advice? What will happen if your business runs into difficulties?

19. The relationship between franchisee and franchisor may, in a few cases, prove difficult to maintain at a harmonious level. What are the lines of communication? Do you think that you will be able to build a good relationship with this particular franchisor?

20. If it is a good franchise, you will face competition from other would-be franchisees. So you should expect a grilling. And if you are not subjected to close investigation, this may indicate that the franchisor is short of buyers.

21. Many points on which you need information before you tie up an agreement with a franchisor are listed throughout the rest of this chapter. Make sure you cover them in your discussions, and check the franchisor's response.

## HOW A FRANCHISE WORKS IN DETAIL

In this section, the following topics are examined:

- Cost (p. 122)
- Finance (p. 124)
- Territory (p. 124)
- Premises (p. 125)
- Operations manual (p. 125)

- Training (p. 126)
- Opening (p. 126)
- On-going support and supervision (p. 126)
- Finding and buying a franchise (p. 128).

COST

The cost to you could be made up of one or more of the following charges. There will be the initial cost of the franchise, which includes the initial fee, and most likely there will be a continuing fee (also called royalty or service fee). There may also be an advertising levy, a mark-up paid on goods or equipment supplied by the franchisor and a mark-up if you lease premises from the franchisor. You need to look out for any hidden costs of financing, if the franchisor obtains a commission on introducing you to a business providing finance or to a leasing company, if you lease equipment. It is only a cost to you, of course, if you could have arranged cheaper finance elsewhere.

- *initial cost:* the average initial cost of the franchise is about £16,000. But this does not include fast food franchises (for example, beefburgers). With these, the average cost is much higher, perhaps as much as £475,000. But the range of prices for all franchises is wide; it could be as little as £2,500, for example. Usually, the initial fee which goes to the franchisor is between 5 and 10 per cent of the total investment.

There is no typical start-up package, but below is an example of the sort of items which could be included in the initial cost:

| | |
|---|---|
| Shopfitting | £13,000 |
| Equipment | 15,000 |
| Initial stock | 8,000 |
| Initial franchise fee | 4,000 |
| TOTAL | £40,000 |

The initial franchise fee is what you are paying to be given the right to use the brand name within a certain territory and to be trained and provided with advice.

- *service fee:* the service fee payable can also vary quite a lot, from nil up to 20 per cent of sales. The average for members of the British Franchise Association is around 11.5 per cent. The service fee could be paid weekly or monthly. The fact that the service fee is nil does not necessarily mean that all you are paying will be the initial start-up cost. Franchisors can also be paid by using mark-ups on products and equipment.

A low service fee is not necessarily an advantage for you. It is crucial that the franchisor retains an on-going interest in promotion and improvement of the business format, and that will only be achieved by the reliance on some sort of continuing payment from the franchisee.

The franchisor prefers to base the service fee on sales rather than profits. This is because monitoring the franchisee accounts to ensure that the franchisor is receiving the proper amount can be time-consuming and expensive. If the fee is based on profits rather than sales, the monitoring has to apply to costs as well as sales, doubling the difficulty of the task.

However, a fee based on sales can be disadvantageous to the franchisee. If the costs of the enterprise prove to be higher than forecast, paying the service fee could be an onerous burden for the franchisee.

You should not underestimate the size of the service fee, because it is based on sales not profits. If, for example, your costs are 60 per cent of your sales value, a service fee of 10 per cent of sales translates into a service fee of a quarter of the profits you make. Work out the figures before you sign.

One point to watch out for is what happens at the end of the original franchise contract if you want to renew. Does the contract allow the franchisor to increase the size of the service fee? Try to negotiate on this, as you do not want a bigger percentage of your hard work to be passed over to the franchisor.

● *advertising levy:* a number of franchise packages charge an advertising levy as well as the service fee. This is usually calculated as a percentage of sales and paid at the same time as the service fee. The existence of an advertising levy could be regarded as an advantage for a franchise if promotion of the brand name is a very important part of the franchise success. If an advertising levy is made, look to see if this will be audited separately in the franchisor's accounts so that you can see that it has indeed been used for that purpose and that alone, not just disappeared into the franchisor's pocket.

If there is no separate advertising levy, the franchisor may undertake to spend a certain proportion of the service fee each year. The other common alternative for advertising is that the franchisor will undertake to advertise as and when needed. With some franchises, the franchisee is expected to advertise as well as, or even instead of, the franchisor. This could lead to promotions which are at odds with each other – and may mean that the prestige of the franchise name deteriorates.

● *mark-ups:* one apparent advantage of grouping together can be that buying in greater bulk can mean bigger discounts and cheaper supplies. This should also apply to franchises, where supplies are often an important part of the cost of the enterprise. However, some franchisors put on mark-ups which deprive the franchisees of any benefit from bulk purchase.

● *hidden costs of financing:* it is not unusual for companies to pay commission to someone who introduces a new customer to them. This does not necessarily mean that you will get a bad deal if your franchisor helps you to arrange finance. But it does mean that you should shop around to satisfy yourself that you cannot organize a more attractive deal elsewhere. In practice, you may find it difficult to arrange finance except through the franchisor, but you should examine the possibility.

## FINANCE

Raising money to finance the purchase of a franchise is treated in the same way as raising money to start any new business. All the clearing banks have specialist franchise units and, on the whole, they appear to look more favourably upon the average franchise application than on the average start-up. This is because a franchise is believed to offer lower risk to a lender.

However, any bank will require that a prospective franchisee contributes a proportion of the start-up capital, around 30 per cent. The remaining 70 per cent could be financed by the bank.

Any loan will need to be repaid by the end of the franchise term; however, there may be some leeway on the initial repayments of capital. For example, a repayment holiday could be arranged until the business is showing a profit.

If the bank requires security this could be provided by a charge on the business assets, such as premises or equipment, but only if you run the franchise as a limited company. If you remain a sole trader, a mortgage on your house may be acceptable.

## TERRITORY

The interests of the franchisor and franchisee may clash when it comes to the allocation of territory. The franchisor would like the option to introduce another franchisee to the area if the original franchisee has not made a success of it. The franchisee, on the other hand, does not want to be competing with another business on the same patch, selling identical goods.

Note that the franchisor has had to register the agreement under the Restrictive Trade Practices Act if exclusive rights were granted. This has been acceptable to the competition authorities and was not a major deterrent. There have been, however, moves afoot in the EEC which may lead to some changes in the franchise contract.

Whatever is granted in terms of rights, it is important to have clear identification of the territory. Check that it is clearly specified in the contract. The delineation of the territory should also be relevant to the particular trade. If it is a shop, perhaps a certain number of miles from the site would be relevant. If it is a service franchise, perhaps Yellow Page division of territories would be more suitable.

It is also important to ensure that the territory is large enough to support a business of the type proposed. If you have any doubts, do not buy.

## PREMISES

There is no set practice on whether the premises are owned or leased by the franchisor and sublet to the franchisee or the premises are owned and leased by the franchisee. It varies from franchise to franchise. Controlling the premises has advantages either way. If the franchisor owns the site, and if the franchise is not renewed, a valuable, well-placed site is not lost, as far as the franchisor is concerned. Conversely, if you are the franchisee and the premises are in your name, when it comes to renewal, you can use the site for another business if you would prefer.

Whatever the position about tenure, the location of a site, especially if it is for a shop, needs to be examined carefully, in exactly the same way as for any other business (p. 187). Do not take the franchisor's word for it.

## OPERATIONS MANUAL

This is where the franchisor puts all the know-how of the business; it should incorporate the essence of the business format you are buying. One of the terms in the contract will be that you must adhere to the manual.

It will include details on everything: accounting systems, recruitment, how to carry out the actual process of the business (for example, grill a hamburger, print a leaflet or unblock a drain), reporting systems and so on. You should see a copy of the manual before you buy. Make sure you understand what is in there; it is how you will have to behave in your business while you own the franchise.

An indicator of the on-going interest of the franchisor can be how frequently the manual is updated. Ask how often this has been done.

TRAINING

Training is an important part of what a franchisor is offering. Before you sign the contract, you need a clear idea of how much training there will be and how long it will take. You should expect training on all the basic business skills you will need to run a business. This includes financial methods, stock levels, operating the equipment, carrying out the process of the business, working out accounts and PAYE, employment law, VAT and so on *ad infinitum*.

OPENING

The franchisor should help you to start your business. If it is a retail business, once the premises have been found, the franchisor will help organize the shopfitting. Indeed, it may be part of the agreement, as it may be that the shopfitting has to conform to the brand image: the colours, style of counter, type of shelves and so on.

Additionally, there will be advice available (it may even be a requirement to follow it) on the equipment and amount and mix of opening stock you should have. Find out before you sign what the franchisor's policy is on this and satisfy yourself that you are not being cornered into a policy of over-equipping and over-stocking.

To have a successful opening day, you will need publicity and perhaps an opening ceremony; you should get help and advice on how to advertise and arrange media coverage. Find out the franchisor's level of commitment on this.

ON-GOING SUPPORT AND SUPERVISION

This could consist of six elements:

1. refresher training (see above)

2. continuous product and business research and development (see right)

3. troubleshooters and supervisors who give regular visits (see right)

4. updated operations manual (p. 125)

5.  advertising the brand as a whole (p. 123)

6.  advice on an individual level about promotion (see below).

Products do not last forever. So for any business there needs to be continuous assessment of the product to see how well it meets its customers' needs, not just in the past, but now and in the future. Any market trends need to be taken into account and the product may need altering over the years to meet the new criteria. Or, a completely new product may need to be evolved. For a franchise to be successful, the franchisor should devote some energy to this. Check what your franchisor's policy will be on this before buying.

The downside to this is that any innovations or alterations could end up being costly for the franchisee. Try to establish what the future plans of the franchisor will be and check what the agreement says about implementation of any new developments.

Another element of support and supervision by the franchisor is the help available if you or the business are in difficulties, for example, are there troubleshooters to provide guidance? The sort of questions you want the franchisor to answer include:

- how often will support visits be made and what is the calibre of the support staff?

- if the business is struggling to break even, does the franchisor have special troubleshooters? If not, what sort of help will be available?

- what happens if the equipment does not work properly? Are there maintenance facilities and what is the response time?

- if you are ill, is there an emergency staff team available to take over?

As well as the positive side of providing support, you must recognize that the supervisory team also fulfil the role of monitor for the franchisor. You will have to accept that they will want to examine your records and books on a regular basis, check that you are not understating sales (or whatever it is that the service fee is based on) and ensure that the service fee is paid on time.

A final element of support which you need to investigate before you buy is the advice available on promotion of your business. While it is a better arrangement for the franchisor to carry out the advertising and promotion of the product name on a national basis, you may feel that there are opportunities which allow you to boost your business by advertising and promoting locally. The franchisor may be able to advise on this. In fact, the franchisor may insist as part of the agreement that you promote locally. For example, is the amount of expenditure specified and will it prove onerous?

### FINDING AND BUYING A FRANCHISE

There are around 300 franchises currently on sale. Of these, about eighty are full members of the British Franchise Association and twenty or so are registered associates. A full member has to have operated a successful pilot scheme for at least one year and to have at least four franchisees operating for at least a year. Generally, to be a registered associate, the franchisor must have operated a successful pilot scheme for one year and to have at least one franchisee who has been franchising for a minimum of one full year.

To start your search for a franchise you could write to the Association asking for their list of members. The BFA has a Franchise Information Pack, which includes a list of members and registered companies; this costs £8, including post and packaging. Another source of names, addresses and telephone numbers is a book *Taking up a Franchise*. The details are given on p. 406.

There are a number of organizations operating as franchise consultants who say they will give advice on finding a franchise. Before you use one, be absolutely certain that it is not an organization concerned solely, or even mainly, with finding franchisees for one or two franchise companies. If this were the case, the impartiality of the advice can be discounted.

Work out some rough guidelines for the sort of business you would be happy to be in and the sorts of areas of the country you would be prepared to move to. Estimate the sort of price you could pay, bearing in mind that you should be able to invest at least 30 per cent, while borrowing the remaining 70 per cent is a possibility.

Write to a shortlist of five or six franchise companies, asking them to send you the details you need. This should include projections of the likely level of business and a draft contract, as well as the areas where the company currently has a franchisee vacancy.

Once you have received the information, the hard work begins. Consult your solicitor and accountant. Carry out your own very thorough research investigating among other aspects, marketing, advertising, product lines, financial aspects, supervision. Use the step-by-step guide on p. 119. There are also a number of other books and publications which have comprehensive checklists and questionnaires (see p. 406 for details).

It is important to remember that if the franchise is a good one, the franchisor will be able to pick and choose from applicants. Treat the negotiation with the franchisor from two points of view:

● the need to investigate and assess the worth of the franchise thoroughly

● the need to sell yourself as an ideal applicant to the franchisor.

For a good franchise, you will need to provide references along with much more information about your suitability as a franchisee.

While you are negotiating, you may be able to reserve a particular territory by placing a deposit. The amount of the deposit and whether it is partially refundable or not varies from franchise to franchise. Sometimes the deposit is set against the initial fee on signing. Check the terms and the franchisor's references before you pay it.

## THE CONTRACT

This is the kernel of all franchises. Once you have signed it, it will rule your life. Do not skimp on independent legal advice. The contract will attempt to ensure that you run the business along the lines specified by the franchisor.

The contract should cover these areas:

● the type of business, its name and the use to which it can be put

● the territory for which the franchisee will have the rights to use the name

● how long the franchise will run

● what the franchisee will have to pay (the initial fee and service fee)

● if the franchisee wants to sell

● if either the franchisee or franchisor wants to end the agreement

● what both the franchisor and franchisee have agreed to do.

### THE TYPE OF BUSINESS, ITS NAME

This part of the contract will describe the franchise. It will indicate that the franchisor has registered any relevant trade mark or patented any invention. The franchisee will probably have to agree not to handle any trade mark, product or service belonging to a competitor of the franchisor.

## THE TERRITORY

The contract may specify that the franchisee will have the sole and exclusive right to run the franchised business in a particular territory. In return, the franchisee will agree not to sell outside that allocated territory, as that will be the province of another franchisee. There may also be certain restrictions on the type of customer, for example, that you cannot sell to government organizations.

## HOW LONG THE FRANCHISE WILL RUN

The typical length of a franchise is five years. But it could be as short as three or as long as twenty. Normally, you can renew the franchise at the end of the original agreed period, but this may be subject to satisfactory performance. You should certainly want an option to renew and you should try to ensure that the legal wording about what constitutes a 'satisfactory performance' is clear to you, fair to you and can be enforced by you. This is essential, because unless you have the lease on the premises, you would have very little to show for your work at the end of the period. You would not be able to sell the business as a going concern, because you would no longer have the rights to the name or to use the business format, and without these there is little goodwill to be attached to the business.

Some contracts specify that if you do not wish to renew, the franchisor will buy the business from you, including a value for goodwill. The value put on the business will be set by an independent accountant.

If you have an option to renew, the contract may specify that certain sums of money are spent to update the premises and smarten the business. The details of this commitment need to be buttoned down in the contract. In any case, the option to renew may well be to renew on the terms currently on offer to franchisees; these may be less favourable to a franchisee than the terms on which you originally signed.

If you have decided not to look for another agreement with the franchisor, the contract may restrict your activities. It may specify that you cannot carry on a similar or competing business for a certain length of time.

## WHAT THE FRANCHISEE WILL HAVE TO PAY

The contract will specify the amount and the nature of the fees which will be paid, that is, the initial fee, the service fee (or royalty) and, if applicable, the advertising levy.

## IF THE FRANCHISEE WANTS TO SELL

Most agreements include some arrangement whereby the franchisee can sell their business during the course of the term. The contract may specify that the franchisor will be entitled to first refusal. Additionally, one of the conditions may be that the franchisor has to agree that your buyer is properly qualified to run it. Your buyer will have to receive training and probably have to be prepared to sign a new agreement. However, in reality, it will be difficult to give the same sort of rigorous vetting that the franchisor can do for the initial holder.

Watch out for the sort of agreement which allows the franchisor to charge high transfer (or other) fees on a sale. This sort of condition could effectively block any sale you might make, except to the franchisor on poor terms.

A contract should also include the terms and conditions which apply if you die during the agreed period of the franchise.

## IF EITHER THE FRANCHISEE OR THE FRANCHISOR WANTS TO END THE AGREEMENT

It is possible that you may want to end the agreement, if you find that the business is hard going, for example. In those circumstances, it may be difficult to find a buyer. On the other hand, it is not especially in the franchisor's interests to insist on keeping you to the agreement if you are not making a success of it. The contract should deal with what can be done in these circumstances. You need to satisfy yourself that the contract would treat you fairly.

The contract will also specify the conditions under which the franchisor can end the agreement. This could occur if you break the agreement which you sign and fail to meet your obligations under it.

A few of the more stringent conditions may be:

- minimum performance target
- agreement to purchase minimum amounts of goods and merchandise
- the requirement to bring your unit up to standard, if necessary.

Experience is now indicating that, with a good franchisor, renewals are made and some are now on their third or fourth terms.

## WHAT BOTH THE FRANCHISEE AND FRANCHISOR HAVE AGREED TO DO

The contract will stipulate what both of you must do to keep your side of the bargain. For example, for the franchisor the rules about training, supervision, advertising, support and maintenance and management services etc. should be specified.

The franchisee will have to operate according to the manual and allow the franchisor's staff to monitor the business activities. There will be a requirement not to handle the trademarks, products and services belonging to any competing business of the franchisor's or possibly to trade in any other area allocated to another franchisee.

## SETTING UP AS A FRANCHISOR

This aspect of franchising is beyond the scope of the guide, although your interests can be interpreted from what is said about the franchisee's interests. Here are a few brief guidelines:

● you need to have proved in practice that the business format works. This is done by establishing a pilot operation which should be run exactly along the same lines as the proposed franchise. All the systems and products should be tried out here and all the wrinkles ironed out before selling any franchises. Ideally, the pilot should have run for two years. It goes almost without saying that the pilot has to be successful, otherwise you will not be able to sell any franchises

● the business format needs to be distinctive in its image and/or its way of operating

● it must be possible to pass on the format successfully to others

● the format needs to be capable of earning high enough profits to give both the franchisee and franchisor an adequate living.

## SUMMARY

1. The main advantage of starting a business by buying a franchise is that a lot of the initial start-up problems have already been sorted out; this

means there is a greater chance of survival than starting a business from scratch yourself.

2. The main disadvantages are that there is a loss of independence because of your commitments to a franchisor; you also lose the possibility of earning exceptionally high profits, because the profits are divided between the two of you.

3. Use the step-by-step guide to choosing a franchise on p. 119 to help you sort out the good from the bad.

4. The franchisor should provide support and development throughout the franchise.

5. Because of uncertainty about what will happen at the end of the initial agreed period of the franchise, your decision to buy or not should be based on the initial period only.

6. Use your own advisers, for example, bank, solicitor and accountant, and carry out your own research into finance, the market, the product, the franchisor, the location and the detailed terms of the franchise. Do not rely on the word of the franchisor.

OTHER CHAPTERS TO READ

# 11. THE RIGHT NAME

At an early stage in your planning, the question will come up: 'What am I going to call my business?' or 'What am I going to call my product?' You may be tempted to spend a couple of minutes and then plump for your own name or your initials, and move on to other more important planning tasks. But this would be a mistake.

Choosing a name is a long-term decision, which is all wrapped up with working out what you are trying to sell and identifying why customers will buy from you rather than your competitors. Your company or product name should encapsulate a message to potential or existing customers. This will not happen overnight; it takes many years to build up a name to carry the message you want. But one thing is for sure, you cannot change horses mid-stream. The name you plump for now should be the name you still have in five, ten years time.

## CHOOSING A NAME

Before you start the search for a name, there is quite a lot of background thinking you need to do about your marketplace, your competitors and your product.

### WHY DO PEOPLE BUY FROM YOU?

If you analyse why people buy a particular product or service, the list might include things like:

- it is cheaper
- the product has a special feature which others do not have
- the service is near by and is very convenient
- its running costs or maintenance are less
- there is 24-hour-guaranteed service.

These are all rational reasons, capable of proof. If your product or service has one feature, or more, which are like this you have a primary benefit. You may be able to achieve your sales on this alone.

The list of reasons why people buy a product might also include things like:

- it is better

- it looks good

- the quality of the service is high

- it is believed to be very reliable

- it is better value for money

- the design is excellent.

These are all emotional reasons, which may be real or imagined. But they reflect how customers feel about a product.

A combination of the emotional and the rational reasons gives a product its reputation (or *brand image*).

### HOW DOES YOUR PRODUCT RATE?

Your product or service may have some unique element; if so, you are probably unusual. The chances are that there is nothing that much different or better about what you are going to do than your competitors. But that does not mean you will not be more profitable, make more sales and get a bigger share of the market than someone with a product which does have unique features.

Creating a 'good feeling' among buyers about your product can give you a better general reputation, can make you better thought of and more widely known. Giving your business an identity can make you successful.

However, creating an image of quality and reliability for a utilitarian product can lead to a downfall if your product or service does not live up to it. The product must be good, if it is not *the* best; the service must be reliable, if not *the* most reliable.

### WHERE DOES NAME COME IN?

You want to get the name of your business or product into the position that it summarizes all the emotional and rational feelings about the product. So, if a potential customer hears the name, it instantly gives a good connotation. On day one of your business, this will not happen. You must plan carefully to achieve it over a number of years.

Your first step is to select a name which does not, by itself, cause any feeling of antipathy. Ideally, the name on its own should give a clue to your image, but this is a counsel of perfection. You should at least aim for the name to generate neutral feelings in the early stages, until you have built the image from scratch.

## ONE NAME OR TWO?

Should your business and product share the same name? There is no clear-cut answer to this one, and for a small business it may not be very important. You will not have the resources to create two brand images, one for the product and one for your business. In any case, it could be confusing. So, even if you do have separate names for the two, you will be promoting only one.

## IF I'M SELLING TO INDUSTRY, DO I BOTHER WITH IMAGE?

Yes. You may be selling to a buyer from an industrial firm but, with the other hat on, the buyer is also a normal human being. This means that he or she will probably have the same amount of prejudices as a member of the general public buying soap. It is as important to create a good feeling about your product with an industrial customer as with a domestic one.

## IF MY PRODUCT HAS A UNIQUE FEATURE, DO I HAVE TO BOTHER WITH IMAGE?

Yes. You may have some original feature, but once you have launched it on the market, your competitors will be beavering away to make sure that it does not stay unique for very long. And, on the whole, you cannot patent an idea, only a mechanism, so you may not be able to rely on protection (p. 142).

If you do not concentrate on the image of your product, and your competitive advantage is subsequently eroded because other products are improved, the future of your business may not look so rosy. Building an image for your product is a low-risk safety route.

## WHAT IMAGE DO YOU WANT TO CREATE?

This is all linked up with the market research you will have done (p. 28), a crucial stage of your planning. When you analyse the market for your product, you will find that there are sectors within the market. For example, if you were considering opening a picture framing business, you might find the following sectors:

- do-it-yourself

- speedy service

- mail order
- high-quality frames
- a service with advice from a designer or artist.

Your research will identify the size and growth of each sector, where the competition lies, and what are the prime demands by customers in each sector. In turn, your decision will be to go for one or more sectors, to look at your service compared to the competitors and to focus on what your customer wants. This will give you guidance on what sort of image to build for your business.

LOGO – A NO GO?

A logo or logotype may be nothing more than a word, the name of your company or product, always shown in the same typeface or in the same colour, or, perhaps, within a simple shape. It could also include an unusual or memorable shape; one which people will recognize quickly, and eventually come to associate with all their perceptions of your product.

Using a logo can emphasize your name and get greater customer awareness. If you can afford to do it, do it. But, do not rely on your printer. Paying an adviser, such as a design consultant, may be worthwhile (p. 210). In your dealings with an adviser, specify that the logo must be cheap to reproduce, as once you have got it, you will use it on everything you can. So you do not want to end up with a beautiful logo, which costs you an arm and a leg every time you want new quantities of stationery.

Do not make snap decisions on logos; if you can, try a little bit of market research on potential buyers to assess their reaction or possibly ask colleagues, family or friends.

TIPS ON CHOOSING A NAME

1. Made-up words can make good product or business names. They may not arouse any positive feelings about your business, but they are also unlikely to create negative ones. If you are going to register that name as a trade mark, you will stand a greater chance of success in doing so, if it is a made-up word (p. 147).

2. If you are going to use an existing word, if possible try it out on potential buyers to check that you will not create a bad impression simply because of the name.

**3.** Use brain-storming sessions with family and friends as well as colleagues to produce a list of names for consideration.

**4.** Check that the name you prefer is not used by another product or business in the same or similar market.

**5.** Avoid initials; it is difficult in the short term to create a comfortable feeling about a business or product with initials.

**6.** If you think that some of your business will come from people searching through Yellow Pages or other alphabetic listings, choose names beginning with A.

**7.** Check that the name you choose does not mean anything nasty in a foreign language (for example, look it up in dictionaries in the library).

**8.** Very complicated words need careful consideration. If a customer has to ask you to spell the word when it is first mentioned, this can be a positive reinforcement for recognition in future. But, if it is just too difficult, it may be a disadvantage.

**9.** A name which uses all capital letters, for example, FLAG, can stand out in a chunk of written text, giving the name prominence.

**10.** Finally, ask yourself, does the name seem right for the image you want to project.

### WHAT THE LAW SAYS ABOUT NAMES

If you are forming a limited company, you will not be allowed to register names:

● which are identical to that of an existing company

● could be considered offensive or illegal.

There is also a range of words, which if you want to use them, you have to have the agreement of various bodies. Examples are Abortion, Building Society, Royal, Windsor, National and English. There are around eighty of these words altogether. There are other rules about company names, so advice from your solicitor would be helpful.

If you are a sole trader and want to use a business name, other than your own surname, there are certain rules you have to observe. Your own name and address must be stated legibly on all business letters, on written orders for goods and services and on invoices. You must also display your name and address prominently at your business premises or at any place to which your customers and suppliers have access.

## BUILDING YOUR REPUTATION

Once you have selected your business or product name, your next strategy is to devise means of getting your name noticed by as many of your target customers as you can. Obviously, you do not want your name to be associated with any bad news, so you may find that you do not want to take up every opportunity to publicize your business name. What you should aim for is that your business or product name comes instantly to mind in your potential buyers, but with a favourable impression.

### ADVERTISING

This can prove expensive for small businesses and there may be other low-cost alternatives. Nevertheless, it is useful to have some idea of what advertising can achieve (p. 150).

### PUBLIC RELATIONS

This can be a low-cost way of increasing public awareness of your business and products. But it does need skilful handling, so it doesn't backfire and produce the wrong sort of attention. This is also covered in Chapter 13. 'Getting the message across' (p. 150).

### LETTERHEADS

This is the single most important way for most of the self-employed and small businesses to create some sort of image about themselves. Poor quality paper suggests cheap, poor quality service. Spend more on the paper to create that good impression.

It is tempting, especially if you know little about marketing or design, to play safe and choose white paper with black type for your letterheads. But consider experimenting with some draft versions before making your choice; it may cost a little extra, but if it helps create the image you are seeking you should do it. Your local instant print or photocopying shop can be very helpful, either printing small-run samples of different types or positions, or at least letting you re-arrange elements (name, logo, address) and photocopying the permutations.

Consider:

- different colour paper

- different colour type
- try positioning your business name in the centre or to the right
- different typefaces for name and address
- try big-sized and small-sized typefaces.
- adding a line to give a more finished appearance
- consider the typeface, what impression does it give you?

Once you have settled on your letterhead, look carefully at your other stationery needs. If your work is the type where you send out few invoices for large sums of money, you may not need separate invoices, but can use ordinary stationery. Will you need compliment slips, or will business cards suffice if you will only need them for a few occasions? Whatever stationery you do require, the colour and typeface should be uniform throughout the range. If you have a logo, it should be included in all your stationery.

If you are in retailing, you may decide that letterheads are not an important tool for you in creating an image. While this may be so with customers, letterheads are still needed to create that right image with suppliers, on whom you rely for credit.

LABELS AND STICKERS

If you can see any opportunity for using labels and stickers on your products, seize it. These can also carry the message you want. There must be continuity with your chosen letterheads; colour, style, typeface and logo – if you have one – all identical to your stationery. In a shop, you might consider having price stickers done like this. In garments or other material items like rugs, tablewear and so on, labels should be sewn in.

PACKAGING

The package says lots about the goods, so take the opportunity to reinforce the message you are sending to customers. The style of the packaging should be consistent with all the other items for promoting your image, and with your chosen image itself. Packaging is an extension or even an integral part of your products.

OTHER IDEAS

These can all help build your reputation:

- cleanliness of vehicles

- appearance of sales people
- how you answer the telephone
- vehicle liveries, that is, the colour or markings on them.

## SUMMARY

1. People buy particular products or services for rational and emotional reasons.

2. You should aim to create a 'good feeling', a brand image, a reputation, about your product among customers. Make sure that your product can live up to this.

3. Industrial or unique products still need brand images.

4. Analyse your market and your customer requirements to decide on your image.

5. A business or product name will be built up over the years to summarize what your image is all about.

6. If you can afford it, have a logo designed for you.

7. Try to encapsulate as many pleasant (or positive) associations in your name as you can.

8. Letterheads are a most important way of projecting messages about your business. Keep the style consistent with labels, stickers and packaging.

OTHER CHAPTERS TO READ

# 12. BEATING THE PIRATES

Successful small businesses do not need to be founded on an invention or an original design. The Eureka syndrome can play a very small part in the success of a business. A much more important factor is that there is a market there which wants to buy your product, and this may not be the case with every new idea. The ultimate in good indicators for success would be a strong market and an original product. But so often this is not so; there is unlikely to be a ready-built marketplace waiting for inventions. You may need to educate customers. This can be expensive as well as time-consuming.

However, if you have thought of an invention, a trade mark or an original design which could form the kernel of a successful small business, is it worth trying to protect it with the law? Almost certainly, yes is the answer. If the idea, for example, can be turned into profits, someone else may try to copy it and you should obtain the best protection you can, so that *you* make the profits, not the imitator.

The law cannot protect alone. First, you have to be vigilant in watching out for infringements. Second, and more importantly, the best protection of all is guaranteed by carrying out effective marketing: this can turn a product based on an invention, for example, into the leading product and establish your business as the market leader (p. 182).

WHAT IS IN THIS CHAPTER?

- What to do with an invention (see below)

- What to do with a design (p. 146)

- What to do with a trade or service mark (p. 147)

- Getting help and advice (p. 148)

## WHAT TO DO WITH AN INVENTION

WHAT IS AN INVENTION WHICH CAN BE PATENTED?

There are four requirements for something to be regarded as an invention for patent purposes. These are that it must:

- *be new:* it must not have been published or made known anywhere in the world previously

- *involve an inventive step:* by and large this means that it must not be obvious to another person with knowledge of that particular subject

- *be capable of industrial application:* an idea which cannot be made or used will not be counted as an invention

- *not be excluded:* there are various categories of ideas which are excluded by law. These include something which is a discovery (that is, you found out about it, but did not invent it), scientific theory or mathematical method, mental process, literary, artistic or aesthetic creation, playing a game, presentation of information or a computer program.

Other ideas which are excluded are anything which would be regarded as encouraging offensive, immoral or anti-social behaviour, a new animal or plant variety or a method of diagnosis or surgery for animals or humans.

## WHAT IS A PATENT?

A patent of invention is granted by a government body. It gives the owner of an invention the right to take legal action against others who may be trying to take commercial advantage of the invention without getting the owner's permission. This right is granted in return for complete disclosure by the owner of his invention.

The body which grants the UK patent is the Patent Office (see p. 406 for address). A UK patent can last up to twenty years from the date on which you first hand over documents to the Patent Office. After the first four years you have to pay a yearly fee to keep it in force. Note that the four years start from the date you first applied for the patent. A national patent only gives protection for the country in which it is granted.

If your invention is of a type that you believe you may want to exploit throughout Europe, not just in the UK, it could be cheaper to take advantage of the European Patent Convention. This allows you to obtain patent rights in a number of European countries. You need to make only one patent application, whereas if you applied for a UK patent first, you would then need to apply for patents in each of the individual countries which you thought important.

To file a European patent application, if you live in the UK, you apply at the Patent Office in London (see p. 406 for address).

## CAN YOU GET A PATENT?

The main criterion for granting a patent is whether or not the invention meets the four guidelines about what an invention is (p. 143).

One area you have to be particularly careful about is that you should not tell anyone (apart from in confidence to a patent agent, which would be a good idea) or publish information about your invention before you file your application at the Patent Office. This may mean that, even if no one else has thought of your idea, you will not be able to get a patent.

Occasionally, even if you have been granted a patent, you may find that someone challenges it. This would be on the grounds that someone else had already thought of the invention and had made details of it public before you filed your application for your patent. The other person may have decided not to bother to apply for a patent. Making details of it public would include describing it in a trade journal or exhibiting it or selling it.

## WHAT DOES IT COST?

When you first file your application, you have to enclose a fee of £10. Within a year, you will have to pay a fee of £80 for a preliminary search and examination. If you still decide to go ahead with your patent application there is another fee of £95. To keep the patent in force for the maximum twenty years, there is a yearly renewal fee, which increases each year.

However, many inventors use a patent agent (p. 149) to help with the application, as it can truly be a complicated and very lengthy task. You would have to check the fees before employing one.

The cost (in official fees up to grant of the patent) for a European patent is more – in total around £1,500, compared with the UK patent of around £200. After the patent is granted, national fees are payable to each of the designated countries.

## A STEP-BY-STEP GUIDE TO OBTAINING A PATENT

(This is a guide to UK patents)

1. Keep mum about your invention, except in confidence to a patent agent (p. 149).

2. Complete and file patents form 1/77 in the Patent Office, together with the necessary fee. With the form should be sent a

description of the invention. This description must be drafted in accordance with the rules laid down by the Patent Office which specify the exact format it should take. It must describe the invention fully and clearly enough so that a competent person could follow the description and build it or carry out the process. Enclose two copies, preferably typed and on A4 size paper.

**3.** You will receive a receipt with the date of filing and a number. This gives you your priority date which gives you precedence over the same invention being filed later. But this is no guarantee that the same invention has not already been publicized elsewhere by another person (see left).

**4.** During the next year, examine the commercial possibilities of your invention and decide whether to press on with your application or let it lapse.

**5.** If you make an improvement to your invention, you cannot add it to your first application but would have to file a new one. However, as long as you do this within a year of the priority date, that date will apply to whatever is in the new application, which was also in the first application. The first application can now be allowed to lapse.

**6.** Within a year of the priority date you need to file a request for a preliminary search and examination on patents form 9/77, together with the required fee. If you do not do this, your application lapses.

**7.** Once the search has been carried out by a Patent Office Examiner, a search report will be issued. This is a list of relevant documents so you can compare your invention with others and decide whether your application is likely to be successful.

**8.** If you do not withdraw your application at this stage, your application will be published by the Patent Office without any changes.

**9.** Within six months of publication of the application, you have to file the next form (Form 10/77), plus the required fee. There is now a much more detailed examination of your invention.

**10.** As a result of this substantive examination, amendments may be required by the Examiner. If these are carried out satisfactorily and within the required time, the patent will be granted.

## WHAT TO DO WITH A DESIGN

### WHAT IS A DESIGN?

An industrial design is not a unique work of art; as protected by registration under the Designs Act, it is the outward appearance of an article.

### IS IT PROTECTED BY THE COPYRIGHT ACT?

Copyright gives the right to protect yourself if others copy your design. However, it is quite possible that someone could independently come up with a similar design and, in this case, copyright gives no protection.

Copyright arises automatically; you do not have to register your design. However, it is very important to keep a note of your original drawing, even if a very rough sketch, and date it.

The copyright for designs which are entirely functional lasts for your lifetime plus fifty years. However, if the design is for a product which appeals to the eye and has been registered under the Designs Act, the protection lasts only fifteen years.

### WHAT IS A REGISTERED DESIGN?

You can apply to register your design with the Designs Registry (part of the Patent Office) and searches are carried out to see if similar designs are already registered. The design must be of the type which appeals to the eye, and also must be new and original, otherwise registration will not be granted. For this reason, it is important to keep the details of the design secret before you register; if you have not done so, it will not count as new.

Registering your design gives better protection than copyright, because it allows you to have complete control over the use of your design, even if someone else has come up with a similar design independently.

The protection lasts up to fifteen years, although you have to renew it every five years by applying for renewal and paying a fee.

### WHAT DOES IT COST?

The fee to the government is £40. However, if you use a patent agent, the cost will be more. Check the agent's fee before asking for help.

## A STEP-BY-STEP GUIDE TO REGISTRATION OF A DESIGN

---

1. Keep mum about your design, except in confidence to a patent agent (p. 149).

2. Tell the Designs Registry what the design is and what is going to be made from it. You must do this with a copy of the design, for example, a drawing or a photograph, in accordance with the rules laid down by the Designs Registry. Remember to send the required fee.

3. The Registry carries out searches and assesses whether the design is original and new. If it is, registration is granted.

---

## WHAT TO DO WITH A TRADE OR SERVICE MARK

### WHAT IS A TRADE MARK?

A trade mark is something which identifies a product in the eyes of the consumer. The consumer will know who has manufactured the goods or who is selling them. A service mark is something which identifies a service. Trade and service marks are closely linked with the idea of building loyalty among customers, so that they will choose your product or service over another similar one.

A trade or service mark can be a word or a symbol, such as a logo. Obviously, what you use as your trade mark should be carefully considered, as it needs to fit in with the image of your product and business which you are trying to put across.

### HOW CAN YOU PROTECT IT?

You can register a trade or service mark with the Trade Marks Registry (part of the Patent Office). To be possible for registration, the mark must be distinctive. A made-up word or a new symbol would be considered distinctive. Ordinary words would not; although after a number of years, with the advertising you put behind such a trade mark and the reputation for the product and business which you build up, the mark can acquire distinctiveness. Consumers will now recognize what was formerly an everyday word or name as identifying your product.

Registration entitles you, and only you, to use the mark. It gives you the right to take action against someone else to prevent them from using the mark.

There are also some simple steps you can take to help protect the mark yourself. For example, put TM beside the mark when you use it in advertisements or sales literature. It can also help to include a sentence like 'Microtops is the trade mark of Matthews Computer Stores'.

## WHAT DOES REGISTRATION COST?

It depends on whether other people challenge your mark during the registration process. The cost can be somewhere between £100 and £200. However, this would only be for one class of goods, and there are thirty-four altogether. If you intend to use your mark on more than one product, you may need to apply for registration in more than one class.

## A STEP-BY-STEP GUIDE TO REGISTERING A TRADE OR SERVICE MARK

> **1.** Consider whether the mark will distinguish your product from another. Is it similar to another mark? Could it confuse consumers about the nature of the product or service? Even if the mark is an ordinary word or name, do you believe that your reputation has built it up into a distinguishing feature for your product or service?
>
> **2.** Apply to have the mark filed at the Registry. Include the required fee and a description of the goods on which your mark will be used. This must be done in accordance with the rules laid down by the Registry.
>
> **3.** The Registry considers the application; if there are any objections you will be told, so that you can decide if the situation can be redeemed or if you should choose another mark and start again.
>
> **4.** After about fifteen months from the application, the Registry will advertise the mark in the Trade Marks Journal. If there is no opposition, the trade or service mark is registered.

## GETTING HELP AND ADVICE

There are a number of organizations and associations which inventors and designers can join. These provide publications and hold meetings.

To get help with the actual process of patenting an invention or registering a design or trade mark, you can approach a patent agent or trade mark agent, who should be a member of the Chartered Institute of Patent Agents or the Institute of Trade Mark Agents.

Help and advice may also be available from local innovation centres. Inventors should beware of organizations which demand a sum of money before any help is given.

The names and addresses where you can contact the various organizations are on p. 406).

## SUMMARY

1. The strongest way of protecting an invention, design, service or trade mark is to use effective marketing (Chapters 2., 11. and 13.) to build up a reputation among customers for your product.

2. Patents and registration can provide protection; but the law cannot achieve this alone. You need to be vigilant in following up infringements of your rights.

3. With inventions and designs the crucial factor to remember is to keep quiet about them before you apply for a patent or design registration. If you have not, the invention or design is no longer new and you will achieve no protection.

OTHER CHAPTERS TO READ

USEFUL PUBLICATIONS

*Introducing patents; a guide for inventors*
*How to prepare a UK patent application*
*Introducing design registration*
*Applying to register a design*
*Applying for a trade mark*

These titles are all published by the Patent Office, London.

# 13. GETTING THE MESSAGE ACROSS

Do you know what message you want to say about yourself, your product, your business? If you do not, how can your customers know? But knowing the message is not the end of the story. You have to decide who to send it to and how you are going to do it. If your message is not received loud and clear, your customers will not understand why they should buy from you or what it is they are getting. If they do not know the reason for buying, there will be no sales; if they have the wrong reason for buying, there will be dissatisfaction.

If you do not manage to communicate effectively the benefits of your product or service, your business will fail. The message, and getting it across, is crucial. But think carefully; the obvious solution is advertising, but advertising can swallow up a lot of money. There are other techniques that may work as well, and be cheaper.

WHAT IS IN THIS CHAPTER?

This chapter concentrates on written communication about your product to your potential market.

First, it helps you to define your message. Second, the chapter looks at what your advertising should aim to achieve. And it explains the main types of promotion which could be useful for a small business or the self-employed. These include:

- Brochures and leaflets (p. 153)

- Public relations (p. 153)

- Mail shots (and see the step-by-step guide to organizing one) (p. 154)

- Advertisements (p. 157)

- Directories (p. 159).

Finally, it gives brief hints on how you make your promotional choice.

# THE MESSAGE: WHO, WHAT, HOW

## WHO IS THE MESSAGE TO?

If you do not know what your target market is, you really do not deserve to succeed. You need this information at your fingertips from a very early stage of planning your business, see Chapter 2. 'Who will buy?' (p. 28). Defining the target market necessitates sorting out its characteristics: the number, the location, the spending power, the class structure (if consumer).

Knowledge of the target market is needed to help refine the message *and* to select the most useful way of communicating the message to that particular group.

## WHAT IS YOUR MESSAGE?

You need to work out what message you want to send to customers. The two main constituents of your message are:

1. *the long-term reputation* you want to build for your product or business. This can be things like good quality, good service, reliability, quick service, good value and so on. There is more about the reputation you want in Chapter 11. 'The right name' (p. 134).
2. *the specific message* you want to get across now. Of course, this may simply be part of building your reputation, as above. Or it could be that you want to describe your product, giving customers the information they need to make a buying decision. Or it could be some specific offer you have available. Or it could be an item of good news about your business. The potential list is endless, but you must know the specific objective you want each communication to achieve.

## HOW TO SEND THE MESSAGE

There are numerous ways of trying to get across your message to your target market. The trick is to select the most cost-effective way of reaching your group. The cost of communication should be measured by what you have to spend to reach each potential customer or, if possible, by the number of sales leads each pound spent generates. Obviously, any cost-conscious small business has to look at the total figure, too. But it would not make good sense to plump for a way of sending the message on the grounds that the overall cost is least, if few customers are reached. What matters is how many possible buyers receive the message compared to the total expense.

Very broadly, you can communicate with your customers by:

- *speaking the message:* this includes direct selling to customers, carrying out demonstrations, and attending exhibitions. This is covered in Chapter 14. 'Selling' (p. 162)

- *writing the message:* this includes advertisements, brochures and mail shots. These might be loosely called advertising and are described in this chapter

- *implying the message:* this does not give any specific details, but gives an impression about your business or product. For example, the quality and design of your letterhead, a business gift or van sign send an implied message to anyone who sees them. You should recognize that all ways of communicating the message, such as selling and advertising, also include an element of this. An advertisement does not simply have a picture and some words describing a benefit; the whole adds up to more than this, or it should. It should build up the general impression you want.

## WHAT CAN YOU EXPECT ADVERTISING TO DO FOR YOU?

Sell more. Unfortunately, it does not seem to work quite like this. The direct link between spending money on advertising and generating more sales is rather difficult to establish; the linkage is there, but measurement is fraught with problems. Advertising is an investment decision, as are all the other ways of trying to get your message across. Spend money now in the hope of more sales later; but the outcome and the return are not certain.

Your advertising strategy should aim to help the potential customer from a state of ignorance about your product to a desire to purchase it. It should:

- get attention for your product
- help them understand the product or service
- get them to believe in the benefits
- establish a desire for the product
- generate action
- improve the reputation and general impression of the product.

You should not expect one particular form of advertising carried out at one particular time to achieve all this. To expect it might be counter-productive, if it leads you to cram too many objectives into one small piece of advertising. Your strategy should be to use a mix of different forms to achieve these aims over a long period of time.

And if you can sell as much as you want by personal contact, do not waste your money on advertisements, PR or literature. With large-value items sold to a few buyers, spending more on direct selling might be a better use of your money.

Apart from the obvious form of advertising – advertisements in newspapers and magazines – there are other forms which small businesses will probably find more useful.

## BROCHURES AND LEAFLETS

Brochures and leaflets can be used to send out in response to sales queries or as mailings to generate interest. They can be given out by sales people to reinforce the sales message and shown to suppliers to give credibility about your business. They are relatively cheap, although it is important that they should look consistent with the image you are trying to build. So they should not look tatty and the style should follow on from letterheads, packaging and labels.

A brochure can be used to describe your product as well as drawing attention to the benefits. Beware of filling a brochure with a mass of technical details; if the only recipients are going to be highly technical people, consider cheaper forms of advertising, such as leaflets. If necessary, keep the brochure jargon-free and tuck a one-page sheet in the back with all the technical details.

Leaflets are cheaper still, as they may be only one or two pages or a foldover. But again, the style should be consistent and the leaflet should not look low-quality. A leaflet can be used more widely than brochures, given out at exhibitions, sent out in mail shots or dropped through letter-boxes. As with brochures, a leaflet should not be crammed with technical detail, unless it is specifically for technical people; instead, it should try to attract attention and increase awareness of your name and product. What is likely to catch a target reader's eye will be the benefit which can be obtained from using your service or product.

## PUBLIC RELATIONS

This can be a low-cost method of getting across a message to the marketplace, although it can be time consuming. The basic aim is to get information or news about your business in magazines or newspapers, in the form of an article or news item. If you can achieve this, such items are seen as very credible and 'true', in a way that advertising is not, because readers place greater trust in the objectivity of journalists. Sometimes the newspaper or magazine will only accept editorial material if it is accompanied by an advertisement, which obviously you have to pay for.

The main ways of achieving this use of the press are to:

- *issue press releases* when there is a news item. You will have to write this yourself, or pay someone else to do it. If you do the latter, you are losing one of the benefits of public relations, which is its low cost.

To write a press release yourself, keep to the facts, brief and salient. The length of the press release should be as short as possible and summarize all that you want to say in the first paragraph, as this may be all there is room for in the journal. Somewhere on the press release, put a name and the telephone number, where editors and journalists can speak to someone about the release.

If there is a good quote which you can include from yourself or person in your business responsible for this item, this can be an excellent way of lightening the copy and making it more readable. If there is any other personal or human angle, which might appeal to the public, do not forget to introduce that. Do not be too optimistic about the chances of getting your press release in – hundreds will be sent to the journal or newspaper each week.

Press releases stand a better chance of publication if there is a photograph attached. It can be a good investment to have some interesting photos of you and the business, which can be appended to the release

- *get to know the editor or journalist*. In this way, if you have a story, you could ring your contact before issuing a press release, to see if they would be interested because it is 'exclusive'. This may well be a more successful way of publicizing your story than issuing press releases

- *try writing suitable small articles*, for example, for trade or technical papers, and sending them in.

## MAIL SHOTS

There are many ways of trying to ensure that your communication reaches your target market in the most efficient manner possible. These are:

1. Using a mailing list and sending leaflets or a letter through the post.

2. Putting an insert in a trade or regional magazine.

3. Delivering by door-to-door distribution agencies, such as postmen, free newspapers. Look in Yellow Pages for Addressing and Circularizing Services and Circular and Sample Distributors to find the names of agencies. Alternatively, you could see if teenagers or retired people might be interested in the work.

4. Sending direct mail shots with other companies. This would work if you are doing a joint promotion, or, if you are not competing with the other company but are aiming at the same target market.

5. Leaving your leaflets or whatever at a sale outlet, for example, a shop, to be picked up by customers.

6. Delivering your communication by a salesperson. This is very expensive.

The most personalized method in the list above, apart from delivering by sales staff, is sending your message through the post using a mailing list. The other methods might work best for fairly general notices to raise awareness of the existence of the business or product.

The success of a mail shot depends on:

- the accuracy of the mailing list, or other means of distribution

- the impact of what you have written.

To have a successful mail shot by sending to customers through the post, the accuracy of the mailing list is paramount. Why waste the postage and cost of printing letters or leaflets to send to customers who have died, moved away or gone out of business?

Here are some steps to help you organize a mail shot:

---

1. Build up your mailing list from all past, present and potential customers. You can get names from personal contacts, through existing customers, following up requests for information, from exhibitions and so on.

2. Add to your mailing list by checking trade directories, members of trade associations, in fact, any likely place for finding potential members of your target market.

3. Consider renting or exchanging mailing lists with other

organizations. If you can buy a list it means you can use it as often as you like, but few organizations sell them. If you are going to rent or exchange, the other organization may insist on using a specialist mailing service, so you cannot copy the list. The organization may also want to see what you are going to send out, so that they can approve what is going to their customers. If necessary ask a list broker to help find suitable lists for a fee.

**4.** Weed out all 'gone aways', 'cannot be founds' and 'died' from your mailing list. To achieve this you need to keep working on your mailing list on a regular basis and feeding in any information which comes in. But keep a separate note of old sales leads that appear to have gone away, in case they resurface.

**5.** Find out the name of the most suitable individual to receive your message. If you are sending to businesses, do not simply send to a company or to a position, for example, the chief accountant. Finding out names may mean telephoning the company first.

**6.** Always include a letter addressed to the individual and, if possible, signed personally by yourself or someone in your business, not pp'd (that is, signed by someone else on your behalf).

**7.** Remember what image you are trying to build. Choose good quality literature, paper and envelopes. Make the style consistent with all your other correspondence.

**8.** Look carefully at what you are sending. If it is a letter, do not make it too long; probably one or two pages is the maximum. Nor should it be too cluttered with jargon. Try to grab your reader's attention in the opening sentence or headline. Make sure that the letter ties up with any other material, such as leaflets, catalogues. If you are making some special offer, make sure it is understandable.

**9.** Consider how you can increase the response. Would reply cards or coupons be a good idea? Could you use Freepost for replies? The charge for this is $\frac{1}{2}$p on top of normal postage, but you have to pay a licence fee of £20 and there is a minimum charge of £25.

**10.** Test your mailer first, if you think it necessary. Learn from your mistakes and improve your full mail shot.

**11.** Work out the cost. Try to assess your likely response rate. Only one and half per cent is considered to be a normal response. A poor mailing list could mean even less inquiries. Calculate the cost for each response by dividing total expenses by number of likely inquiries or follow-ups. Is this a cost-effective way of reaching potential customers?

If the mail shot is expected to achieve awareness rather than instant sales, this could only be checked for cost effectiveness by researching afterwards. This could be done by contacting a sample of the mailing list to see if the mail shot was received and to get a reaction.

**12.** Do not forget to find out about any cheap rates on offer to new businesses and for large postings from the Post Office

## ADVERTISEMENTS

You can advertise in:

- local and national newspapers
- national, technical or special interest magazines
- reference handbooks, trade directories
- local radio
- cinema or TV

However, small businesses are unlikely to find that advertising in this way meets their needs, apart from advertisements in technical or special interest magazines or local newspapers.

Before embarking on an advertisement, every small business has to decide six things:

1. Which newspaper or magazine?
2. What size and position of advertisement?
3. What goes in the advertisement?
4. When do you advertise?
5. How often do you run this, or any other, ad?
6. Advertising agency or not?

1. *Which newspaper or magazine?*
Choosing the right place to put your advertisement is crucial. To be cost-effective, the ad must be placed where it reaches the biggest possible section of your potential customers. The journal or paper must be read by the people or businesses you want to talk to and by people at the right level in the organizations or in the right class grouping in the population.

Two important statistics you need to find are the number of copies sold and what is the readership. Larger magazines have their circulation figures independently audited by the Audit Bureau of Circulations (ABC), although it may be necessary to rely on publishers' claims for smaller magazines. Rates charged for space usually bear some sort of relationship to circulation. Do not assume that the cheapest or the most expensive will be the best bet. Try to estimate the cost per reader for any ad you want to put in.

A listing of magazines and journals accepting advertising, together with the prices charged for space can be found in British Rate and Data (BRAD). Look in your local reference library.

2. *What size and position of ad?*
Clearly the cost of your ad is affected by its size and its position; the bigger the ad and the better the position, the more expensive it will be. For example, an ad on the front page will be seen by more readers and an ad which does not have to compete with others on the same page will be more easily seen, too. There is no clear-cut advice which can be given about whether to go for bigger and better.

In a trade magazine, a good rule of thumb is:

- in first third of magazine
- on a news or editorial page
- on a right-hand page, and
- one third the size of the page.

3. *What goes in the ad?*
Here are some general guidelines, none of which are sacrosanct:

- have a clear, straightforward message
- do not be afraid of white space in an ad
- use as few words as you can to get your message across

- steer clear of humour; readers may not share your sense of what is, or is not, funny

- do not copy other people's ideas

- remember you are speaking to your customers, not competitors or yourself

- the reader is more interested in the message, than in your name, so do not put your name at the top of the ad

- an ad is easier to read if the words go from left to right and from top to bottom.

### 4. *When do you put the ad in?*
There may be seasonal fluctuations in your business and an advertising strategy may need to take this into account, using ads at the start of the summer for summer goods and at the start of the winter for winter ones.

### 5. *How often do you run this, or any other, ad?*
One isolated ad on its own may, frankly, achieve little. If that is all you can afford, you may be better concentrating on the other ways of getting your message across. To achieve objectives such as increasing awareness, generating further action or reminding existing buyers, an ad may need to be repeated several times. A different ad may be required to follow the first one up and to consolidate the improvement in awareness, and, ultimately, in sales.

### 6. *An ad agency or not?*
You do not have to use one, but your objectives are more likely to be achieved if you do select one. There are lots of small agencies who are willing to work for small businesses, and you may be able to find one you can work with and can afford. Negotiate what fee is payable before you commit yourself. Very often, what you pay is based on a percentage of the advertising space you take in newspapers and magazines. But the agency may require a minimum fee. There may also be a percentage charged on the cost of items like brochures and leaflets if the agency is involved in helping you design those.

### DIRECTORIES
It may be important in your type of business to pay for entries in various directories, the commonest of which is Yellow Pages. Before you commit yourself to paying for an entry, investigate how many copies of the

directory are sold and to whom. The longer-established diectories may be the ones with the biggest usage by potential customers. Directories tend to be published once a year and entries need planning a long time in advance. For example, if you want to be in Yellow Pages, you need to apply many months before it actually appears.

## DECIDING THE ADVERTISING STRATEGY

For most small businesses, the single most important determinant of what advertising is done is the cost. If you cannot afford much, there is one area which should not be skimped on: good letterheads, good quality paper, labels, product packaging and, possibly, this should be extended to include a professionally designed logo. Other ideas you should consider are the effect of van liveries, uniforms and premises.

Once you have established this as a priority, what advertising forms part of your strategy will vary depending on the nature of your business. However, it would be a mistake to think of each type in isolation from the other.

A successful strategy will include a mix of advertising. Each form of communicating your message will support the other forms, and will be consistent with the image of your product or of your business which you hope to sustain. A strategy should also be considered as extending over a long period of time, rather than isolated actions.

## SUMMARY

1. To communicate your message about your product's benefits, you need to know who you want to talk to, what your message is and the best way of getting your message across.

2. Advertising can create attention, inform, remind, prompt sales and improve the image of your product. But the return from advertising is uncertain. It costs more and takes longer than you think.

3. Advertising which is most suitable for small businesses includes brochures and leaflets, public relations, mail shots, advertisements in technical magazines and entries in directories.

4. Do not rely on one form of advertising to achieve your objectives. If you can afford it, use a mixture and try to organize a spread of advertising over a period of time (unless you have specific timing to consider for your product).

5. The advertising must be consistent with the impression of your product and business which you are endeavouring to foster among potential buyers.

OTHER CHAPTERS TO READ

2. 'Who will buy?' (p. 28)
11. 'The right name' (p. 134)

# 14.  SELLING

The simple truth is that if you do not make any sales you do not have a business. This chapter looks mainly at direct selling: the face-to-face encounter, the telephone conversation or the demonstration.

However, one important rule for you to remember is that every part of your business will be involved in selling, in the search for more sales. This extends from answering the telephone, to your notepaper and literature, to any person or activity in your business which may one day come into contact with an existing or potential customer. Train everyone who answers the telephone in the correct way to do it; they must be prompt, polite, friendly and helpful. If necessary, provide them with a script to follow. But also read Chapter 11. 'The right name' (p. 134) which gives lots of useful tips on building your reputation: from choosing the right name, to the right notepaper. Chapter 13. 'Getting the message across' (p. 150) gives some simple and cheap ways of getting your company or product message across to potential buyers. You should not think of selling as confined to your sales representative or whoever does the direct selling.

The first step in gaining sales is to plan and organize. You will need to keep records of your present customers, as well as keeping track of your negotiations with potential ones. If you do not record what has happened, possible sales can drop through the cracks, for example, if you fail to follow up an initial contact or forget to provide something which is promised.

Sales records are needed for another reason: to help in business planning. For example, you will need to know week by week what is the likely level of your sales so that you can forecast what working capital you will need to fund.

The second step for effective selling is to brush up personal selling skills. If you are going to do the selling, and it has not been your job previously, it is vital to have well-thought-out dialogues and presentations. It could well be worthwhile to spend some time acquiring some training in selling skills by attending a specialized training course.

## HOW TO INCREASE SALES

Probably the quickest and easiest way to increase sales is to persuade existing customers to buy more of your product, more frequently. You may even be able to convince them to buy other products you offer. But a business will not prosper on current customers alone; you must be able to broaden your base and sell to new businesses or buyers.

### EXISTING CUSTOMERS

When a new customer signs an order, this is not the end of the selling story. You should aim to build up a long-term relationship, because, in most businesses, you will be hoping for repeat orders or for additions to the original order. These will not come to fruition if you do not follow up orders, see they are delivered on time, or, if they are going to be late, warn your customer in advance. You need to give prompt attention to any problems or criticisms.

If your business depends on a few sizeable customers, it will be important for you to establish a network of contacts in the customer's business, not just the buyer.

Another important reason for building up a good working relationship with your present customers is that they can often be the source of your new business, too. They may be able to suggest others in the same line of business who may be considering buying a similar product to yours. They may even be willing for you to use their name as an introduction. If the customer is very satisfied with your service or product, they may be willing to act as a reference for you, although obviously you must ask first. A reference means that you can give their name to potential customers and they will be prepared to discuss your business with them.

At some stage, preferably before your business has really got going, you should plan a way of recording information about your present customers. The record will need to be tailored to your individual business or product, but more than likely should include:

- name, address and telephone number of business

- customer's type of business

- what the customer has bought from you, how frequently and in what amounts

- the name of the decision-taker, plus his position and the names and positions of other contacts within the firm

- the customer's credit-rating or information about paying

- a record of visits

- any complaints and how they were resolved.

## NEW CUSTOMERS

The first stage in acquiring new customers is to work out a possible list by market research and other methods. You may, for example, start with the raw list which you use for doing mailings (Chapter 13.). But you could not possibly follow up and sell direct to everyone on this list; your efforts would not be effective because you would not be pinpointing those most likely to buy. So the list needs narrowing.

This is done in many ways:

- *following leads:* leads are those people who have approached you, either as a result of your advertising or mailers or having seen your business at an exhibition. They may have asked for your literature or for a demonstration or simply expressed interest

- *using referrals:* ask your existing customers if they know of other businesses who might be interested in your product or service. On the whole, referrals are more likely to lead to a successful sale than a lead, because you have several advantages. You already have an introduction, you know something about the person you are trying to sell to and your existing customer may have already expressed satisfaction with your business

- *by qualifying potential customers:* when you are first starting up your business, you may not have any referrals or leads to follow. All you may have is a list you have built up from market research. To reduce the list to the best prospects for you, you need to qualify. Find out the name and position of the decision-taker. Look for information about the potential customer's business. Work out what are likely to be the main factors which mean a business is likely to buy your product or service. This could be volume of sales, numbers of employees, location. You also need to know if the potential customer is considering buying a product like yours or has recently bought one. Your market research will identify what the key factors are for *your* product or service.

Two important aspects of sales organization are:

1. recording the information you have about each potential customer.

2. devising a strategy for following up at regular intervals those potential customers who are not interested in buying just now, but may do so in the future. Keeping in touch is important.

## HOW DO YOU SELL?

There are six possibilities:

- You, directly as a salesperson
- Sales representative
- Agent
- Distributor
- Mail order
- Over-the-counter.

## YOU

When you are first starting your business, or if it is a very small one, it is more than likely that you will be selling yourself. If you have not previously worked in this role, the prospect may be fairly daunting. But you are likely to start with one major advantage – complete product knowledge – which is very important for selling. It is possible to acquire and develop many of the personal selling skills which you need. There are many courses available which can help you do this.

If you are doing the selling, it would be a mistake to think that you do not need to organize and plan because you have stored it all in your head. You need the same information, sales systems and records as any sales rep, see below.

## SALES REPRESENTATIVE

At some stage you may decide to employ someone else to carry out or help with the selling. To enable a sales rep to work effectively, you need to make several decisions:

- how will the rep be paid?

- how much training is needed?

- what sort of back-up organization and systems will be needed?

- how to control the rep's activities.

### Pay

Most sales people will have an element of business-related remuneration. The purpose is two-fold. Firstly, commission or bonuses can be a motivator for sales people to achieve greater sales. Secondly, it allows you to keep your overheads lower by not having to pay a greater fixed salary.

Three of the possible combinations of salary and commission are:

- basic salary, plus commission on all the sales the rep makes. The rate of commission could vary depending on the volume of business already achieved, that is, the more sold the greater the rate. Commission could be based on value of sales, or if there is some discretion on pricing, possibly the amount of gross profit (p. 300) achieved by each sale

- basic salary, plus commission on sales once a certain level (or quota) has been achieved

● commission only, that is, no basic salary and every sale made triggering commission payments.

## Training
Unless you yourself as the business owner are a sales specialist, it would be unusual for a small business to take on someone who needs basic training in selling skills. If you do employ a trainee, you need to be prepared to wait for a long period before the person is achieving a good level of sales.

However, even if you employ experienced salespeople only, you may find it difficult to employ someone who knows your particular market and product in great detail. You must be prepared to provide good product training, plus detailed analysis of the strengths and weaknesses of competitive products. If you fail to do this, your sales are likely to be disappointing.

## Back-up organization
There need to be a number of systems and records in place to enable the sales effort to work effectively.

1. Sales staff spend a lot of time out of the office. This is incompatible with the need for existing and potential customers, as well as new leads, to be in contact. There needs to be a well-organized way of recording phone calls, for example, name, position and company of caller; date and time call received; brief message about purpose of call and what response was promised at your end. It goes without saying that any good sales rep will keep in touch with your office to ask what calls have been received and to follow those up.

2. Every sales rep needs a comprehensive and up-to-date price list, plus copies of any literature, press releases or publicity material.

3. If yours is the sort of business which has to issue quotes to customers, try to standardize these as much as possible. This cuts down the amount of time the rep has to spend on paperwork. This also applies to any other sales job which can be standardized. Word processors and micro computers will help. Sales letters, follow-ups to those not currently buying, and terms and conditions of the sale can be standardized. Terms and conditions can be printed on the back of the order form.

## Control
You need to exercise effective control over your sales staff. This can be difficult if they spend most of the time out of the office. You must insist on

a weekly sales meeting with prepared information, such as number of phone calls or sales visits made, demonstrations carried out, quotes issued and orders received. The sales rep should be able to give you an estimate of the probability of receiving an order from each potential customer and when it is likely to be received.

The information provided by sales people is crucial in helping you to plan your business. You may be able to produce 'conversion ratios' to help you predict your likely level of sales. This would be something like:

- a percentage of initial phone calls which become a sales visit

- a percentage of sales visits which move to the quote stage

- a percentage of quotes which turn into orders.

## AGENT

Agents are not employees. They are in business on their own. They are likely to be agents for several products, but you should insist that they are not agents for any competing products. They work for commission on each sale, often between $7\frac{1}{2}$ and 15 per cent. The agent does not buy the product from you; instead, you invoice the customer direct.

The advantage of an agent is that you do not have to fund the overheads: no salary, car, office space and so on. The disadvantage is that you may find it difficult to control the agent's activities and the effort put in to sell your product. If you have a continuing responsibility for your product or service, you need to be particularly careful that the agent does not sell to unsuitable customers.

To mitigate the disadvantages, you need a written agreement which you should enforce carefully. The agreement should include the details on territory, products the agent will sell, the type of customer the agent can sell to, the rate of commission and the duration of the agreement.

## DISTRIBUTOR

Wholesalers and distributors are not the same as agents. They are your customers. They buy direct from you. When they sell on to their customers, they expect to be able to put on a mark-up of at least 30 per cent, if not more. If you choose this route for your business it cuts out most of the costs of direct selling, as you will probably deal with only a few distributors. However, you have no control over their selling effort.

MAIL ORDER

You can sell your product direct to the end-user, cutting out the middlemen, by selling through mail order. This can be done either by advertising a particular product in a magazine or newspaper and asking customers to buy the product direct or by producing a catalogue which consumers use to make their choice. If you are selling a product direct, make sure you meet the requirements of the Newspaper Publishers' Association's Mail Order Protection Scheme. Your advertisement should also conform to the Advertising Standard Authority's code. The addresses are on p. 406.

Selling by mail order can work well if you are selling to a specialist niche and can use the appropriate magazine for your advertisement. The product should also be relatively small and relatively high-priced, otherwise the cost of postage and packing makes the whole thing unattractive for the consumer. However, response can be unpredictable, with consequent problems for you in deciding the right level of stock.

OVER-THE-COUNTER

If your product is a specialist item, for example, a craft item, you can sell direct to shops, who in turn sell to consumers. To persuade the retailer to stock your product you need to be able to convince him or her that it will sell to that shop's customers.

On the other hand, if you are the retailer the sales process is quite different from some of the others discussed in this chapter. You cannot approach a potential customer in the same way as a salesperson selling direct. Instead, you have to tempt them into the shop before the sales process can begin.

## PERSONAL SELLING SKILLS

Many people regard salespeople as liars, cheats and commercial vultures. Some salespeople may be like this; while others can be more successful by being honest and responsible, but by paying attention to every small detail and developing their own selling style to match the product, as well as their own character.

What you need to do to improve your selling skills is develop a sales strategy, which can be simple but which should be applied to every sale. One approach is to produce a series of lists. These should include:

• main features of your product

- major benefits it offers
- most likely objections and your planned response
- advantages and weaknesses of competitive products
- the key characteristics of your potential customer
- in what ways your product meets the customer's needs or wants.

There are also simple rules you can follow which will vastly improve your selling ability:

- know your product
- listen to your buyer
- relate what you are selling to your customer needs and wants
- plan your sales strategy for each prospective customer, so that you know what you want to achieve at each stage of the negotiation
- have clear and well-worked out sales presentations, demonstrations or even telephone calls
- make sure at all times that you know who the decision-maker is in your prospective client's business.

## DEVELOPING YOUR OWN SALES APPROACH

The first time you try out your selling approach should not be in a potential customer's office. It is important to feel confident in your dialogue and handling of the client. This means practice. Ask a relative or a colleague to take part in a role-playing session. The best practice for you will be obtained if the customer is played by your relative or colleague as hostile, vindictive and uncooperative. Try to carry out role-playing sessions many times before you come face-to-face with a genuine customer so that you can develop confidence in your style.

## THE STAGES OF A SALE

There are three stages to making the sale:

- opening stage (often a telephone call making an appointment to visit)
- building the sale (including sales presentations, demonstrations and dealing with objections)
- closing the sale (recognizing buying signals and asking for the order).

*Opening stage*

Your objective at this stage will usually be to make an appointment to visit a prospective buyer of your product and commence the negotiation. Obviously, you do not want to spend the time doing this unless you have already qualified this potential customer and satisfied yourself that there is a chance of selling your product.

The most efficient way of arranging appointments is to do so by telephone. The first hurdle may be to get past the buyer's secretary. Do not allow your name and phone number to be taken with a promise of ringing back. Instead, ask when your prospect will be free to take a telephone call.

The purpose of the phone call is to make the appointment, not sell your product at this stage. Try to keep it fairly brief and plan ahead what you are going to say. It may run along these lines:

1. an opening statement

2. any qualifying questions you would like to put (such as 'Are you likely to buy this product in the next three months if it meets your requirements?' or 'What is your budget?')

3. why your prospective customer should arrange a meeting to see you and your product

4. be prepared with a list of answers to the possible objections your prospect might throw out

5. offer alternative times for the appointment

6. finish the phone call.

Jot down the important parts of the conversation while you are speaking on the phone or straight afterwards.

*Building the sale*

You must plan in advance any sales call, presentation or demonstration. Carefully analyse your potential customer's needs and requirements and decide the relevance of your product or service to these.

The opening phrase is important. First impressions are important to make sure that your appearance fits in with your customer's, as well as being neat and clean. Do not waste too long on social trivialities but establish why you are there and awaken your listener's interest in your product. Before making your detailed sales pitch, ask about the customer's needs, so you can sell to these.

Important points you want to communicate to your listener are:

● the good reputation of your business, product and yourself

● the benefit your potential buyer will gain if your product or service is purchased.

This suggests that you are talking while your possible buyer is listening. But this is unlikely to achieve your sale. Salespeople have a tendency to talk too much. Instead, you should spend over half the sales call listening to your prospective customer. If you do not do this, you cannot qualify how high is the chance of making the sale and you cannot relate your product to the customer's needs. You must be able to see yourself, your product and your company through your prospective customer's eyes. This involves listening.

It also implies that your prospective customer will talk. Some try not to, which can be disconcerting. Prepare a number of open questions which you can put during the sales call. An open question is one which cannot be answered by 'yes' or 'no'.

References to other customers who are already dealing with you can be very powerful, as long as your buyer sees the reference as relevant. So the reference must be a comparable business and use.

At some stage, the subject of your competitors may be raised by your buyer. The traditional stand-by advice is 'Don't knock the competition!' On the whole, the advice is sound; criticizing the competition may have an adverse effect on your listener, because it tends to make you sound rather weak. However, do emphasize any benefits which you know your competitors do not have, as long as they are important to your buyer.

Demonstrations can be an effective selling device. You must take great care in preparing the demo. Make sure everything works before you leave your office for the appointment. Handle the equipment carefully during the demo and if it is possible involve the buyer in using and handling it during the demo.

With some products or services, quite a lot of investigation needs to be done by you before you can suggest a solution and give a quote. If yours is this sort of complicated sale, before you make a proposal you should carry out the following steps:

● make sure you are investigating the right problem

● ensure you have assembled all the facts you need by speaking to everyone involved

- keep an open mind about the solution you will propose

- keep in touch with the decision-maker and talk through your proposed solution before committing yourself to paper.

The sales proposal should simply be a restatement of what has already been said.

Little has been said so far of your potential client's reactions. If there is to be any chance of making a sale, at some stage objections will be raised. Do not view these negatively as a nuisance. An objection displays that your listener is interested in the negotiation process. An objection should be treated as a request for more information. It would be a mistake to respond to sales resistance by becoming too persistent or pressurizing too much.

There are some general guidelines to follow:

- do not contradict or argue and remain calm at all times

- do not allow the objection to become too important by spending too long replying to it or making several attempts to reply

- if possible, anticipate the objections and prepare a response

- the best way of dealing with an objection appears to be either to turn the objection into a sales benefit or to agree with the prospect, but counter with a benefit.

*Closing the sale*

It is important to ask for the order at the right psychological moment. This could be after overcoming an objection or if your potential buyer is showing buying signals. These might include asking about delivery terms or financial terms, arguing about price or asking about extras available.

If your prospective customer is hesitating, extra pressure is unlikely to be effective. Instead try to create a relaxed atmosphere to have a discussion and assume the decision will go your way. Talk about what will happen in the future and assume that there will be a continuing relationship between the two businesses.

Once you have got the order verbally, do not relax – you can still lose it. Do not count it as an order until you have received written confirmation; in particular, do not order materials until you have the order in writing. If it is a new customer, it is prudent financially to take up references or find out credit ratings before you accept the order. The last thing you want is to do all the work and find that you will not be paid.

## SUMMARY

1. Do not neglect your existing customers as a way of increasing sales. You will need to achieve a good long-term relationship to exploit their full potential.

2. Existing customers can be a useful source of new leads and you can use them as references in your negotiations with prospects.

3. Qualify all potential customers to avoid wasting time and effort. Narrow down your list to those most likely to buy from you.

4. If you employ salespeople, you will need some back-up organization and system. You need to be able to record information about customers to help with negotiations and to help you plan, control and forecast your business.

5. If you are doing the selling, try to develop personal selling skills. There are some hints about starting sales negotiations, developing them and closing the sales on pp. 169–73.

OTHER CHAPTERS TO READ

# 15. HOW TO SET A PRICE

There are four ways you can increase your profits. You can cut your costs, you can sell more, you can change your product mix or you can increase your prices. Clearly your aim should be to set your prices initially at the level which gives you your highest profits possible. Needless to say, as with everything else to do with your business, it is easier said than done. There is no clear-cut or agreed method of establishing a price for your product or service.

Some people use the level of costs as a way of fixing price. This may seem a fairly straightforward calculation, but it has drawbacks. For example, if your costs are very low, does it automatically mean that your prices should be low too? And even working out the cost of your product can be fraught with possible errors.

Other people argue that the price should be set by what the market can bear. But there are no quick and simple calculations which can tell you what this should be. Instead, you have to establish the price by looking at the market you are in and the particular part of it your product appeals to. How does your product rate against others competing in the same marketplace? There are also different strategies you can adopt depending on whether your product is a new or old one. Often overriding all your plans can be the effect which your competitors' pricing policy has on yours.

It is probably more realistic to think in terms of a range of prices. The lowest price you should consider setting will be fixed by the cost. On the whole, you should not go below this price; if you have to, it would be better not to be in business at all. There are a couple of exceptions, of course, where temporarily it may make sense (p. 178). The highest price will be the highest the market can bear without sales disappearing altogether. Between the two will be the price which will give you the highest possible profits.

WHAT IS IN THIS CHAPTER?

- The price range (p. 176)
- The highest price (p. 176)

## THE PRICE RANGE

There is a range of prices open to you to charge for your product or service. Your aim should be to get as near as possible to the price which is going to give you the highest profit. But this is a long-term strategy; there may be short-term considerations which imply that another price could be more appropriate at that time.

## THE HIGHEST PRICE

This strategy means you have decided to go for the cream at the top of the market. In marketing jargon, it is called price skimming or prestige pricing. You are pricing your product to appeal to those of your potential customers with the highest incomes or those seeking the snob value of buying a very high-priced item. You can also carry out this price-skimming policy if you have a product with a genuine technical advantage or if it has novelty value.

Adopting a price-skimming policy implies usually that you are accepting that you could make bigger profits if you lowered the price, because you would sell correspondingly more. Nevertheless, this sort of strategy can be very appealing to small businesses. To sell more you may need to invest in bigger production facilities, or employ more staff if you are offering a service. This could involve raising funds to be able to do so. And you may find that this bigger business is harder for you to control. Creating a specialist niche could be ideal for the self-employed and small business owner. While it may not give the highest possible profits, it could make you a very acceptable living.

A pitfall to watch out for is that high prices attract competitors. Your profitable niche may soon be invaded by those offering lower prices or a better service or product. You need to allow for this competition in a price-skimming strategy. This particularly applies if you are adopting a price-skimming policy because your product is new with a technical innovation. It is unlikely to remain unique for long. Your strategy needs to involve either reducing prices in the longer term or concentrating on other advantages or benefits, so that your product establishes its own image. This allows it to carry on commanding a higher price even when the technical advantage no longer exists.

## THE LOWEST PRICE

The lowest price you should consider accepting for your product is the one which covers your direct costs and contributes something to the cost of your overheads. But this must be regarded as a last resort and not to be accepted if you can obtain business at a higher price.

### HOW IS IT WORKED OUT?

You need to find the direct costs of your product or service. Direct costs are the costs which you would not have if you were not producing that particular item. Your business will also have other costs, indirect costs or overheads. You will still have to pay for these whether you produce the item or not.

*Example*

Sidney Smith knows that the cost of producing his stationery pads is as follows:

| | |
|---|---|
| Direct materials (paper, glue) | 10 pence |
| Direct labour | 5 pence |
| Total direct costs | 15 pence |

Lowest price Sidney should consider accepting for his stationery pads is 15 pence plus something towards the cost of his overheads, for example, 16 pence a pad.

Note that the terms direct costs, indirect costs and contribution to overheads are explained in much more detail in the section BREAK-EVEN POINT on p. 299.

### WHEN SHOULD YOU USE THIS PRICE?

As little as possible, must be the answer. You would need to sell very large volumes of your product to have enough contribution to cover the cost of your overheads, never mind make a profit.

The main circumstance in which you can justify selling as cheaply as this is if you have spare capacity in your business, with very little prospect of using it for product or services selling at a higher price. If this is the case, anything you sell which helps to contribute to the cost of your overheads should be considered.

However, making this decision can have longer-term effects which must be considered. If you are operating in a market which is very competitive or in one in which your customers tend to be in contact, you may find that you are being forced to sell all your products or service at this very low price. If your customers talk to each other, it will soon become an established fact that you can be forced to sell at this low price. Raising or maintaining your prices can be very difficult in these circumstances.

Selling your product at the lowest price, even on a one-off basis, can have an even worse effect on your business if it triggers off price-cutting by your competitors. This could well occur if customers use your low price to force the competition to lower their prices.

The moral is only sell something at this contribution price if it is a one-off product, perhaps not part of your normal range of goods, and if you are very confident that it will not lead to secondary effects on your other product or the competition. You must only consider this price if you have spare capacity. If you do not have any spare capacity, choose the price which gives you the biggest contribution.

## CAN YOU GO LOWER THAN THIS PRICE?

Only in exceptional cases, such as if you need to clear excess stocks or low-selling lines. If this is the case, try to clear these outside your main selling channels, so it can have no counter-effect on your normal selling activity.

## WHY YOU SHOULD NOT USE COST AS A BASIS FOR ESTABLISHING YOUR NORMAL PRICE

Many businesses work out their prices by calculating what it costs to make the product or service and adding on what they consider a suitable profit margin. But this approach is not satisfactory for two reasons:

• it is surprisingly difficult to work out what it costs to produce an item

● the cost of an item tells you nothing about whether customers will buy it at that price at all or whether they would have paid much more.

There are various different ways of working out the cost of something. But very often businesses use some variation of a standard costing system. Typically, it looks something like this:

| | |
|---|---:|
| Direct materials | £100.00 |
| Direct labour | 75.00 |
| Indirect materials (50 per cent of direct materials, say) | 50.00 |
| Indirect labour (30 per cent of direct labour, say) | 22.50 |
| General overhead (40 per cent of direct labour, say) | 30.00 |
| Total cost | £277.50 |
| Profit margin (add 20 per cent) | 55.50 |
| Price | £333.00 |

Of course, there may be various discounts offered on this price.

The problem with this system is the difficulty of working out how much of the indirect costs and overheads should be added to each product to work out the cost. To be able to attribute a certain percentage to the product, you need to have:

● some idea or forecast of the total amount of overheads and indirect costs for the year, and

● some idea of the total amount of your product you will sell during the year.

In other words, a pricing system based on cost is based on your best forecasts. Obviously, forecasts can be wrong. You may find that you have not sold at a price high enough to cover the cost of overheads, because either your sales are lower or your overhead costs higher than your forecast.

The problem is multiplied if you have more than one product or service. How do you decide how much of the indirect costs and overheads should be apportioned to each product? There is no clear-cut answer.

## SETTING A PRICE

There are several influences which will determine how near the top or how near the bottom end of the price range your product should be placed. These are:

- how your product compares to competitive products
- the lifecycle of the product, that is, how new or mature
- how price sensitive are your customers
- what price conveys to your customers
- what position in the market.

## HOW YOUR PRODUCT COMPARES TO COMPETITIVE PRODUCTS

Assuming that you face competition in your chosen market, it is realistic to assume that the price you can place on your product will, to a certain extent, depend on the competition. This does not mean that if your competitors price very low, you have to follow suit. But it does mean that you should analyse your product carefully in relation to the others. The sort of characteristics you should look at include:

- what your product looks like and how it performs compared to the others
- how it is packaged and presented
- what is the availability?
- is your delivery and after-sales service better or worse than competitors?
- how do customers pay? (easy payment terms are a form of price discounts)
- has your product a better image or reputation?

If your product compares favourably with the others, you may be able to justify a higher price than the competition, even if you are relatively new into the market. Do not be afraid of putting a higher price than the competition. If your product does really have benefits, such as better delivery and service, or a better image, the marketplace may well accept that your price should be higher.

## WHAT STAGE IN ITS LIFECYCLE?

If it is a new product, one not before produced, such as video recorders a few years ago, there are two possible strategies to adopt. One possibility is a price-skimming policy (p. 176), which goes for an initial high price. The other possibility is to try to secure a very large share of the market for your product before the competition appears on the scene. This would be achieved by setting the price fairly low, known as penetration policy (p. 184).

## HOW PRICE SENSITIVE ARE YOUR CUSTOMERS?

If you put up your prices, do you have any idea how many of your existing customers would switch to another supplier? Or if you dropped your prices how many new customers would you acquire? How great an effect changes in prices have on the amount you sell is called price sensitivity (or elasticity of demand). If customer response to price changes in your product are not that great, you can push nearer the upper end of the price range.

Broadly speaking, if your product is not bought that frequently, that is, one purchase will last quite a long time, the sales of it will not be so sensitive to price changes. On the other hand, if it is bought at regular intervals, sales may react much more strongly.

If it is difficult to differentiate one product from another in your market, this also implies that it will react much more strongly to price changes. If, on the other hand, your product can be differentiated from others by perceived benefits such as image, delivery and so on, sales will be more resistant to price changes.

## WHAT PRICE CONVEYS TO YOUR CUSTOMERS

Price alone can conjure up ideas about your product in your potential customers' minds. The consumer often associates higher quality with a higher price; paradoxically, a high price can help the image or reputation of your product. If this applies to your market, a lower price will not generate more sales.

In general terms, a product which has the greatest market share is unlikely to be the cheapest. These products may generate high sales, because despite their high price they are thought by consumers to offer the best package of benefits (or best value for money).

## WHAT POSITION IN THE MARKET?

Often, your ability to set prices may be limited by the market in which you operate. There may be a going rate established in the market, and unless your product becomes the market leader (p. 182) or is definitely a better product, it may be difficult to establish any other price.

The price of your product needs to fit the market position planned for it. This is the place that the product occupies, compared to competitive products, in the eyes of your existing or potential customers.

## A STEP-BY-STEP GUIDE TO SETTING PRICES

---

**1.** Analyse the position your product holds in the market. Are your target customers those who are looking for reliability? Has your product already achieved an established image in the eyes of the market? Do buyers view it as good quality, prompt service, stylish, say?

**2.** Analyse your product. Are you planning modifications or alterations which could alter its reputation or relative position in the marketplace?

**3.** Analyse the competition. How do their products rate against yours? What is the relative price structure in the market?

**4.** Decide your pricing strategy. Where in the price range are you going to pitch your price? Is it going to be average for the market, 5 per cent less than the average, 5 per cent above the average or a premium price, 25 per cent above the average?

**5.** Choose some specific prices. Estimate volume of sales, profit margin and costs to forecast the level of profits for each price.

**6.** Choose your price.

**7.** Would you be able to test market the price in a small area of your market? This would allow you to gauge customer reactions.

---

## PRICE NEAR THE TOP END OF THE RANGE

There are two possible reasons why you may be able to justify a price near the top end of the range:

- the product is market leader

- the product is set apart from the competition by non-price benefits.

### MARKET LEADER

The market leader will be the biggest selling product in the market. There are several advantages to being the market leader, and so it is a position worth aspiring to. The advantages include being able to charge a higher price than the average, making greater sales, having more power over your suppliers and competitors, and being less risky in poor economic conditions.

There is, of course, no easy way to become the market leader. Some of the guidelines to achieve the premier position include:

- try to be one of the first into the market

- develop, by careful marketing, selling and advertising, what is different about your product or business

- be ruthless about efficiency and costs

- be sensitive to changes in the market

- compete intensively on all sales

- look for profits over a long period, not the short-term fast buck – so lengthen your horizon.

## NON-PRICE BENEFITS

The price you put on the product tells prospective customers something about it. On the whole, a higher price implies high quality, a lower price low quality. You are unlikely to build a business offering a low quality product at a high price; on the other hand, you are throwing away profits if you offer high quality at a low price. You have to decide where your product is placed in the market compared to competitors and price accordingly.

You will be able to justify a higher price, near the top end of the range, if you decide to offer a high-quality product. You must not be frightened into thinking that the only thing that matters to buyers is price; they are interested in other aspects of your product, too.

In your marketing and selling, build an image or reputation for quality, efficient service, reliability, prompt delivery, effective sales and technical literature. This will allow you to raise prices and generate higher profits.

## PRICE NEAR THE BOTTOM END OF THE RANGE

There are three main reasons why your pricing policy might be near the bottom end of the range:

- fear (because you mistakenly believe that the main factor in buying is price – but see above)

- a strategy of grabbing market share

- severe price competition.

## MARKET SHARE

A legitimate strategy for a business is to sacrifice the level of profits in return for an increased market share. To achieve this, you would pitch the price near the low end of the possible price range (in marketing jargon, a penetration price) in return for selling more of the product. The intention in the strategy is to increase your market share, to consolidate your position, to increase your prices gradually while retaining the share you have established. Essentially, the aim is eventually to become the market leader with higher unit sales at a higher price.

There are a number of dangers inherent in this strategy:

- you may find it exceptionally difficult to raise your prices, without demonstrating an improvement in the product in compensation

- you may find that your new customers do not remain faithful to your product when you move the price upwards; instead they return to their original supplier

- you may trigger off a price war with your competitors.

The likeliest use of the strategy occurs when you are introducing a new product to the market, and the competition is weak. In this case, you can establish a large market share without attracting strong competition because of the large profits to be made.

Few small firms will have the financial and managerial resources available to achieve this strategy of establishing a large market share successfully; it is really too risky to be considered. Instead, they should look more closely at devoting the available resources to promotion or advertising.

## FACING SEVERE PRICE COMPETITION

Low prices or a price-cutting war is an advantage to very few people: you do not want it, other small competing firms do not want it; in the long run, customers do not want it, if it means a reduced number of suppliers and less choice. It may only be in the long-term interest of a large company, if that is your main competitor. So whatever you do, try to avoid triggering it off.

If one of your competitors cuts prices, what should you do? Try to avoid the instant reaction of following prices downwards. Instead try to concentrate your customers' minds on the non-price benefits (p. 183) of doing business with you. If you have carried out some market research you will know which are the non-price factors which buyers rate most highly, and these can be emphasized.

However, if you operate in a market which is very price sensitive and does not differentiate between products, there is little choice but to match the price cuts. In this case, your survival will depend on savage reduction in your costs.

## PRICING WITH MORE THAN ONE PRODUCT

If you have more than one product, the sales could be interlinked if they are:

- competing with each other, or

- complementary to each other.

You need to ensure that your pricing policy is consistent across the range of your products. With competing products, the prices need to make sense. There needs to be a recognizable gap in the prices, if one is a high-quality product while the other is lower quality.

The pricing considerations are different if your products are complementary, that is, if you sell one, you are likely to sell the other. Once your customer is hooked, there will be lots of scope for charging high prices on a complementary item, as long as it is not so blatant that it puts off buyers from the starting product.

## SUMMARY

1. There is a range of prices which you can charge for your product or service.

2. The lowest price is set by the contribution to overheads that it makes. Never go below this price. Only accept this price if you have spare capacity and there is no prospect of selling your product or time at a higher rate. If you have little or no spare capacity, choose the sale which gives you the biggest contribution.

3. Do not use costs as the basis of setting your prices, at least not without trying to price the product according to what customers will pay.

4. If you go for the highest price possible in the market, you will restrict the amount you can sell. It will not give you the maximum possible level of profits. However, a specialist niche of this type can be attractive to a small business.

5. When it comes to setting a price you have to compare your product with others, establish how responsive sales are to a change in prices, work out your strategy if it is a new product or coming to the end of its life, analyse what price conveys to your customers and decide what position your product is aiming for in the market. Use the step-by-step guide on p. 182.

6. The market leader has several advantages; the main ones are that it means you can achieve more sales at a higher price than the competition.

7. Justify a higher price by stressing non-price benefits, such as quality, reliability, delivery and so on.

8. Avoid pitching your price too low through fear or misunderstanding what buyers are interested in.

9. A strategy of increasing market share through low prices is dangerous for a small business.

10. If you are facing severe price competition, try to distract attention from price by emphasizing the product benefits.

OTHER CHAPTERS TO READ

# 16. CHOOSING YOUR WORKPLACE

One of the jokes that can be made about someone starting a small business is that the first thing they want to do is search for premises. It is an understandable desire, as premises are tangible proof of the creation of an enterprise. However, if the business is to stand any chance of success, it is *not* the first step. There is a whole host of other jobs to be done first, researching the market, positioning the product or service, drawing up the business plan and so on.

Nevertheless, finding a workplace is a very important step to take. It can also prove to be extraordinarily difficult to find the right premises at just the right location for just the right price. It is a problem which is particularly acute for those starting in the UK, especially in the South-east. If your business was transported to the US, the problem would seem much less immense. But the UK is densely populated and land values and hence property values are proportionately high.

The problem looms even larger for those businesses where premises are critical to success or failure, such as a retail business. If you are planning to start a shop, a large part of the setting-up process *will* be devoted to a search for a good location. And you cannot afford to compromise and take premises which with a bit of luck will be OK. You have to be satisfied that they meet all your criteria; if they do not, carry on the search until they do.

WHAT IS IN THIS CHAPTER?

The important steps to take are:

- Where is your business to be located? (p. 188)

- What sort of premises do you need? (p. 191)

- Searching for premises (p. 193)

- Investigating and negotiating (p. 195).

## WHERE IS YOUR BUSINESS TO BE LOCATED?

An important first exercise would be to start with a blank piece of paper and think about location from first principles. What is the ideal location for the type of business you have in mind? At a later stage, you can introduce the constraints placed on location, such as home and family. You should know the ideal location so you can estimate the effect of concessions you are making to these outside non-business constraints. There may be further business constraints, such as the lack of finance, which may cause you to compromise and choose a less than perfect location.

### COMMUNICATIONS

How dependent is the success of your business on communications: road, rail, air, bus? This could be important if your business falls into one of the following categories:

- you deliver your product
- your business is service-based to particular areas of population
- you sell your product direct, using salespeople
- your business is dependent on import and export.

In these and other categories of business, an ideal location would allow easy access to the relevant parts of the country. For example, if import/export is your trade, a location within reach of a major airport could be an advantage. Or, if you direct sell to the whole country, you need to be on the motorway system.

### LABOUR

If your business is dependent on the use of certain skills, you may find that one part of the country is more abundantly endowed with potential employees who have already acquired those skills than other parts. On the other hand, skills may be irrelevant; what you may need is a ready pool of unskilled labour, in which case some areas have higher unemployment than others.

### CENTRES OF POPULATION

Your business may need to be located near particular centres of population. If you are trying to sell your product in large volume, being in a large centre of population may be an advantage. Or you may want to choose an area with a specific structure of population if your product or service is sold only to particular sectors. For example, if you plan to open a bookshop, you need a town or population area of a certain size. You also need a population well endowed with the particular characteristics of those who buy books. Your market research will help you identify what those characteristics are.

SUPPLIERS

Your business may depend on supplies of a particular raw material or some other product. Costs would be lessened if your business was located near the source of supply. This could either be the main distributor of the item or it could be where the item is grown or produced.

GOVERNMENT AND LOCAL AUTHORITY ASSISTANCE

Your business may be location-independent. Thus you can look at some of the deals which the government and local authorities produce to stimulate the founding of new businesses in particular areas, in the hope of increasing employment.

Best known of these initiatives are enterprise zones. The government has set up a number of these zones, which will last ten years from the date they were started. The starting date varies from 1981 to 1984. The size of the zones ranges from around 120 acres to over 1,100 acres, but they all contain land suitable for development.

The present zones include:

*England*
Corby, Dudley, Glanford (Flixborough), Hartlepool, Isle of Dogs (London Docklands), Middlesbrough, North-east Lancashire, North-west Kent, Rotherham, Salford/Trafford, Scunthorpe, Speke (Liverpool), Telford, Tyneside, Wakefield, Wellingborough, Workington

*Wales*
Delyn, Milford Haven Waterway, Lower Swansea Valley

*Scotland*
Clydebank, Invergordon, Tayside

*Northern Ireland*
Belfast, Londonderry

Setting up in an enterprise zone brings the following benefits, which last for the life of the enterprise zone (ten years from the date it was started).

These are:

- no rates to pay on industrial and commercial property (this does not extend to water rates)

- no development land tax to pay

- capital allowances of 100 per cent can be claimed in the first year (p. 351)

- exemption from paying industrial training levies and from the requirement to supply information to Industrial Training Boards. You may, however, still be entitled to get grants from the Boards

- a greatly simplified planning regime. If what you plan to do conforms with the published scheme for the zone, you will not need to obtain individual planning permission

- planning applications, if needed, are speeded up. Most enterprise zone authorities have set themselves the target of accepting or rejecting planning applications and building regulation approvals within fourteen days

- applications from firms in enterprise zones for certain customs facilities will be processed as a matter of priority and certain criteria are relaxed

- government requests for statistical information will be reduced.

Other initiatives exist to encourage the growth of new businesses and jobs in certain locations. One example is in Irvine, which has been designated as having development area status. Irvine offers among other advantages:

- a business development unit, which provides guidance to new businesses

- regional development grants which are paid for capital expenditure or for the number of new jobs created by a project

- selective assistance, which can be paid as well as regional development grants. There are two main forms available: a project grant for capital expenditure and jobs and training grants

- rent-free period for premises, up to two years in general

- discounts of up to 40 per cent on the rates

● business support grants. First, there are better business services grants, which are paid to improve the structure and performance of existing small companies. Second, there are better technical services grants to help small companies develop new markets, improve products and production efficiency. Third, there are employment grants which assist companies in providing employment for registered unemployed workers.

Irvine is not alone in providing these incentives. Other areas which are also designated as having development area status will offer similar packages of incentives. Contact your local Department of Trade and Industry regional office who can advise you on the location of development areas.

### THE FINAL CHOICE OF LOCATION

It would be unrealistic to assume that domestic constraints are not important in locating a business. The extra benefits gained from moving to another area may simply not outweigh the domestic upheaval and cost of moving house when you want to start your business.

If you decide not to move your home, it then makes sense for your offices to be close to your home, as long as other business considerations do not apply. If it would not adversely affect your business to be near your home, it can be an advantage as it cuts down on your wasted travelling time from home to office when you probably need all the time you can get to solve initial business problems.

## WHAT SORT OF PREMISES DO YOU NEED?

After settling on a location, your search can home in on the premises you need. There are two aspects. First, you need a tighter specification of location, for example, town, district, neighbourhood or even street. This very tight specification mainly applies to retail business. Most of the considerations you need to take into account are explained on p. 101. The second aspect is the type of premises.

The factors which influence your choice of premises include:

● appearance. If customers and suppliers are likely to come to your offices, the appearance of your premises can affect your credibility and your image

● cost. You obviously want to keep your costs as low as you can, consistent that is with achieving your business objectives

192 · CHOOSING YOUR WORKPLACE

- size and layout. Your business activity may impose constraints on the amount and exact physical layout needed

- physical environment needed for maximum work efficiency. Cold, noise, dirt, dark can all mean people do not operate at their best.

The type of business may well dictate your choice of premises among office, factory, workshop or warehouse, for example. But there are a number of specialized options open to small businesses.

### HOME

Many small businesses will start off in the back bedroom. Some, especially if they are part-time businesses, may stay there permanently. The big advantages are cost and convenience. But there are a number of disadvantages or even obstacles. Introducing a business into the home can disrupt family life; it may also mean that it is difficult to leave your work cares and worries behind at the end of the working day. Another disadvantage of using your home as working premises is the poor impression it could create on customers if they need to visit you.

The obstacles which could exist include the possible need to get planning permission. This may occur if your business breaks town planning regulations because you have made a 'material change in the use of land'. Unless your business is very noisy, annoys your neighbours or means that there is a large increase in the number of visitors coming to your house, you may find that planning permission is not necessary. The moral is: keep a low profile.

Other possible obstacles include:

- the existence of restrictive covenants on the land (check with your solicitor)

- the existence of a mortgage (check with building society or bank or whoever holds the mortgage)

- restrictions on insurance (check with insurance broker or company)

- the possibility that capital gains tax may become due on the sale of your home (check with accountant and see p. 356).

### MANAGED WORKSHOPS AND SMALL BUSINESS CENTRES

Springing up all over the place are centres designed especially for small businesses. These provide small offices, workshops or factory space. There may well be an element of joint services thrown in, for example, telephone answering service, secretarial facilities. There could even be the existence of an advisory team to help you with initial management problems.

Sharing accommodation in this way with other small businesses has its attractions; there can be mutual support and business introductions, for example. You may also be able to run a more efficient business because of the shared facilities than from an office on your own.

## SCIENCE PARKS

Finding premises in a science park has its attractions for the high-tech businesses. Most science parks are attached to universities or polytechnics. The theory is that by grouping innovative businesses together and in close proximity with the research facilities of the university or polytechnic, this will provide a breeding-ground for new ideas. Whether this happens or not, your business may be able to project a high-tech image as a result of being located in a park.

## SEARCHING FOR PREMISES

There are two aspects to searching for premises. First, you have to find out about premises which are vacant. Second, you have to decide whether any of the premises you see meet your needs.

There are several places to look to find out about vacant premises:

- local newspapers

- estate agents. You will find that not all estate agents handle commercial property. The estate agent dealing with a particular property may not be local at all, but could be based many miles away. Nevertheless, find out which of the local agents do deal in commercial property and ask for a list

- contact the local authority. Many of them keep lists or registers of vacant industrial or commercial property within their boundaries. Indeed, it can be worthwhile having a discussion with the local authority, for example, the industrial development officer, as there may be special schemes to help you within certain areas of the authority

- local enterprise agency

- a number of national agencies or organizations who provide premises, especially in areas of high unemployment (see p. 407 for names and addresses).

194 · CHOOSING YOUR WORKPLACE

Once you have gathered together information about premises for renting or buying in the area, the next step (before you go to see any of them) is to draw up a checklist of the priority points your premises need:

1. *Space*  How many sq ft do you need? For offices, allow roughly 100 sq ft per employee.
   Office _____
   Storage _____
   Factory _____
   Retail _____

2. *Working environment*  What is the importance of these factors:
   Appearance for customers and suppliers _____
   Light _____
   Noise _____
   Cleanliness _____
   Smells _____
   Fire hazards _____
   Neighbours (type of work) _____

3. *Ease of access*  Do the premises need:
   Good access for pedestrians _____
   To be near to bus stop or railway _____
   Good parking facilities _____
   Delivery facilities _____

4. *Services and facilities*  Would you like already-installed:
   Partitions/fittings _____
   Telephone _____
   Burglar alarms _____
   Central heating _____
   Lighting/electricity points _____
   Air conditioning/ventilation _____
   Cooking/refrigeration _____

5. *What about cost?*
   Rent per sq ft _____
   Rates per sq ft _____
   Maintenance _____
   Running costs _____
   Rent reviews _____
   Premium for getting in _____

Rent-free period    _____
Decoration    _____
Fittings needed    _____
Phones, electricity, security etc.    _____
Length of lease    _____

When you have worked out a shortlist of properties which you want to see, it can be useful to draw a quick sketch-plan of the premises. At your leisure, you can mark where the various parts of the business will be put and get some idea of how comfortably your particular business fits into those premises.

## INVESTIGATING AND NEGOTIATING

Before you sign anything, there are several steps to take to investigate the premises further. These steps are:

- to estimate costs

- to check structure of property

- to investigate the legal side of things, and

- to look at local authority requirements.

### TO ESTIMATE COSTS

There are a few things to investigate before estimating costs. First, do not rely on the measurements given by the estate agent or landlord. Measure the premises yourself. There is a chance that the area is less than said which could mean lower rent for you, if you have been quoted a rent per sq ft.

Second, it would be a good idea to look at the premises a number of times on different days and at different times of the day. This should allow you to get a better idea of decoration, heating, lighting or noise insulation needed.

Third, make sure you estimate or allow for all the running costs as well as alterations and improvements you would need to make.

It is always worthwhile trying to negotiate a lower rent and, in particular, asking for a rent-free period of three, six or twelve months.

### TO CHECK STRUCTURE OF PROPERTY

Many leases make the tenant responsible for the repairs and maintenance

196 · CHOOSING YOUR WORKPLACE

of the premises. It would be advisable to ask for a survey from a member of the Royal Institute of Chartered Surveyors (p. 407). You can also use a survey to negotiate that the landlord pays for certain improvements before you take the premises.

## TO INVESTIGATE THE LEGAL SIDE OF THINGS

Your solicitor should be asked to undertake a perusal of the lease. The sort of points to look out for are:

- can the premises be used for the type of business you have in mind?

- how long is the lease? Commonly, a lease is between three and twenty years

- are there rent reviews and what are the arrangements for these? When are the rent reviews?

- can you sublet part or all of the premises?

- who is responsible for the repairs and the insurance?

- is the lease actually owned by the person trying to sell it?

- are the premises likely to be affected by any road or town improvements or alterations?

- who is paying for the landlord's legal costs? It is general practice for you to pay them, but it is always subject to negotiation. At any rate, agree beforehand that you will only pay a reasonable amount

- is it possible to rent the premises on a weekly agreement, rather than sign a long lease? This gives you flexibility, but you lose security. An informal arrangement like this may be possible at times when there is a glut of vacant property

- does the landlord want you to give a personal guarantee? Your solicitor should spell out to you the implications of doing so and help you to negotiate to try to avoid this.

## TO LOOK AT LOCAL AUTHORITY REQUIREMENTS

A simple step you can make for yourself is to call the planning and building control officer to find out what is the current approved use for the premises. If your intended use is the same, you may need to do nothing more. If a change of use is required, your solicitor should be able to help.

Depending on the nature of your business, you may need to consult:

- town planning and building control officers
- environmental health officer
- fire officer
- health and safety executive.

## SUMMARY

1. Look at location with an open mind. Would your business be off to a better start moving to a different part of the country? Enterprise zones and locations with development area status can offer considerable benefits.

2. As well as conventional premises, small businesses can also look at shared workshops and offices, use of home as a place of work and setting up in a science park.

3. Before you inspect any premises, draw up a list of what you think your business needs.

OTHER CHAPTERS TO READ

17. 'Getting equipped' (p. 198)

# 17. GETTING EQUIPPED

One area which is infrequently covered by books and training courses is how you get your business equipped. Equipment is a very loose term to cover the infrastructure of your business. Obviously, if you are a manufacturing business, the equipment you need for the production line is very specific to the type of business. This may also apply to the equipment you need for an office.

The infrastructure of your business ranges from cars to phone systems, from office furniture to computer systems. One part of setting up your working environment is to select what you need, at what level of sophistication and for what price.

WHAT IS IN THIS CHAPTER?

The topics covered in this chapter include:

- What to consider when choosing equipment (see below)
- How to protect yourself against the computer wolves (p. 201)
- How to pay for equipment (p. 203).

## WHAT TO CONSIDER WHEN CHOOSING EQUIPMENT

There is equipment which is important to choose correctly and there is equipment which you are likely to spend a long time choosing. In the former category comes:

- the right telephone system
- the right furniture.

In the second category comes:

- the right car
- the right computer system.

THE RIGHT TELEPHONE SYSTEM

Installing a telephone system which is suitable for your business is a high-priority task. Of course, if it is a one-person business, you need nothing more sophisticated than a telephone with a very efficient telephone answering machine to cover when you are out. However, you must realize that using a machine is making it clear to all callers that you *are* a one-person outfit, which may lower credibility.

Once your business is growing beyond this stage, spend some time researching to find a telephone system which meets your requirements. Failing to find one that is adequate can lead to inefficient working and great frustration.

THE RIGHT FURNITURE

Choosing the right furniture for your business depends essentially on the type of business. Cheap, second-hand desks and chairs may not be good business sense. If you think it likely that customers or suppliers are likely to visit your premises at regular intervals, it is crucial to select furniture which projects the image (p. 135) you have planned for your business. People are very affected by appearances, even other business people. Choosing good-quality furniture can suggest to customers that your business is good quality, too. And if exports are likely to play a big part in your business, smart offices are crucial.

Suppliers, too, can be affected by appearances. Well-planned and smart offices suggest that this is how you run the business and can help in your negotiations on credit terms and prices. In the case of furniture, cheap may mean expensive in the long run. However, what you choose is obviously determined by what you can afford and so you must look for ways in which you can give the impression you want without necessarily paying very high sums of money. Tidiness and cleanliness play an important role in appearances.

THE RIGHT CAR

A car can arouse great emotions. It is one of those peculiar purchases where it can be difficult to disentangle desires from needs. The car you drive somehow projects something about your own personality; it is often regarded as an extension of it. Nevertheless, caution is needed before personal desires get confused with business needs.

It is often argued by business owners that a prestige car is needed to project an image of credibility, for exactly the same reasons outlined above for furniture. But a cool, hard look is needed at that claim. Will customers and suppliers really see you driving into their car parks? To project the image that is needed, is the souped-up version essential? Will not the same effect be created by the slightly cheaper version? The argument that one car will only cost £50 more a month to lease than another is weak. You need to look at the cost over a longer period of time, say two years, or however long you intend to keep the vehicle. It would, of course, be a mistake to swing too far in the opposite direction and choose a second-hand car which is rusting or requires excessive maintenance.

Delivery vehicles provide an opportunity for advertising your company name and message which should be seized.

## THE RIGHT COMPUTER SYSTEM

The first question you need to ask is whether a computer would be helpful in your business. The sort of tasks which can be carried out are:

● *word processing:* a computer can be invaluable if in your business you send out a lot of routine letters, such as sales letters, quotes, mailing shots. A word processor or a computer with a word-processing program can be time-saving and produce a higher-quality service than an ordinary typewriter

● *accounts:* there are a number of computerized accounting packages. But you might find it worthwhile to consider these only when the number of transactions has grown

● *financial control and planning:* the programs range from cash management to sophisticated systems for working out forecasts and updating them at regular intervals. Again the importance of these depend on the size and complexity of your business. Ask your accountant for guidance

● *database-type work:* if you have a large list of potential customers and send out mail shots, storing the information could be time-saving

● *stock control:* this can be important for retail outfits. Some computer systems link up to the cash till, so that levels of stock and need for re-ordering are worked out automatically.

A computer system is made up of:

● the hardware, that is, the computer and the terminals, which you attach to the computer so that more than one person can use the computer at the same time

● the software, that is, what makes the computer carry out the jobs you want doing.

There are two sorts of software: the operating software which makes the computer go and the application software which does the specific job, for example, cash management, word processing. This software can either come as a 'package' or be designed especially for your own needs and systems. A small business cannot really afford to have software specially designed for it to carry out the basic business tasks.

Both aspects of a computer system are important, although with the development of cheaper and better hardware, choosing the software becomes the prime task. You can buy computer systems from several sources:

● high-street stores sell cheap computers

● computer dealers who specialize in business computers and software, but may be dealers for a limited range

● software houses write custom-built software from scratch.

From November 1987, if you have a computer system, you must comply with the requirements of the Data Protection Act. If you acquire a computer on which you intend to hold computerized personal data, you will need to register at once as a 'data user' with the Data Protection Registrar. You will need to obtain further information from the Data Protection Registrar's Office (see p. 407 for address).

## TIPS ON HOW TO PROTECT YOURSELF AGAINST THE COMPUTER WOLVES

**1.** Decide what you want the computer and the software to do, before you ask anyone for advice. But remember that a computer will not solve management problems caused by flawed systems. It is not a super-hero.

**2.** Ask the National Computing Centre (NCC) for a list of the leading software which does what you want and the names of local suppliers. The NCC is not a free source of advice, but is independent. The address is on p. 407.

**3.** Ask the suppliers to come in, set out for them what you want to do, and ask for detailed proposals and installation plans.

**4.** Do not be overwhelmed by jargon or be drawn into discussions about the number of bytes or the operating systems. Insist that the suppliers explain what the computer system will do for your business.

**5.** Ask the suppliers for a full customer list, so you can take up references. Be suspicious of anyone who will only tell you the names of two or three customers. Take up the references fully and carefully.

**6.** Ask the supplier these specific questions: 'How many systems identical to this one have you installed?', 'Are the businesses similar in operation and size?'

**7.** Ask to see everything and anything you need working. If there are any excuses, however plausible, do not commit yourself to any order. You must see it all working and doing what you want.

**8.** Always buy software packages; never agree to have anything which will need to be designed from scratch. If necessary, bend your system to the package. Building software from scratch on a customized basis can prove to be expensive and unpredictable in timing.

**9.** If an important part of what you need is not ready yet and 'is coming in a couple of months', delay buying until it has come and been fully demonstrated to you. Do not be the 'first' buyer of any computer system. You have your own business to run without pioneering for the computer industry.

**10.** Be prepared to spend more now to install the right-size system with the right back-up. If you choose the cheapest version, you may well find that you up-grade the system within a short space of time and the cost could be much higher than doing it right in the first place.

**11.** Remember the binary law of computing; it will do half as much, cost twice as much, take twice as long, as the salesman says or you think.

## HOW TO PAY FOR EQUIPMENT

There are four main ways you can pay for equipment. Two of them involve buying the equipment, so you become the owner; the others do not, the ownership being retained elsewhere. The ways are:

- buying outright
- hire purchase
- leasing
- contract hire.

# 18. PROFESSIONAL BACK-UP

Luck can make a lot of difference to the success or failure of an enterprise; but you cannot sit around waiting for luck to land on your doorstep. You must take all the steps you can to ensure success. Weaknesses in specific skills must be covered; you may be able to obtain advice and guidance from an enterprise agency. But there may still be some skills for which you must seek outside professional help.

The time to seek out and engage professional advisers will be fairly early in the planning stage. Thus their expert advice can be taken before your plans are firmly formulated. If the adviser is good, this should help you avoid making the sort of expensive errors and misjudgements which could mean your business begins with a permanent disadvantage.

The sort of advisers who could be helpful to you include:

- Accountant
- Bank
- Solicitor
- Surveyor/estate agent
- Designer/design shop/design consultant
- Corporate finance adviser.

This chapter discusses for each of these advisers:

- The advice available
- How to choose
- Cost.

## ACCOUNTANT
### THE ADVICE AVAILABLE
The advice accountants may be able to give ranges from the very basic services, such as book-keeping, to the more sophisticated, such as tax planning or raising funds. Not every accountant will offer every sort of

advice. For example, a big firm of accountants is unlikely to undertake weekly book-keeping functions; a sole practitioner may not have the expertise for help with raising funds.

Some of the areas of advice include:

● accounts: doing the book-keeping, setting up accounting systems, advising on computerized accounting packages, auditing for a limited company

● finance: managing cash, helping to raise finance and to negotiate with the bank manager

● business purchase: investigating possible acquisitions, analysing franchise opportunities, negotiating purchase prices

● tax: preparing income tax and VAT returns, carring out PAYE and national insurance requirements for employees, personal and business tax planning

● general business advice: preparing business plans, budgets, forecasts and advising on the form of your business, that is, whether you should be a sole trader, in partnership or form a limited company.

Quite a lot of accountants, particularly the large firms, also have management consultancy divisions, which can advise on the setting up of internal systems, computerization and so on.

## HOW TO CHOOSE

The term 'accountant' does not necessarily mean that the person so described has any formal accountancy qualification. If you want to employ someone who is a member of a recognized body, you should look out to see if there are letters after the name. The two main organizations which will be of interest to you as a small business are:

● Institute of Chartered Accountants (p. 407), whose members put ACA after their name

● Association of Certified Accountants (p. 407), whose members put ACCA after their name.

What you gain by using a member of one of these bodies is the knowledge that a required course of training has been followed and certain exams passed. In addition, if you run a company and what you want to do is to appoint an auditor, you must appoint someone who is a member of one of

- selecting what your employees wear and what your vans look like (livery specialists)

- using letterheads, logos, brochures and leaflets (pp. 137, 139, 153)

- packaging.

Using a design shop can be a more cost-effective alternative than an advertising agency for a small business, especially as you are likely to adopt other means of getting your message across than straight advertisements (p. 160).

You may find that some printers have designers working with them, and this could be the most cost-effective of all. However, cheapness is not the best option, if you fail to achieve your objectives because of the poor quality of advice. You must still assess how good the advice is.

Before you approach a designer you should have a clear idea of what you want, although be prepared to listen to suggestions. You should ask the designer to show you a wide range of ideas in what is called 'scamp' form, which is a very cheap way of letting you see what sort of impression the idea will give. Settle on two or three ideas that you think are consistent with your product or business and ask the designer to work in more detail on these.

HOW TO CHOOSE

The best way of finding a designer whose advice you value is to ask friends and colleagues for recommendations. Another approach is to keep an eye open for work you admire which other businesses have, for example, a logo you think good, an effective premise fitting and so on. Most businesses will be flattered if you ask who helped design it.

There is also a book, *The Creative Handbook* (p. 407), which lists advertising agencies, designers and public relations firms. Whichever way you choose of finding some names of designers, ask for references and see examples of the work done.

COST

There are two elements of cost:

- the idea

- carrying out the idea into production.

A designer should be able to give you a quote.

## CORPORATE FINANCE ADVISER
**(or venture capital sponsors)**

This is a new profession emerging; they have developed the role of intermediary between those wanting funds and those with money to invest, such as venture capital funds. Their emergence coincides with the growth in availability of venture capital.

### THE ADVICE AVAILABLE

A venture capital sponsor will look into a business plan and proposal, and their sponsorship of it should carry some weight with the funds; but this only applies if their reputation is sound.

There are four ways they may be able to help you:

- advice on the marketing strategy

- advice on the organizational structure, in particular whether there are gaps in the top management and how the structure can be strengthened

- a check on your projections

- advice on how much money you will need and the best way of raising it.

### HOW TO CHOOSE

As with any new profession, there are those who are very good and those who are awful. Unfortunately, there is no clear-cut way of finding the name of a good sponsor as there is no organization or recognized qualification. Probably the best way is to ask other people how they raised the funds and if they would recommend the person who helped. A magazine, *Your Business*, which is aimed at those running small businesses, may have articles about who has raised money and how much. Contact the MD of the firm who raised the funds and ask for a recommendation. However you get the name, always ask for references.

During 1987/8, a new regulation system of investment advisers is being introduced. These corporate finance specialists or venture capital sponsors will register as a member of a self-regulatory organization probably either FIMBRA or the Stock Exchange, even though they are not stockbrokers in the traditional sense. Do not consider using anyone who is not an authorized member of a self-regulatory organization.

use of an agreed number of the specified type. The length of the agreement is usually shorter than the estimated life of the equipment. Use of the vehicles can be provided with or without the maintenance.

## SUMMARY

1. Choosing the right phone system can be important for the efficiency of your business.

2. The furniture and fitting out of your premises can have an impact on your credibility with customers and suppliers.

3. The car you drive may affect the image of your business less than you believe.

4. Follow TIPS ON HOW TO PROTECT YOURSELF AGAINST THE COM-PUTER WOLVES on p. 201.

5. There are four main ways of paying for equipment: buying outright, hire purchase, leasing and contract hire.

OTHER CHAPTERS TO READ

BUYING OUTRIGHT

This does not necessarily mean buying it with your own money; you could use a bank loan or overdraft to finance the purchase of the equipment. The advantage of buying outright is that you own the asset, which will be entered in your balance sheet. This will make your balance sheet stronger. The disadvantage is that it uses up large lumps of cash, maybe at a time when you are short of funds.

HIRE PURCHASE (OR CREDIT SALE)

Ultimately, you will own the asset outright at the end of the hire period. This means that hire purchase confers some of the same advantages as buying outright. As with outright purchase, you can claim a capital allowance from the time you start using the equipment, and you will be able to take the equipment into your balance sheet as an asset, with what you owe as a liability on the other side.

Using hire purchase also means that you are not laying out such a large sum initially, compared with buying outright, which can be helpful for cash flow. However, the payments you make will consist of capital, as well as interest. You only get tax relief on the interest part of the payments.

LEASING

If you lease equipment, you never become the owner of it. The company who organizes the lease remains owner. The main advantage of leasing is that there is no capital outlay, so it can be a big help to cash flow.

You do not claim the capital allowance for the equipment; the company organizing it claims the allowance, although you should get some benefit such as reduced rental. However, all the payment you make is treated as an expense and so you get full tax relief on it.

There are different sorts of leases. If the lease is a closed-ended one, it means there will be a fixed period of one to five years. At the end of the agreed period, there may be an option to take a further lease for a nominal rent. Or you may be able to buy it. An open-ended one means you can end it when you like after the expiry of an agreed minimum period. Yet another type of lease is a balloon lease, which allows you to make part of the capital payment at the end of the lease.

CONTRACT HIRE

This is a form of leasing, mostly used for financing a fleet of vehicles. In this case, what is in the contract is not a specific vehicle or vehicles, but the

COST

A venture capital sponsor will probably charge between 2½ and 4 per cent of the money raised. But there may also be demands for shares or options on shares or directorships.

## SUMMARY

1. You can improve your chances of success by using professional advisers with their expert knowledge. Select your advisers at an early stage in your business planning.

2. Agree with your advisers at the outset what work they will do for you. Make sure you both understand and agree the scope of the work.

3. Take up references and ask for estimates of costs before the work begins.

OTHER CHAPTERS TO READ

# 19. GETTING THE RIGHT STAFF

Deciding when to take on an employee is a delicate balancing act. On the one hand, if you increase your manpower, you might not be able to cover increased costs straightaway. On the other hand, extra manpower could free you to spend more time on other activities, such as marketing or planning, which should, in the end, mean increased profits.

A useful rule of thumb for choosing the best time to increase your manpower is to ask yourself if you can generate enough extra sales to cover the cost of taking on that extra employee. If you will not be able to increase your sales straightaway, you could still employ someone; but, in this case, you will need to be able to keep your business going until you have been able to build your sales up to the new level you need. It all sounds straightforward, but in practice it is very tricky. It is like being on a seesaw. One step in the wrong direction can tip the balance against you.

If you are clever enough, or lucky enough, to get your timing right, you will not want to throw away your advantage by employing the wrong person. The whole process can take several months; so finding you have made a mistake and having to recruit again can throw your business off its planned course. Nor should you underestimate the emotional problems of getting rid of an unsuitable employee, which can unnerve the toughest of businessmen and which can unsettle other employees.

WHAT IS IN THIS CHAPTER?

This chapter looks at the cost of employing someone and what effect it will have on your business. It then looks at how to recruit. It should help you to answer three questions:

- Do I know what I'm looking for?

- Will I recognize it when I see it?

- Can I make sure that, if I offer the job, it will be accepted?

To answer these questions, there are sections on the job that needs doing (p. 216), the employee you want (p. 218), getting the right person to apply for the job (p. 221) and interviewing (p. 225). The legal aspects of employment are included in Chapter 20. 'Your rights and duties as an employer' (p. 234).

## THE COST

The costs can be divided into two groups:

● one-off costs of employment, such as advertising costs and increased use of telephone. As well as these costs, there is also the time you spend interviewing or sifting through applications and the time spent on training a new employee – although these do not involve you in spending any cash

● continuing costs of employment, such as salary, employer's national insurance contributions, fringe benefits you offer and extra office equipment. There will also be the extra costs created by the person carrying out the job; these may include more stationery, petrol, telephone or whatever. Later in this chapter, on p. 230, there is a checklist which you can use to work out what these costs will add up to.

### WHAT IS YOUR BREAK-EVEN POINT?

Your break-even point is the point at which your business is making the right amount of sales to give you enough profit to cover your overheads, which include rent and rates, heating and lighting. Sometimes employee costs are overheads and sometimes they are not. It all depends on what they do. If what the employee does is related to the level of sales, their costs will be called *direct* and are not part of overheads. Examples would include staff whose time is paid for by customers, or employees who are directly involved in making a product. But if the employee's job is something like accounting, marketing or general clerical duties, their costs will be included in *overheads*. In your business there may be a grey area in which it is difficult to decide whether the employee's costs are direct or not.

The purpose of finding your new break-even point is to work out how many extra sales you need to make to cover the cost of your new employee. You can see how to work out the break-even point in more detail in Chapter 24. 'Staying afloat' (p. 298). And there is an example showing how to work out the effect of adding an extra employee later in this chapter on p. 232.

## THE JOB THAT NEEDS DOING

Before you plunge into adding that extra employee, look carefully at the work to be done. It is very important to sort out in your own mind what the job entails. Once you have done this you can define the type of person you need. If you fail to do this preparatory work, you might find yourself employing someone who does not fit in your organization and does not carry out the work that is necessary. This list of topics might help you to organize your thoughts about the job:

● *level of skill:* when you decided you needed an extra pair of hands, was it because you needed work done which you did not feel competent to carry out yourself? If so, it may be that the work you need doing requires a special skill

● *training:* if you have the skill to do the job, but not the time, would it take a lot of training to employ someone without that particular skill and teach them on the job? Would you have the time to carry out that training?

● *length of time:* do you estimate that this extra work will need doing for a long period of time? Or is it a temporary bulge? Watch out for mistaking a backlog of work which can be cleared up quickly for a permanent increase in activity

● *how much extra work:* can you quantify how much time will need to be spent by someone to carry out the work? Is it a full working week? Do not assume that if you find the work difficult and time-consuming, because it is outside your range of skills, a skilled employee will take as long as you to complete the work

● *experience:* do you think the job requires a lot of experience? Would the employee need to be able to make independent judgements or assessments? Or is it intended that the work will be closely directed by yourself or another?

● *responsibility:* how much responsibility will the employee have? Will the employee be required to man the office alone? If the job is selling, will the person be required to go out selling unsupervised? Will the employee handle money? Or be responsible for other staff? To whom will the employee be responsible – yourself or some other member of your business?

• *tasks:* list the things that need to be done by your new employee. Work out for whom the tasks will be done and which tasks are more or less important

• *authority:* work out what your new employee can do without asking you or someone else for permission – for example, making appointments, spending money up to a certain limit

• *contacts:* will your new employee need to deal directly with the general public or your customers? Will the contact be face-to-face, on the telephone or by letter?

• *special circumstances:* does the job involve working during unsocial hours? Will your new member of staff need to do much travelling away from home? Will the working conditions be unpleasant or dangerous?

• *future developments:* consider how the job might develop and expand in the future. You need to assess a job hunter for this potential, too.

Setting out your thoughts in this way may seem like overkill, if the job is relatively simple. But hiring and firing a succession of unsatisfactory people will be more time-consuming and disruptive to your business than spending an hour or so defining the job; and marshalling your thoughts in this way will also help you to decide whether there really is a job that needs doing.

Another way of examining your needs would be to fill out a job description form. Try using the simple one below:

*Example: job description*
Job title:
Purpose of job:
Who does the employee work for:
Who works for the employee:
Main tasks:
   1.
   2.
   3. (and so on)
What authority does the employee have:
   1.
   2.
   3. (and so on)

Duties:
  1.
  2.
  3. (and so on)
Contacts:
  Internal:
  External:
Possible development of the job:

## THE EMPLOYEE YOU WANT

Your next task is to match the employee to the job. Decide if you need someone full-time or part-time. Think about what experience and qualifications the employee will need. And, most important of all, work out what sort of person you and your other employees will get on with.

### FULL-TIME EMPLOYEES?

Conventionally, most employees are permanent, full-time and salaried, but this may not suit your business. Do not ignore other ways of getting the job done. Look closely at the following:

- help from your family

- contract or temporary staff

- part-time staff

- commission-only salespeople or agents.

### YOUR FAMILY

Do not overlook the possibilities of your wife or husband or other relative helping out; and if it is your wife, there is a tax advantage (p. 350). Employing your family may not be the permanent solution you seek, but it may help to tide you over until you are confident that taking on an extra employee is justified.

### CONTRACT OR TEMPORARY STAFF

For quite a number of jobs it is possible to get people who are happy to work on a contract or freelance basis. This means you will pay an agreed fee, but have no responsibility for national insurance contributions, sickness payments or holiday pay. And if the extra work comes to an end, you need feel no responsibility towards finding more work for a contractor, as long as you made it clear that the work was temporary or was a contract for a particular piece of work or period of time, but less than a year.

A further advantage of using contract or temporary staff is that it can be a good opportunity for you and the person to size each other up and see if you could work together, before you offer a permanent job.

There are two main disadvantages of solving your extra workload in this way. First, it can cost you more than taking on permanent staff to get the particular piece of work done. If the job involves a skill which is widely demanded and in short supply, a self-employed contractor's rate is likely to be correspondingly high. And if you are using a temp, you will have to pay a fee to the employment agency that introduces you. Second, while some contractors or temps may be keen and enthusiastic, others may be less so.

Your legal obligations to temporary or freelance workers or to people who contract out their services is rather hazy.

You could also consider whether you may be able to receive some temporary help by using one of the government's schemes. You could provide a place for a youngster under the Youth Training Scheme (p. 225). The MSC also organizes a scheme to second out-of-work executives for a period (see p. 45 for more details).

PART-TIME STAFF

If the work you want doing does not add up to a full working week, consider getting someone in on a part-time basis. Your duties to a part-time employee vary according to the number of hours worked. See Chapter 20. 'Your rights and duties as an employer' (p. 234).

COMMISSION-ONLY SALESPEOPLE OR AGENTS

Do not automatically think in terms of a salaried employee if you are looking to boost your selling effort. You may be able to find someone competent who would prefer to be paid by getting a commission on each item sold. Again this will cut your risks – no sales means no pay. However, you will have to expect that the commission you will pay will be greater per item than to a salaried employee who also gets commission on sales.

WHO IS RIGHT FOR THE JOB?

Try to develop an idea of the sort of person who will fit into the job and your business. Use the groups of characteristics listed below to help you sort out what is important for the job and what is not. You can use this to help you specify what you want before you start advertising the job. You can also use it to help you collect your thoughts while you are interviewing people.

Here are some useful ways of grouping characteristics:

- *physical make-up:* this covers the employee's health, physique, appearance, manner, age and speech

- *achievements:* what education, qualifications and experience do you expect?

- *general intelligence:* this is rather difficult to judge if you are not a psychologist, but what sort of reasoning ability should the person have? How quickly do they understand what you are saying?

- *special aptitudes:* what particular skills do you need, for example, mechanical, verbal, numerical or manual skills?

- *interests:* what are the person's hobbies and leisure activities? Are there any particular hobbies which would be more or less suitable for the person who is needed to do this job? Check how much time is spent on interests. Is this likely to conflict with the job?

- *circumstances:* this includes factors such as where the person lives, if he or she is married or single, number of children (if any) and so on

- *personal characteristics:* this covers the slightly tricky area of whether the person has the right personality to cope with that particular type of job.

For more details on the above, see p. 407.

It would be a good idea to pick out of the list those characteristics which you think are very important and those which would be an advantage but are not crucial for this particular job. It is always tempting to demand very high qualifications, experience and so on, but it is wiser to be fairly flexible in your requirements and not overstate what is needed to carry out the job satisfactorily. In any case you should always remember that employing someone who is over-qualified for a job may lead to a rapid staff turnover, as the employee may soon get bored.

As well as picking out those characteristics which you need or hope to find, it is equally important to sort out those which would be a definite disadvantage to someone carrying out the job.

# GETTING THE RIGHT PERSON TO APPLY FOR THE JOB

Once you have completed the essential preparation and so got a clear idea of whether you can afford to take on an employee, what job you need doing and what sort of person you would like to fill the job, your problem now becomes: how can I find the person I want?

The main ways you can tell job hunters about the job you have on offer are:

- through friends, existing employees and business contacts

- by advertising direct

- through recruitment agencies and consultants

- by recruiting direct from colleges.

## FRIENDS, EXISTING EMPLOYEES AND BUSINESS CONTACTS

This method of finding your new employee is not to be ignored, as it has several advantages. First, it is cheap. Second, if it is through a friend, you will start off knowing something about the new person – background, personality and so on. Third, a new employee recruited in this way may find it easier to fit in your organization, especially if the person who made the recommendation is an existing employee.

The main disadvantage arises if the appointment proves unsuccessful; this can prove embarrassing if the contact was made through a friend and disruptive to a previously harmonious working relationship if the recommendation came from an existing employee.

If you do get a strong recommendation from someone, do not rely totally on the friend's advice. Ask your prospective employee for a curriculum vitae (CV) and give them a copy of the job description (p. 217) and the advertisement you would have used. Observe all the necessary precautions by conducting a full and careful interview, taking up references and insisting on medicals, where appropriate (see more about all this on p. 225 and p. 229).

## ADVERTISING DIRECT

If you have not found anyone suitable through friends or contacts, you could get in touch with the local Jobcentre or Professional and Executive Recruitment (PER) (p. 225), if the vacancy is suitable. Failing this, you can advertise direct in the appropriate newspapers or magazines. This could be tricky if writing is not your strong suit. However, there are certain guidelines you can follow to help you.

Remember that the purpose of the ad is to attract someone who will be able to do the job very well and who will fit happily into your organization. You have to tell job hunters enough about the job to stimulate their interest and make them feel it is worth having a closer look; equally, you want to use the ad as a starting point of the selection process. So you want to make it clear to those applicants who would be suitable that they should apply and to those applicants who would not be suitable that they should not apply. Finally, the ad should be interesting enough to attract attention compared with what else is on offer in that newspaper or magazine the same day.

From the research which has been done on what attracts people to join a company, some of the important points are listed below in order of priority:

- the prospects for interesting and creative work

- the prospects for promotion and pay

- the quality and reputation of the company's products or services

- the opportunity to use 'brains'

- the security of the job

- the company's past financial record

- congenial working environment.

How does your business and the job you are offering rate against these points? In your ad you need to draw attention to your strong points. Most small and new businesses would score high on giving lots of scope for interesting and creative work and the opportunity to use 'brains'. In particular, an employee would be given the opportunity to be part of the whole business and not just in one department. However, if it is a new business, there may be little reputation built up for its products and its financial record may be short.

When it comes to writing the ad, the style could be important in attracting job hunters' interest. Be informal and friendly – but not too friendly. Use 'you' and 'your' when you are speaking about the person needed and 'we' and 'our' when talking about your business; but avoid over-chatty comments and stick to the facts.

CHECKLIST: WHAT SHOULD BE IN THE AD?

• *company name:* put in the name and logo, if you have one

• *job title:* use a title or description which will mean something to a stranger

• *pay:* state what salary can be expected. Job hunters interpret phrases like 'salary negotiable' as meaning a low salary

• *place:* state where the job is. If you are not offering moving expenses, this is very important. In any case, people like to know what the environment of the job is

• *the work:* describe the work to be done and say what authority the job has

• *the company:* state what your company does and what size it is. Avoid clichés about dynamism, fast-growing and so on; all companies use them

• *the person:* state your requirements, such as experience needed, qualifications, age and other personal qualities

• *how to apply:* name the person to write to, not just the job title. Tell the job hunter how you want them to give details of experience and qualifications – for example, send in brief CV, apply for application form and so on

• *when to apply:* give a closing date for applications, if possible allowing two to three weeks from the appearance of the ad

• *the law:* check your ad is not breaking sex or race discrimination law (see Chapter 20. 'Your rights and duties as an employee' (p. 247)). And make sure the information is accurate, as the ad may form part of the contract between you and your new employee.

HOW TO APPLY

Asking for too much information from job hunters can deter people from applying, and you should remember that your business is competing with all others for the best talents. Keep your demands to a minimum. Asking applicants to write in has the advantage of letting you see what their written work is like – important, if that is an element of the job. It will also be less time-consuming for you at this stage. If you do give a telephone number that job applicants can ring, make sure it is always manned – and by someone who knows what they are talking about. You can use the

224 · GETTING THE RIGHT STAFF

telephone to sift out people, as well as to give them information. This can be done by preparing a short list of key questions, which you can ask over the phone.

An application form has the advantage of allowing you to compare information presented in an identical format. On the other hand, drawing one up would take you some time and may not be worthwhile, unless you are considering employing many people.

## WHERE TO PUT THE AD

It depends on the job. Different newspapers and magazines will give you the response you need for different jobs. There are trade magazines which may have cornered the market for job ads in a particular specialization, for example, computing. For jobs which are not so specialized, local newspapers may provide a good response, for example, for clerical staff. A magazine called *British Rate and Data* lists newspapers and magazines and gives details of the cost of advertising and a profile of the readership for each of them. Your local library should be able to tell you where to see a copy.

The best market research about where job hunters look for jobs may be to ask people who work in that field where *they* would look if they wanted a new job.

## THE COST OF ADVERTISING

The bigger the circulation of the newspaper or magazine, the more they charge for advertising. You have to weigh up the cost against the benefit of getting the size of response you need.

## RECRUITMENT AGENCIES AND CONSULTANTS

If you do not have the time to handle the advertising and to sift through all the applications, you can use an agency. Obviously, you have to pay for this, so you must be sure it is worth the extra cost; and do not forget that you will have to spend time in selecting the right agency, so the time-saving may not be as great as you think. Nor can you afford to skip any of the preparatory stages; you will still have to decide what the job is and what sort of person you want, so that the agency can do their job.

There are several different types of agencies:

- Jobcentres and employment offices

- Professional and Executive Recruitment (PER)

- private employment bureaux (Alfred Marks or Brook Street, for example)

- candidate registers

- selection consultants

- search consultants (or headhunters).

Using a Jobcentre is free and can be a useful source of applicants for manual and clerical jobs, but do not expect too much from the screening process. With PER you can advertise in their newspaper, *Executive Post*. Or you can use their selection service. If the job is filled, you are charged the equivalent of 10 per cent of the employee's first year's earnings.

The other agencies charge varying amounts ranging from 6 per cent of first year's earnings up to 20 per cent, depending on the agency and the type of job to be filled.

You can get a list of members of the Federation of Employment Services to help you pick out an agency (see p. 408 for the address and telephone number).

### RECRUITING DIRECT

If you are looking for someone who does not need experience in your particular field or skill, you could try colleges and other organizations direct. The sorts of skills you might be able to recruit direct in this way include secretarial, hotel and catering, retail management and so on.

If the type of job you have in mind could be done by a young school-leaver to whom you could give on-the-job training, it could be worthwhile finding out about the government's Youth Training Scheme. Your local Jobcentre can give you information. The government will pay you a grant towards the cost of employing and training each young person.

## INTERVIEWING

An interview has two purposes:

- it helps you choose your new employee

- it helps your new employee choose you.

It is important to remember that you should structure the interview process to enable you to find out what the applicant is really like *and* to allow the job hunter to find out about you and your company and decide that this is the job he or she wants.

Before you get to the interview stage you will have to sift the applications and decide who to select for a closer look.

## WHO SHOULD YOU SEE?

If your ad was successful, the sifting process will not be a case of eliminating totally unsuitable candidates; rather it will be to rank the applications according to how close they match your ideal. If you are tempted to see someone who does not fit the bill but looks interesting, think twice. It means either that the requirements you set for the job were not the right ones or that you will be wasting your time on an unnecessary interview.

Once you have ranked them, choose to see the top five, say. If you do not find anyone in that group, you could try the next five. After that second-ranking group, if you still have not found the ideal person you may have to accept that your ad has been unsuccessful. You will need to reconsider how to find the person you want.

## GETTING READY FOR THE INTERVIEW

There are two stages. First, you must gather together the essential information you will need to give the job applicant. This can be conveyed in written form or verbally, in which case you need the facts at your fingertips if you are to sound organized and efficient to the job hunter.

The questions you might be asked could be about aspects of the job such as:

● holidays. You need to be able to say how many weeks, when they can be taken and any restrictions you intend to impose

● illness. Explain what will happen if your employee is away from work because of illness

● starting date of the job, if this has been decided

● hours of work

● salary matters, such as when they are paid, any rules on overtime, bonuses or commission, if applicable.

The second stage of preparation is to work out what key questions you want to ask. One type of question would give you comparable information about the people you see. This could be a test question, such as describing a typical event in your business and asking what each person would do in those circumstances.

The second type of question is to help you pinpoint each candidate's strengths and weaknesses. The only way this can be done is by good preparation, reading the candidate's CV or whatever. There is no short cut. What you should look for is anything which seems odd or is not a smooth progression. Watch out for any unexplained gaps in the person's story; this may give you hints about poor health, unsatisfactory jobs or character. Notice very frequent job changes as this could raise questions in your mind about job success, as could a failure to match in employment the level of achievement suggested by educational qualifications.

## HOLDING THE INTERVIEW

Some thought needs to be given beforehand to where the interview should be held and who should be present. The person you are interviewing will feel more relaxed if the interview is private and uninterrupted, so try to find somewhere where the interview will not be overlooked or overheard. If you are not going to be the new employee's boss, perhaps the person who is should sit in on the interview. The disadvantage is that if two of you are present, you may not be able to establish a relaxed relationship with the job hunter. It may be a good idea for you and the new person's superior to see the candidate separately, before deciding to offer the job.

## WHAT SHOULD HAPPEN IN THE INTERVIEW

Roughly a useful interview could run along the following lines:

1. Spend a few minutes putting the applicant at ease, for example, talking about his or her interests

2. Ask open questions which the person you are interviewing will have to answer with more than a yes or no. The questions you ask should allow you to get some idea of the person's character and attitude – see below for a list of useful questions

3. Also ask closed questions designed to test a candidate's knowledge and skill, specific questions such as 'On what date . . .' and hypothetical questions 'If you were . . .'

4. Try using silence sometimes as a way of getting the person to expand. For example, once the person has finished explaining something, do not always leap in with another question but remain silent. Sometimes, the person being interviewed will be prompted to say more, which may be revealing

5. Keep in control of the interview while doing little talking, perhaps less than a third of the total time

6. Concentrate on listening and observing your applicant. This helps you to judge the replies and to pinpoint areas where you need to probe more. You should also reflect on what the person has said and feed it back to them

7. Be flexible; do not stick rigidly to a planned script. Try to develop what your interviewee has said

8. Take notes. They do not need to be very comprehensive, but sufficient to jog your memory when assessing the interview afterwards

9. Give a little detail about the job and how it fits in your business. You can miss out this and the next stage, if you have already concluded that the person is not suitable and thus save wasting time. It is important not to do this stage before asking the questions. If you do, you may have fed the person with sufficient information, so that he or she knows how to answer your questions

10. Ask the job applicant if there are any questions, or if he or she wishes to tell you anything else about suitability for the job, which has not been brought out by the questions

11. If the person seems promising, spend some time making sure that the job would be accepted if it was offered. After all, the person is selecting a new job in the hope that it will last for a while and will want to be confident that your job is really the best choice.

## USEFUL INTERVIEW QUESTIONS

1. What is the best part and worst part of your present job?

2. What bit of your work do you find difficult and what bit the easiest?

3. How do you rate your present boss?

4. Describe your ideal boss.

5. What do you consider to be your greatest success and why?

6. What do you consider to be your greatest failure and why?

7. When were you last angry at work? What caused the anger? What form did your anger take?

8. What is most important to you about the job you are looking for?

9. What will your family and friends think of your new job?

10. What are your greatest strengths?

11. What are your weaknesses?

12. What worries you most about the job?

13. What excites you most about the job?

These are all examples of the kind of open question which should prompt the candidates to reveal a bit more about themselves; use whichever seems most appropriate. As well as these questions, there are more straightforward ones about the present job, the career, education and so on which need to be asked.

AFTER THE INTERVIEW

You should summarize the interview straight afterwards while your memory is fresh. The aim of the summary will be to allow you to look back when you are choosing between the candidates, and to judge how closely each person matched up to the job you want done. In particular, you will want to remember later the person's strengths and weaknesses.

There are some other important actions to be taken before someone joins your staff. First, always take up references. It can be much better to speak to a referee direct on the phone than to interpret what the written word may be hiding; people can be much more unguarded 'off the record'. Second, if the job is an important one, consider having a medical done. It might throw up a problem which you would want to know about before hiring. Third, if the job involves driving, always ask to see the driving licence; do not be fobbed off by excuses.

MAKING THE OFFER

Always make sure your written offer letter is conditional upon satisfactory references and medical, if applicable. Remember that this letter (and the ad) forms part of an employee's contract of employment (p. 238).

WHEN THE NEW EMPLOYEE JOINS

A new employee will feel more positive when starting a new job if presented with a planned induction and training period. It is well worth the extra effort on your part to prepare this in advance.

IF IT ALL GOES WRONG

Sometimes you can make mistakes. If it is a really bad one, you will need to know how to deal with it. In Chapter 20. 'Your rights and duties as an employer' (p. 252), there are details about the law on dismissing staff.

It could be worthwhile to interview a job leaver to see why it did not work out from the employee's viewpoint. You can learn from your mistakes and make a better choice next time.

## THE EFFECT OF STAFF OVERHEAD ON COST AND BREAK-EVEN POINT

Here we give you more help on working out what it will cost you to employ that extra person and what effect it will have on the profitability of your business. Below there is a checklist to help you sort out costs.

CHECKLIST: how to work out the extra cost of employment

| | THIS YEAR £ | FULL YEAR £ |
|---|---|---|
| Salary or wages | ... | ... |
| Employer's NI contributions | ... | ... |
| Estimated commission, bonuses, overtime payments | ... | ... |
| Other possible costs or benefits: | | |
| • employer's pension contributions | ... | ... |
| • use of car | ... | ... |
| • payment of subscriptions to professional societies | ... | ... |
| • cost of sick pay insurance | ... | ... |
| • others _____ | ... | ... |
| _____ | ... | ... |
| _____ | ... | ... |
| _____ | ... | ... |
| Additional office space required | ... | ... |
| Additional equipment needed | ... | ... |
| Extra use of telephone, stationery, heating, lighting and so on | ... | ... |
| TOTAL | £ ... | £ ... |

*Notes*

1. Most small businesses will not be providing many fringe benefits, but you may need to consider doing so if you want to employ an experienced and skilled member of staff, for example, an accountant or salesman.

2. You will need to break down these costs into monthly expenditure for your budget (p. 264).

3. This breakdown of costs assumes that you rent, lease or hire any additional equipment, rather than buying it outright. For help in deciding which is the right way for you, see p. 202.

### BREAK-EVEN POINT

First, you have to find what your gross profit margin is. This is your gross profit as a percentage of sales. You work out gross profit by deducting the amount of your direct costs from the value of your sales. Direct costs will be the purchases you need to make to supply your service or product and the costs of any labour directly associated with your sales.

Once you have worked out your gross profit margin, your second step is to work out the amount of your overheads (for example, rent, rates, heating, lighting or labour costs, such as secretarial or book-keeping).

To find your break-even point, your third step is to divide the amount of your overheads by the gross profit margin. This will give the level of sales you need to make to cover your overheads.

There is an example of working out your new break-even point on p. 232; break-even point is described in more detail on p. 299.

## SUMMARY

1. Work out the costs of employing an extra person and watch the effect on your break-even point.

2. Make sure there is a job to be done.

3. Look to see if the work can be carried out in a non-permanent way, for example, temporary staff, contract or freelance worker.

4. Draw up a job description, no matter how simple or low-level the job seems.

5. Get a mental picture of the person for the job. Do not overstate your requirements. Pick out the characteristics which would be a disad antage in doing the job well.

232 · GETTING THE RIGHT STAFF

Jeremy Jones works out his new break-even point

Jeremy Jones needs help in his business. He needs someone to act as a secretary, book-keeper and sales assistant. He uses the checklist on p. 230 to work out the extra cost involved. For him the calculation is quite simple (no fringe benefits, for example) and looks like this for the full year:

| | |
|---|---|
| Salary | £6,000 |
| Employer's NI contributions | 540 |
| Extra use of telephone etc. | 350 |
| TOTAL | £6,890 |

Jeremy now works out how it will change his break-even point:

He has estimated sales of £35,000 for this year with direct costs of £15,000. This gives a gross profit of:

$$£35,000 - 15,000 = £20,000$$

And his gross profit margin is

$$\frac{£20,000}{£35,000} \times 100 = 57.1\%$$

His overheads, without taking on an assistant, come to an estimated £5,000 and after would come to £11,890 (£5,000 + £6,890 — see above).

Jeremy finds his break-even point before he employs someone. This he gets from the following sum:

$$\frac{\text{overheads}}{\text{gross profit margin}} \times 100 = \frac{£5,000}{57.1} \times 100 = £8,757$$

of sales to cover his overheads. If he employed an assistant, the break-even point would become

$$\frac{£11,890}{57.1} \times 100 = £20,823 \text{ of sales}$$

Jeremy needs to increase his sales by £20,823 − £8,757 = £12,066 to cover the extra overhead created by employing his new assistant. As he has estimated his sales at £35,000 (compared with the £20,823 he needs), he goes ahead with employing an assistant.

6. Ask friends, contacts and existing employees if they know the person for the job.

7. You can save money by drafting your own ad. Use our checklist to make sure you include the necessary information.

8. Prepare thoroughly for interviews.

9. Ask open questions to get the job applicant to talk.

10. Don't forget to insist on a medical, if necessary; check all references and see the driving licence if driving is part of the work.

11. Work out an induction and training programme. Do not put all the effort into finding the right person for the job and then fail to ensure that they can function properly in your business.

OTHER CHAPTERS TO READ

# 20. YOUR RIGHTS AND DUTIES AS AN EMPLOYER

The idea of employment law can conjure up images of the Gorgon. You, as an employer, turned to stone when faced with the legal pitfalls of employment. The myth is that you cannot sack anyone and you cannot exercise your own preferences in employment. Well, it is not true.

By and large, you can employ whoever you want. You can set up your own criteria about who you want to employ. But there are some rules imposed on you, including what you can say; for example, you cannot put in an ad 'no blacks' or 'no whites'.

You can normally dismiss unsatisfactory employees. But the law sets out that it should be done fairly. Even if you fall foul of the law, you can usually still successfully sack someone, if you are prepared to pay some money in compensation.

To put the law on unfair dismissal into perspective, a quick look at the statistics will provide encouragement:

• less than 10 per cent of dismissals result in claims to an industrial tribunal of unfair dismissal

• over two-thirds of unfair dismissal claims are settled without going to a tribunal; they are either withdrawn or settled by voluntary agreed compensation

• only in 30 per cent of the cases going to a tribunal was the dismissal found to be unfair. This is less than 10 per cent of all the claims of unfair dismissals

• and the amount of compensation ordered in the cases which were held to be unfair dismissal is not huge. In 1984, half the cases found to be unfair received £1,345 or less.

Nevertheless, it is still worth your while to find out about how to deal with employees in a legal sense, because arguments about dismissal, for example, can be time-consuming. The effect can also be debilitating on other employees. A little bit of planning on your part before you decide on some employment action could save you a lot of time and anguish in the future. This chapter should give you some guidelines about how:

- to take on an employee (p. 237)

- to pay staff (p. 240)

- to provide a safe and healthy working environment (p. 245)

- to avoid discrimination (p. 247)

- to treat an employee if pregnant (maternity) (p. 250)

- to dismiss them if unsatisfactory (saying goodbye to an employee) (p. 252)

- to treat part-time staff (p. 255).

## BIRD'S EYE VIEW OF YOUR RIGHTS AND DUTIES

In general terms, apart from what you agree in the contract of employment, what can you expect from your employees and what can they expect from you?

### YOUR RIGHTS

1. Your employees should be honest and obedient and not act against your interests.

2. They should not disclose confidential information about your business to others.

3. They should take care of your property.

4. Any patents, discoveries or inventions made during working hours belong to you.

5. Your employees should be competent, work carefully and industriously.

### YOUR DUTIES

1. You should behave reasonably in employment matters.

2. You should practice good industrial relations, such as clear disciplinary procedures and grievance procedures.

3. You should pay your employees when you agreed to do so.

4. You should take reasonable care to ensure the safety and health of your employees.

As well as these general rights and duties, your employees acquire certain rights by law. Some of the rights in the LEGAL LIFE-CYCLE OF AN EMPLOYEE (see below) refer only to full-time employees (working over sixteen hours a week). If you have a part-time employee, working at least eight but less than sixteen hours, these rights will be acquired, in the main, after you have employed them for five years (see p. 255 for more details).

There has been a proposal to raise the number of hours worked to twenty before an employee is regarded as full-time and to raise to twelve hours the number of hours worked before rights are acquired after five years.

### IF YOUR BUSINESS EMPLOYS MORE THAN FIVE EMPLOYEES

There is an additional requirement. An employee may have the right to return to work after pregnancy, and this applies if she has been employed by you for two years or more (p. 250).

### WHAT IS IN THE REST OF THIS CHAPTER?

The rest of this chapter fills out the details. But it cannot cover every single employment possibility. The Department of Employment produces very useful booklets to give guidance on employment matters. The appropriate booklets are listed throughout this chapter. You can get the booklets from employment offices, unemployment benefit offices and Jobcentres.

## LEGAL LIFE-CYCLE OF AN EMPLOYEE
**(if your business employs five people or less)**

| HOW LONG EMPLOYED | WHAT YOU MUST DO |
| --- | --- |
| new starter | 1. Do not discriminate on racial grounds (p. 248) |
| | 2. Pay equal pay to men and women (p. 243) |
| | 3. Do not discriminate because of trade union membership (p. 249) |
| | 4. Give an itemized pay statement with pay (p. 241) |

5. Give paid time off for ante-natal care (p. 250)

6. Consult recognized trade union about redundancy (p. 254)

7. Do not discriminate on grounds of sex (p. 248)

after one month

8. Give the minimum notice periods required by law (p. 254)

9. Pay guaranteed pay if you have no work (p. 243)

within thirteen weeks

10. Give a written statement of the main terms and conditions of employment (p. 238)

after six months

11. Give written reasons for dismissal, if requested (p. 253)

after two years

12. Do not dismiss unfairly (p. 252)

13. Do not dismiss because of pregnancy (p. 250)

14. Pay maternity pay (p. 251)

15. Pay redundancy money (p. 254)

16. Give paid time off work to look for work in redundancy

17. Give job back to employee on maternity leave, unless original job or alternative job not available.

## TAKING ON AN EMPLOYEE

The most important part of employing someone is to select the right person for the right job in the first place. The techniques of job description, advertising the job, selecting for interview and interviewing are covered in Chapter 19. 'Getting the right staff' (p. 214). However, there are certain legal points to look out for to ensure that you and your employee get off to a happy start.

WHAT YOU MUST DO

Broadly:

1. Keep racial and sex discrimination out of ads, interview and job descriptions

2. Tell your tax office when you take on an employee

3. Give your employee a written statement.

STARTER RULES

You should be careful that sex or racial discrimination do not creep into ads or interviews. Avoid using job titles which imply one sex or the other – foreman, for example. If you use this sort of job title, include in the ad a note that you welcome applications from both sexes. Avoid using 'he' or 'she' to describe a job applicant in an ad as it suggests you want applications from men only, if you use 'he', or women only, if you use 'she'. In an interview avoid asking women about their husband or their marriage.

The job should be described accurately in the ad and in the letter offering the job. These two can form part of the contract of employment. When you do take on an employee, you should tell your tax office. Remember to get your new employee's P45; if your employee does not have one, fill out P46. When your employee has been with you for thirteen weeks, you must have given your new employee a written statement of the conditions and terms of the job (see below).

It would be wise to take note of the actual day on which your employee starts. The date can determine whether you may be able to dismiss your employee fairly or not, if things do not work out.

WHAT IS THE CONTRACT OF EMPLOYMENT?

The words 'contract of employment' conjure up thoughts of a written document. But the terms of your employee's contract of employment can be made up of anything you write or say. It can include what you say in the ad, in the interview, in the offer letter, when your employee starts work and any subsequent chat you have about the terms and conditions of the job.

The basic contract is offer of employment, acceptance of employment and agreed amount of payment; these can be verbal or written. Anything else makes up the terms.

WHAT YOU HAVE TO PUT IN THE WRITTEN STATEMENT

First, you have to put your name and your employee's name. You have to say when your employee's present job began and when your employee was first employed by you.

Second, you have to give information on various terms and conditions. If you have not made any agreement about a particular point, you should say so. The terms and conditions are:

- pay, including how it is worked out, if appropriate

- when the pay will be made

- hours of work, including normal working hours

- holidays, including public holidays, and holiday pay, including how it is worked out

- arrangements for sickness and injury, including any sick pay

- pensions and pension schemes

- period of notice you and your employee have to give

- your employee's job title.

Third, there has to be a written note giving information about disciplinary rules and grievance procedures. Fourth, you also have to state whether a contracting-out certificate under the Social Security Pensions Act 1975 is in force which applies to your employee. And finally, you have to give the name of a person to whom the employee can apply if he is dissatisfied with any disciplinary decision.

## WHO GETS A WRITTEN STATEMENT

Most employees do unless:

- you have already given your employee a written contract of employment which includes all the above items

- your employee is a part-timer (p. 255).

## BOOKLETS

Inland Revenue (IR), *Employer's Guide to PAYE* P7
IR, *Thinking of Taking Someone On?* IR53
Equal Opportunities Commission (EOC), *Code of Practice*
Commission for Racial Equality (CRE), *Code of Practice*
Department of Employment (DE), *1. Written Statement of Main Terms and Conditions of Employment* PL700

## PAY

There are quite a lot of rules about how you can pay, how much you have to pay and what you have to give with pay.

### WHAT YOU MUST DO

Broadly:

1. Give minimum pay to workers in certain industries governed by wages councils. Young people of twenty-one or under are no longer covered by Wages Orders

2. Act as collector of income tax and national insurance contributions for the government

3. In most cases, do not deduct anything from your employee's pay unless they ask you to do so in writing or if it is in the contract of employment.

### HOW MUCH DO YOU HAVE TO PAY?

In many cases, deciding how much and how often you pay your employee will be negotiated between you and your employee. Whatever is decided will be part of your employee's contract of employment. You can also negotiate the question of bonuses, commission, overtime, holiday pay and sick pay.

But there are exceptions to this, if your business is in one of these industries:

- retail, but not chemists, butchers and some others

- catering, but not canteens or boarding houses

- hairdressing

- clothing manufacture

- toy manufacture

- laundries, but not dry-cleaning or self-service laundrettes.

In these cases, and in some others, you may well find that pay and other conditions of employment for your employees, but not for those aged twenty-one and under, will be regulated by a Wages Council. During 1987 the responsibilities of Wages Councils will be redefined. They will be limited to setting a basic hourly rate of pay, an overtime rate and a limit on charges for accommodation the employer provides.

## WHAT YOU CAN, OR HAVE TO, DEDUCT FROM PAY

You cannot deduct anything from your employee's pay unless it has been laid down by law or unless it has the written agreement of your employee.

By law, you have to act as a tax collector. This means you have to deduct tax and national insurance contributions from your employee's pay (p. 244). And on the rare occasion it happens, you may also have to act to enforce a court order, by deducting sums from an employee's earnings under what is called an *attachment of earnings*. This may occur, for example, for paying maintenance or for paying a fine.

You can, however, make some other deductions, if your employee has agreed in writing. For example, you can deduct a sum of money and hand it over to someone else, such as dues to a union. Another example where deductions are allowed is if you have made your employee an advance against wages, you can deduct the amount of the advance from your employee's pay, but you cannot make any charge, such as interest, for making the advance. A third example is if you provide medicine, the services of a doctor or nurse, fuel, materials and tools, you can deduct an amount equal to the true value; but there are rules about how value can be checked for some of these items.

Finally, under some very stringent rules, you can deduct a fine or a payment for damage to your property, or for negligent work. Remember that for all these deductions to be legal, you need your employee's agreement in writing to their imposition. Again the law is in the process of being changed.

## WHAT YOU HAVE TO GIVE YOUR EMPLOYEE WITH THE PAY

You must give your employees a detailed written pay statement when or before they are paid. You may not have to if your employee is a part-timer (p. 255).

What must be in the written statement is laid down by law. It must include:

• the amount of your employee's salary or wages before any deductions are made

• if you deduct any sums of money, which can vary from pay day to pay day, you must say what the amount of each deduction is and what it is for

• if you deduct any sums of money which remain the same on each pay day, you can do one of two things. Either, you can say how much each deduction is and what it is for on each pay slip. Or, on the pay slip, you can

242 · YOUR RIGHTS AND DUTIES AS AN EMPLOYER

say what the total of these fixed deductions are and separately from the pay slip give a statement of what the sums of money are used for.

This separate written statement must be handed out at twelve-monthly intervals. It must say how much, when and why any deductions are made and you must hand it to your employee before or when they are made. If these fixed deductions are changed you have to give your employee written notice or an amended written statement

- the amount of your employee's pay after all the deductions.

If your employee is paid by more than one method, your pay slip should show how much is paid in each way, half in cash and half by bank transfer, for example.

## DO YOU HAVE TO GIVE HOLIDAY PAY?

No, unless you have agreed to do so, in which case it is part of your employee's contract. The only exception to this is if your employee's employment conditions are regulated by a Wages Council (p. 240).

## DO YOU HAVE TO GIVE SICK PAY?

Yes and no. If you have agreed to give your employee pay while ill, you must do so as it is part of the employment contract. How much pay and for how long should be set out by you in the written statement of employment, which you have to give your employee within thirteen weeks of starting the job (p. 239).

For most of your other employees you will have to give statutory sick pay; but for the first three days of sickness, you do not have to pay anything at all. If your employee is still ill on the fourth day, you will have to pay sick pay if your employee comes within certain categories. The amount of the sick pay is set out by the government; but you can claim back what you have paid by deducting it from national insurance contributions. For an employee earning more than £39 but less than £76.50, the rate is £32.85 a week; for an employee earning £76.50 a week or more, the rate is £47.20.

Briefly, to get the sick pay, your employee has to provide evidence of illness lasting four or more consecutive days, including Sundays and public holidays. Your employee is not entitled to receive sick pay if, for example:

- you pay average weekly earnings of less than the weekly lower-earnings limit for national insurance contributions, or

• if your employee is sixty-five or over (sixty or over if your employee is a woman).

The rules about who does, or does not, get statutory sick pay are complicated and set out in full in a leaflet, the DHSS's *Employers' guide to statutory sick pay*.

You have to pay statutory sick pay for twenty-eight weeks in one period or linked periods.

## IF YOU HAVE NO WORK FOR AN EMPLOYEE, WHAT DO YOU HAVE TO PAY?

For most employees, you will have to pay their salary or wages regardless of how much work you have and regardless of whether something happens, such as a power strike, which means your employee cannot do the work required. But if your employee is paid by the hour or on piece rate, you do not have to pay:

• unless you have agreed to do so in the contract of employment, or

• unless you have to make what is known as a guarantee payment. You may have to make this payment once your employee has worked for you continuously for a month. You have to pay for a workless day whichever is the less:

£10.90 or the number of normal working hours times the guaranteed hourly rate.

You have to make this payment up to five times in a three-month period.

## EQUAL PAY

You cannot pay one employee more than another because one is a man and the other a woman. Simply to say that a man is stronger is no defence to justify higher wages. If your employees are doing the same or broadly similar work or work of equal value, you should pay the same rate to each and give each the same terms of employment. 'Broadly similar' means that the differences between the two jobs are not of practical importance.

You can pay one employee more than another if there is a genuine non-sex-based reason for it. An example would be if one of your employees had been with you for many years and you had a scheme to pay employees a higher rate after you have employed them a number of years.

## HOW TO OPERATE THE PAYE SYSTEM

You have to act as a tax collector for the government. On each pay day you have to deduct the correct amount of tax and national insurance contributions from your employee's pay and you have to send it to the tax collector. Here are the steps to take when you employ someone:

1. Tell your tax office. If it is your first employee, tell your own tax inspector. You will be told which is your PAYE tax office as an employer, which could be different from the office which handles your tax affairs as an individual.

2. Work out the tax and national insurance contributions you have to deduct each pay day. Your PAYE tax office will send you the tax and NI tables you need to calculate this.

3. Fill in the Deductions Working Sheet you have been sent by the tax office. Do this for each pay day.

4. Within fourteen days of the end of each month send the tax and NI contributions to the accounts office. You will have been given pay slips to send in with the money.

5. At the end of each tax year (5 April), you will be sent a return to fill in for each employee. You can use your Deductions Working Sheet to complete the return. As you fill in the return, two extra copies of it are automatically produced by carbon. You give one of those copies to your employee as form P60. The other two copies you send to the tax office, together with a statement you have made summarizing the returns for all your employees.

You will not have to do all this if your employee earns less than a certain amount – in the 1987–8 tax year, the PAYE threshold is £46.50 a week or £202 a month for tax; the lower-earnings limit is £39 a week, £169 a month for NI contributions. But even if your employee earns less than the limits, you still have to tell your tax office.

Your employee should give you a P45 on the first day of the job; if not, you should fill in a P46. You should fill in a P45 when an employee leaves. You send the top part of it to your tax office and give the rest (Parts 2 and 3) to your employee.

## FRINGE BENEFITS AS PAY

Fringe benefits, such as a company car or cheap meals, can often be worth much more to an employee than a salary rise, simply because the tax treatment is relatively light. For example, a 1.6-litre company car can be worth £2,750 or more to an employee who pays basic rate tax. How much of your employee's pay package is made up of salary and how much of fringe benefits is a matter of negotiation.

You have to send in a form P11D each year before 6 May to the taxman, which gives information about fringe benefits and expenses. The form needs to be filled in for:

● higher-paid employees, which for 1987–8 means those earning £8,500 or over, including the taxable value of fringe benefits and expenses. So you might have to fill in a form for employees whose salary is much less than £8,500, if they also have a lot of perks, and

● any directors, unless the director earns less than £8,500, including perks, works full-time for you and has 5 per cent or less of the shares, including what his family and friends own.

BOOKLETS

IR, *Employer's Guide to PAYE* P7
DHSS, *Employers' guide to statutory sick pay* NI227
EOC, *Equal pay for work of equal value*
EOC, *Equal pay for women*
EOC, *Code of practice*
DE, *Payment of Wages Act 1960* PL673
DE, *8. Itemized pay statement* PL704
DE, *9. Guarantee payments* PL724
DE, *The Truck Acts* PL725
DE, *11. Rules governing continuous employment and a week's pay* PL711
DE, *Equal Pay* PL743
DE, *16. Redundancy payments* PL744
DE, *Statutory minimum wages and holidays with pay* WCL1 (rev.)
Home Office, *Sex Discrimination: A Guide to the Sex Discrimination Act 1975*

## A SAFE AND HEALTHY WORKING ENVIRONMENT

You have to carry out your work, as far as possible, in such a way that visitors and the general public are not exposed to health or safety risks.

This applies to everyone whether you have employees or not. And it applies to your workplace as well as your work.

## WHAT YOU MUST DO

Once you have employees there are additional rules. Broadly:

1. Get employer's liability insurance

2. Make your workplace safe

3. Employ competent workers

4. Have a written statement on your policy for health and safety at work (if you have five or more employees).

## INSURANCE

You must have employer's liability insurance to cover you for any physical injury or disease your employees get as a result of their work (p. 258). You must display your latest certificate so your employees can see it.

## SAFE WORKING ENVIRONMENT

You must see that the place where your employees work, and the entrance to it, is reasonably safe. Making a safe place of work includes things like fire exits and extinguishers, electrical fittings, storing material, machinery, hygiene, first aid; the list is very wide and covers all aspects of work.

You also have to take steps to provide a system of working for your employees which will give adequate safety. This includes making sure your employees are trained well enough to carry out the work safely. And you also need to check that the system of working is actually being carried out.

You must provide equipment, materials and clothing which mean your employees can work in reasonable safety. You could be held responsible if there is a defect in the things you give to your employee which causes an accident.

If there is a risk of injury from criminals, you must take steps to protect your employees.

## COMPETENT WORKERS

If you know one of your employees is incompetent, and if one of your other employees is injured as a result of that incompetence, you could be held liable. And even if you do not believe your employee to be inefficient, but your employee behaves negligently while carrying out your work, and another employee or a member of the general public is injured, you can be held liable.

If one of your employees breaks a safety rule which you have publicized, you can fairly sack your employee. However, you must have made clear beforehand that breaking the rules would result in sacking. The reverse side of the coin is that if you do not take reasonable steps for the safety of your employees, an employee could resign and claim constructive dismissal (p. 253).

PAPERWORK

If you have five or more employees, you must have a written statement on your policy for health and safety at work and how that policy is to be carried out. This statement should be displayed so your employees can see it. If you have ten or more employees, you must keep an accident book to record work accidents. If you have a factory, you have to keep a book like this, regardless of the number of employees.

ENFORCING HEALTH AND SAFETY

Your local authority has this job and can appoint inspectors to enforce the health and safety regulations. An inspector has the right to enter your workplace to examine it.

BOOKLETS

Health & Safety Commission, *Advice to employers* HSC3
HSC, *Advice to the self-employed* HSC4
HSC, *Writing a safety policy statement* HSC6 (rev.)

## DISCRIMINATION: WHAT TO WATCH OUT FOR

In general, you cannot discriminate on grounds of sex or race, and in employment, you cannot discriminate on grounds of marriage or trade union membership. But, normally, you can refuse to take on someone who is too old or too young for a job and you can refuse to take on somebody who is gay.

WHAT YOU MUST DO
Broadly:

1. Do not discriminate on grounds of sex or race

2. Do not refuse to allow your employees to join a trade union or dismiss them for trade union activity.

## SEX

Discrimination means less favourable treatment of a man or woman on the grounds of sex. It covers pay and conditions of the job, as well as opportunities for promotion, for example. You cannot discriminate:

- in advertising or interviews for the job

- in the terms in which the job is offered

- in deciding who is offered the job

- in opportunities for promotion, transfer or training

- in benefits to employees

- in dismissals.

You need to be particularly careful that you do not introduce requirements for a job or promotion which are more likely to be met by one sex more than the other. For example, if you insist that the person for the job needs to be six feet tall, you will be discriminating against women. The same could apply if you insist on some technical qualification more likely to be held by men than women. But you can insist on height, technical or other qualifications, if you can show that these are genuinely necessary for the job.

Note that if someone takes a case against you to an industrial tribunal, it is illegal for you to victimize them afterwards.

## RACE

Racial discrimination means treating one person less favourably than another on racial grounds, which includes colour, race, nationality or ethnic or national origins. As with sex discrimination, racial discrimination also applies if you make a requirement for a job which one racial group would find more difficult to meet than another group.

You cannot discriminate:

- in advertising or interviews for the job

- in the terms in which the job is offered

- in deciding who is offered the job

- in opportunities for promotion, transfer or training

- in benefits to employees

- in dismissals.

If one of your employees takes you to an industrial tribunal claiming racial discrimination, it is unlawful for you to victimize the employee.

## TRADE UNIONS

An industrial tribunal will find the dismissal unfair if you sack an employee for:

- trying to join or joining an independent trade union (it is independent if the Certification Office, appointed by the government, says it is)

- refusing to join a trade union, unless you have made a closed shop agreement, which has been approved in a secret ballot of employees in the preceding five years. Even then, the sacking of certain employees will be unfair (for example, those who object to union membership on grounds of conscience or other deeply held personal conviction)

- taking part in trade union activities (for example, meetings) at the appropriate time, which is normally outside working hours. Industrial action does not count as a union activity.

Employees can also complain to an industrial tribunal if you penalize them, but do not dismiss, or if you make them redundant for any of the above actions.

## CRIMINAL OFFENCES

In some cases, people who have been convicted of an offence do not have to tell you about it. If you ask, they can lie about it quite legally. The people who can do this are those who have had sentences of thirty months or less. They can keep quiet about their convictions after a specified time, which varies, but is not more than ten years and not less than six months.
  If you employ someone who is entitled to keep quiet about their convictions and you subsequently discover their past, you cannot fairly dismiss the employee.

## HEALTH AND DISABLEMENT

You can refuse to employ someone if you are unhappy about their state of health. And if one of your employees has absences from work which is interfering seriously with the running of your business, the chances are that you can fairly dismiss the employee. It would be wise to get a doctor to give the employee a complete medical before doing so.

If you employ twenty or more people, you may be required to employ someone from the Disabled Persons Register. There is a required quota of 3 per cent of your workforce.

BOOKLETS

EOC, *A short guide to the Sex Discrimination Act 1975*
EOC, *A guide for employers*
EOC, *A model Equal Opportunity Policy*
EOC, *Code of Practice*
MSC, *The Disabled Persons Register* DPL1
CRE, *A guide for employers*
CRE, *A guide to the Race Relations Act 1976*
DE, 7. *Union membership rights and the closed shop* PL754
Home Office, *Sex Discrimination: A Guide to the Sex Discrimination Act 1975*

# MATERNITY

Pregnant women employees, married or unmarried, have several rights.

WHAT YOU MUST DO

Broadly:

1. Give reasonable paid time off work so that your employee can have ante-natal treatment

2. Do not dismiss your employee because she is pregnant, except in certain circumstances (see below)

3. Give your employee maternity pay (see right)

4. In certain circumstances, give your employee her job back (see right)

DISMISSING WHILE PREGNANT

A pregnant woman cannot complain of unfair dismissal if she has been employed by you for less than two years (see p. 255 for part-time staff).

You can also fairly dismiss an employee because of pregnancy if:

• her condition makes it impossible for her to do her job properly, or

- it would be against the law for her to do that particular job while pregnant.

If either of these apply, you must offer your employee a suitable alternative vacancy if there is one available. If you do not have one, your employee is still entitled to maternity pay and has the right to return to work, provided she otherwise qualifies.

## MATERNITY PAY

You will normally have to pay statutory maternity pay (SMP) to a pregnant employee even if she is not going to return to work for you after the birth of her child. It is normally paid for a period of eighteen weeks.
   You only pay statutory maternity pay if your employee:

- has stopped working for you

- is still pregnant at the eleventh week before her baby is expected

- has average weekly earnings of at least £39 a week for 1987–8

- has been continuously employed by you for the six months or more at the fifteenth week before the baby is due.

For the first six weeks you pay SMP, you give your employee 90 per cent of her average weekly earnings. For the remaining twelve weeks SMP is paid at a lower weekly rate set by the government (for 1987–8 £32.85)

## RIGHT TO RETURN TO WORK

If you had five or less employees at the time your employee's maternity absence began *and* it is not reasonably practicable to take her back in her old job or to offer another suitable vacancy, your employee is unlikely to be able to claim unfair dismissal.
   If you have more than five employees, your employee has the right to return to work if she has worked for you for a certain period (see above in *Maternity pay*). Your employee may lose the right to return to work if:

- her job no longer exists because of redundancy and there is no suitable alternative job (in which case you may have to pay redundancy pay)

- it is not practicable for her to return to her job and you have offered suitable alternative work, which she refuses

- if your employee fails to meet some complicated rules about written notification to you.

BOOKLETS

DE, 4. *Employment rights for the expectant mother* PL710
NI, 257. *Employer's guide to Statutory Maternity Pay*

## SAYING GOODBYE TO AN EMPLOYEE

You have got two years to assess employees, and during that time you can dismiss them without any fear of being taken to an industrial tribunal and accused of unfair dismissal. The only exceptions to this are if you dismiss someone because of sex, race or trade union activity; you would be guilty of unfair dismissal right from the start of the employment period.

### WHAT YOU MUST DO

Broadly:

1. Behave in a reasonable way when dismissing an employee

2. Give your employee the right notice.

### HOW YOU CAN SACK AN EMPLOYEE

After the initial period is up, it is still not too much of a problem to dismiss someone. There are five reasons which may mean a dismissal is fair, although you will also have to demonstrate that you have been reasonable in the circumstances. The reasons are:

• being incapable of doing the job. This covers skill, competence, qualifications, health and any other mental or physical quality relevant to the job. Note that you do not have to prove to an industrial tribunal that an employee is incompetent, merely that you believed it to be so and that you have acted reasonably

• misconduct, for example, theft, insolence, horseplay, bad time-keeping, laziness

• redundancy (see below)

• illegality, if it would be illegal to continue employing the employee

• some other substantial reason, for example, if it is in the best interest of the firm to sack an employee.

As you can see, it is usually quite possible to dismiss an employee if you are dissatisfied. But it is very important to do so in a reasonable way. It can save you an awful lot of time and money if you do because you can demonstrate to an industrial tribunal that you have been reasonable in the circumstances. Follow this plan.

STEP-BY-STEP GUIDE

---

**1.** When you first become dissatisfied with an employee, tell the employee so, preferably in writing.

**2.** Give your employee an opportunity to explain the problem and discuss constructively how things can be improved.

**3.** Consider whether training would help your employee. Look closely at the arrangements for supervising your employee's work.

**4.** After you have allowed a reasonable period for improvement, if things are still unsatisfactory warn your employee in writing of the consequences of no improvement.

**5.** Repeat 2 and 3.

**6.** Tell your employee when you will review the case.

**7.** Consider if there is not a suitable alternative job for your employee.

**8.** If you are still dissatisfied, dismiss your employee making sure you give the correct notice (see below). If your employee has been with you for six months, you can be asked to give your reasons in writing.

---

There is an ACAS Code of Practice which clearly outlines the steps to be taken in dismissals (p. 408).

SACKING SOMEONE ON THE SPOT

It can be done and it is likely to be a fair dismissal as long as you dismissed your employee for gross misconduct, such as dishonesty. But, on the whole, to avoid problems it is best to try to stick to the guide above.

CAN IT BE UNFAIR DISMISSAL IF YOUR EMPLOYEE RESIGNS?

It may seem a paradox, but the answer is yes. It can be unfair, if it is a constructive dismissal. So watch out. If you increase working hours without extra pay, cut your employee's fringe benefits or accuse an employee of something, such as theft, without investigating it properly, it may count as constructive dismissal.

## MAKING AN EMPLOYEE REDUNDANT

You can make an employee redundant if you are cutting down generally on the number of employees or if your need for a particular skill in your business ceases. But you must make the redundancy fair; do not choose all the married women or all the trade unionists, for example. And you must consult the trade union about the proposed redundancy.

If an employee has been with you for two years, you will have to pay redundancy pay. The amount depends upon the age of the employee and varies between $\frac{1}{2}$ and $1\frac{1}{2}$ weeks pay for each year the employee has worked for you.

## HOW MUCH NOTICE DO YOU HAVE TO GIVE?

You must give your employee:

● one week's notice if your employee has been with you for one month but less than two years

● two weeks' notice if your employee has been with you for two years *and*

● an extra week's notice for each extra year your employee has been with you, up to a maximum of twelve weeks' notice.

If your employee's contract specifies a longer notice period, the longer period applies.

These minimum notice periods do not apply to your employee, who by law has to give only one week's notice if employed by you for a month. So, if you want to make sure that your employee has to give more notice, you must put it in the contract of employment.

## WHAT TO DO WHEN AN EMPLOYEE LEAVES

You must fill in form P45. Send Part 1 to the tax office and hand Parts 2 and 3 to your employee. If an employee dies, you should also fill in form P45 and send all three parts to the tax office.

## BOOKLETS

DE, *14. Rights to notice and reasons for dismissal* PL707
DE, *13. Unfairly dismissed?* PL712
DE, *Fair and unfair dismissal* PL714
DE, *The law on unfair dismissal* PL715
DE, *16. Redundancy payments* PL744
DE, *2. Procedure for handling redundancies* PL756

## PART-TIME STAFF

For the purposes of the employment legislation, there are two categories of part-time workers:

- those that work at least eight hours but less than sixteen hours
- those that work less than eight hours.

Your employees who work less than eight hours have very few rights under the employment legislation. If you have employees who work at least eight hours but less than sixteen hours, they can acquire most of the employment rights, but have to wait for five years. After five years, they have the right:

- not to be dismissed because of pregnancy
- to get maternity pay
- to return to work
- to get guarantee payments if there is no work
- to receive an itemized pay statement
- to receive minimum notice of dismissal
- to receive a written statement of the reasons for dismissal
- not to be dismissed unfairly
- to receive a written statement of the main terms and conditions of employment.

All employees, regardless of the number of hours worked, have some rights, such as to be protected from hazards at work by the health and safety provisions.

## SUMMARY

1. Do not be frightened of employment law. On the whole, you can employ who you want and sack them if they prove to be incompetent.

2. Behave reasonably towards your employees, giving them a chance to explain their actions. If you do this, you can cut down the chances of being found guilty of unfair dismissal in an industrial tribunal.

3. Use the step-by-step guide to sacking someone on p. 253. This will

help you defend yourself against a charge of unfair dismissal, because of the way that you do it.

4. Follow the legal life-cycle of an employee on p. 236.

OTHER CHAPTERS TO READ

# 21. INSURANCE

Deciding what insurance you should have must rate as one of the least exciting decisions you have to make for your business. Paying out money to cover you against hazards, which you fervently hope will not happen, ranks fairly low in satisfaction. But it should rank quite high in priority to work out what insurance you need. Failing to get the right insurance might mean the collapse and end of your business.

There are two different categories of business insurance:

- insurance you must have by law

- insurance you could consider to cover risks and disasters.

This chapter looks mainly at insurance for your business needs, rather than your personal needs.

## BUYING THE INSURANCE

Not only do you want the right sort of insurance, you want it at the right price and with the right company. The obvious place to start your search for your business insurance is with an insurance broker. An insurance broker is probably a better source than other people involved in insurance, for example, an insurance salesman or agent, an accountant or solicitor. These groups of people will probably deal with only a few companies and so may not get you the best possible quote from a company which offers a good service and with a good record for paying on claims. A broker can, in theory, deal with the full range of insurance companies, although, in practice, may not do so. Note that the cost of the insurance may vary depending on the location of the business; at the extreme, you may not be able to buy insurance for some areas.

An insurance broker can only be called a broker if registered with the Insurance Brokers Registration Council. To be registered, a broker has to behave in accordance with a code of conduct. The requirements for insurance broking businesses means getting professional indemnity insurance to reimburse customers for losses suffered as a result of the broker's negligence. And there is a compensation fund in case the broker should go bust or commit some fraud. The broker has to keep a separate bank account for clients' money and keep proper accounts. If someone is called an insurance consultant or adviser, the chances are that you will not be dealing with a registered insurance broker. Check by asking the person a direct question; and do not be put off by arguments that being registered is unnecessary. It is one safeguard that you should insist on.

But choosing an insurance broker can still be tricky – as being registered gives no guarantee that a broker will do a certain amount of research work on your behalf to get the best deal possible for you. Other business contacts may be able to help you by recommending someone. You should certainly consider approaching three different brokers and asking them all to make recommendations for you. Then you can choose the best.

The British Insurance Brokers Association (see p. 408 for address) can provide you with a list of brokers in your area. You could also contact your bank who will provide advice and quotations on the cost and type of insurance you need.

With personal financial needs such as pensions and investment-type life insurance, a new regulatory regime is in the process of being introduced. When the process is completed, independent intermediaries who can advise you on these topics will need to be registered with a self-regulatory organization who will authorize them to give advice; the likeliest self-regulatory organization will be FIMBRA. The British Insurance Brokers Association will still be the trade association for these authorized businesses and will be able to provide you with a list of those in your area.

## INSURANCE YOU MUST HAVE

There are certain sorts of insurance you have to have:

### 1. EMPLOYERS' LIABILITY

You must have insurance to pay out for your liability if one of your employees is injured or ill as a result of working for you. The amount of cover (the amount of money the insurance company will pay out if you claim) is generally unlimited.

### 2. MOTOR INSURANCE

You need to get insurance to pay out if you are liable for any injury caused by one of your vehicles to other people including a passenger. This is known as Road Traffic Act only insurance. It is pretty unusual to choose this cover. As a minimum, you should have what is known as third party cover.

Third party cover will include your liability to others (see above) but also:

● your liability for damage caused to other people's property (including accidents happening off the public roads)

● sometimes solicitor's fees for a Coroner's Inquest, fatal injury inquiry or proceedings in a magistrate's court, if these are for an accident covered by the insurance policy

● sometimes legal costs – up to a specified amount – for defending a charge of manslaughter or for causing death by reckless or dangerous driving.

A further addition to third party cover which could be worth your while is fire and theft cover. Finally, if you want to get cover for accidental damage to your vehicles, regardless of who is to blame for the accident, you want a comprehensive insurance policy.

If you have a car or other vehicle for your own private and social use, and you want to use it for your business, you should tell your insurance company. You may need to pay an extra sum to get it covered for business.

Be clear about what the car is going to be used for when you fill in what is known as the proposal form (the form you fill in to apply for the insurance). You will probably have to pay extra money if the car is used for some purposes, such as by a sales rep. Failure to tell the insurance company may mean that it will not pay out if you have an accident.

### 3. INSURANCE NEEDED BY CONTRACTS

Check all the contracts you have (for example, under a lease or hire purchase agreement) to see what insurance you are committed to get.

### 4. ENGINEERING EQUIPMENT

By law, certain equipment, such as pressure vessels and lifting tackle, has to be inspected and passed as safe at regular intervals. You can combine the maintenance with an insurance policy to cover you against the risk of explosion, accidental damage and breakdown.

# OTHER INSURANCE YOU CAN GET

### 1. INSURANCE AGAINST FIRE AND OTHER PERILS

This covers destruction or damage to your buildings and contents through fire. You can also be covered for other risks such as lightning, explosion, aircraft, storm, riot, malicious damage and so on. If you work from your own home, you should check that you are protected by your own household insurance policy.

Worth getting? *Yes*.

### 2. INSURANCE FOR LOSS OF PROFITS

This covers you if your business is disrupted by fire or some other peril. It can pay out money to pay your employees, maintain your profits and pay for the extra cost of your fill-in working premises.

Worth getting? *Depends* on your business. In most cases, yes; but if your business is small with few employees, and you could easily find somewhere to work, for example, your home, you may not consider it necessary. Rather than insure for full loss of profits, you could consider insuring for the cost of finding somewhere else to carry on working.

### 3. INSURANCE AGAINST THEFT

This covers you for loss or damage to the contents of your premises. Theft for insurance purposes means that someone has forced an entry to your workplace, so if you want to be covered against theft by your employees or visitors, you'll have to pay extra.

Worth getting? *Yes*.

### 4. LOSS OF MONEY

Cash and near-cash, such as cheques, stamps and so on, can be insured against theft from your premises or in transit.

Worth getting? *Yes*, if your takings are in cash. Otherwise, no.

### 5. GOODS IN TRANSIT

This insurance covers loss or damage of your goods in your own vehicles, or other means of delivery, such as post, road haulier and so on.

Worth getting? *Probably*, unless you don't sell in this way.

## 6. CREDIT INSURANCE

This protects you against your customers failing to pay. You probably will not be able to get this insurance until you have been in business some time.

Worth getting? *No*, if you deal mainly in cash or payment on delivery. For selling on credit, by the time you can get this insurance, you will be able to work out for yourself how likely a problem bad debts will be. It is probably better to operate good credit control (p. 308) or use a factoring service (p. 312). However, if you have only one large or a couple of big customers, you should have credit insurance.

## 7. PUBLIC LIABILITY AND PRODUCT LIABILITY

This will cover your liability if your business causes injury or illness to a member of the public or damage to their property. Product liability insurance covers you for these risks which occur as a result of the goods you are producing or selling.

You need to make sure that the amount of cover is high enough. Recent damages in the courts have been as high as £500,000. You may need cover for more than this, depending on your business, especially if you do business in the USA.

Worth getting? *Yes*. With product liability, you may not need it if your products are very unlikely to cause any damage or if you are in the service business.

## 8. PROFESSIONAL INDEMNITY

If you are the sort of business where the end product is expert advice, this insurance can cover you against claims from your clients for damages caused by your negligence or misconduct.

Worth getting? *Yes*. These sorts of claims are on the increase.

## 9. LEGAL EXPENSES

This insurance would enable you to pay for legal assistance if you are involved in a legal dispute.

Worth getting? *Probably not*. Most legal disputes are generally in the employment field. It would be far better to concentrate on getting well organized in this area to cut the risk of being taken to a tribunal charged with unfair dismissal.

## 10. KEYMAN INSURANCE

If your business is heavily dependent on one or a few people for its future success, you can get keyman life insurance, for example, for a sum of £250,000, to be paid to your business in the event of one of those people dying.

Worth getting? *Yes*.

## 11. OTHER INSURANCE

There are some other types of insurance which you should consider, depending on your business. These include:

● glass breakage, which is important for shops

● cover for frozen food

● computers and computer records

● fidelity guarantee, which covers you against your own losses which occur as a result of fraud or dishonesty by your employees

● business machines and equipment

● agricultural and fish-farming operations.

## INSURANCE FOR YOU AND YOUR FAMILY

If you and your family are not covered by insurance for various personal mishaps, you may find it difficult to carry on your business, so do not neglect your personal needs. Make sure that you and your wife or husband have enough life insurance to protect you in the event of your early deaths. For this purpose do not go for the sort of life insurance which is really an investment, but go for term insurance, family income benefit, mortgage protection policies and so on.

Permanent health insurance would pay out an income if you were too ill to work and could pay for a temporary manager. You should consider this carefully. And do not forget pensions, which are covered in detail on p. 396.

## SUMMARY

1. Do not delay in taking out the insurance you need.

2. Use a registered insurance broker to act for you.

3. Shop around. Seek advice from more than one broker and ask for several quotes for each insurance you need.

4. Do not neglect personal insurance requirements. Life insurance for your family, permanent health insurance and pensions should be looked at carefully to determine the level you need. Use an independent intermediary who is authorized to advise you on these topics (p. 258).

OTHER CHAPTERS TO READ

33. 'Retirement' (p. 396)

# 22. FORECASTING

Forecasts are the kernel of your business. They are the basis on which you raise money, negotiate premises and order raw materials. These are only a few of the decisions which need to be made in advance with only your forecasts as guidance on how much is needed. Making a wildly inaccurate forecast can, for example, lead to raising insufficient funds. When the business fails to meet expectations and begins to run short of money, it may prove impossible to raise further funds. Lenders are very wary of handing out more when forecasting has proved to be mistaken. The result could be liquidation, or bankruptcy if you are a partner or sole trader, and the end of your dreams.

However, making no forecasts at all is even sillier. You would have no guidance on when to take certain basic business decisions.

Given the importance of attaining a reasonable estimate of future sales, costs and cash balances, it follows that making the forecasts is a process which should not be hurried or treated casually. You must constantly strive to seek information on which forecasts can be based; you must constantly curb your over-optimism which can lead to estimated sales figures that are too high and estimated cost figures that are too low. Question your first forecasts for the realism of their assumptions, before accepting any figure as a part of the final forecasts.

Nevertheless, it is realistic to accept that some of the figures will be nothing more than a best guess given the current state of information available to you. However, your figures should have some grounding in fact, so that when you present your case to your bank manager or other source of finance you can support the figure when challenged.

It is important to make the forecasts in your plan realistic so that if your business idea does not hold water, you can discover this at the planning stage. You do not want to discover two years down the track that your business will not work, after you have committed money, time and effort. Do not underestimate the mental anguish and financial problems which can be caused by a struggling business (p. 326).

WHAT IS IN THIS CHAPTER?

There are three forecasts you need to make:

- Cash flow forecast (see below)
- Profit and loss forecast (p. 270)
- Balance sheet forecast (p. 274).

Finally, at the end of this chapter, there is an example of how a start-up business produces the cash flow and profit and loss forecasts.

## CASH FLOW FORECAST

The first point to note is that cash and profit are not the same thing at all, so the two forecasts may be quite different.

A cash flow forecast is quite simply a record of when you think you will receive cash in your business and when you think you will have to pay it out. In your business plan, you should include monthly cash flow forecasting for at least one, preferably two years ahead. Depending on the size of your business, you may also need to include yearly cash flow forecasts for three years beyond that, totalling five years of forecasts in all.

On p. 266 there is a blank cash flow form, which shows the typical headings and layout of a forecast. Obviously, the headings will vary with the nature of the business. At the end of this chapter, there is an example of how Betty Crop and her partner, Roger Cartwright, produce their cash flow forecast for their knitwear business.

### DETAILED CALCULATIONS FOR CASH FLOW FORECAST

Do the cash flow forecast for your chosen accounting year. If, for example, you choose to end your accounting year at the end of April, your cash flow forecast will run from 1 May to 30 April.

It is important to make realistic assumptions about when you will receive the cash, or when you will have to pay it out. The purpose of the forecast is to throw up when your need for cash is at its greatest, so you can demonstrate what your funding requirements are.

1. *Opening bank balance*
This shows how much is actually in your business bank account at the start of each period. If you owe your bank money (have an overdraft), show this by putting the figure in brackets. If your forecast is made before you start trading, the opening bank balance is likely to be nil.

Your opening bank balance for one period will be the closing bank balance for the previous period.

MONTHLY CASH FLOW FORECAST (for the period 1 January 198x to 31 December 198x)

| | JAN. | FEB. | — | NOV. | DEC. | TOTAL |
|---|---|---|---|---|---|---|
| Opening bank balance (A) | ... | ... | — | ... | ... | ... |
| *Receipts* | | | | | | |
| Cash from sales | ... | ... | — | ... | ... | ... |
| Cash from debtors | ... | ... | — | ... | ... | ... |
| VAT (net receipts) | ... | ... | — | ... | ... | ... |
| Other receipts | ... | ... | — | ... | ... | ... |
| Sale of assets | ... | ... | — | ... | ... | ... |
| Capital | ... | ... | — | ... | ... | ... |
| TOTAL RECEIPTS (B) | ... | ... | — | ... | ... | ... |
| *Payments* | | | | | | |
| Payment to suppliers | ... | ... | — | ... | ... | ... |
| Cash purchases | ... | ... | — | ... | ... | ... |
| Wages/drawings | ... | ... | — | ... | ... | ... |
| PAYE/NIC | ... | ... | — | ... | ... | ... |
| VAT (net payments) | ... | ... | — | ... | ... | ... |
| Tax payments | ... | ... | — | ... | ... | ... |
| Rent | ... | ... | — | ... | ... | ... |
| Rates | ... | ... | — | ... | ... | ... |
| Heating/lighting | ... | ... | — | ... | ... | ... |
| Telephone | ... | ... | — | ... | ... | ... |
| Professional fees | ... | ... | — | ... | ... | ... |
| General expenses | ... | ... | — | ... | ... | ... |
| Capital expenditure | ... | ... | — | ... | ... | ... |
| Bank interest | ... | ... | — | ... | ... | ... |
| Other payments | ... | ... | — | ... | ... | ... |
| TOTAL PAYMENTS (C) | ... | ... | — | ... | ... | ... |
| CLOSING BANK BALANCE (A) + (B) − (C) | ... | ... | — | ... | ... | ... |

## 2. *Cash from sales*

In here would go any cash you expect to receive when you sell your product, not in payment of an invoice you send out. If your business is a shop, most of your sales will be cash ones, and so this would be the biggest element of your cash receipts.

If you are registered for VAT, enter the figure you expect to receive, including VAT.

## 3. *Cash from debtors*

If you sell your product and do not receive payment at once, but instead send out invoices, you would enter here when you expect to receive the cash. Someone who owes you money (for example, has not yet paid your invoice) is a debtor. You should aim to get your invoices paid as quickly as possible, but most of your customers will expect to delay payment of your invoice by at least one month (see Chapter 24. 'Staying afloat' (p. 298) for how to get your debtors to pay).

If you are registered for VAT, enter the figure you expect to receive, including VAT.

## 4. *VAT (net receipts)*

If you are not registered for VAT, ignore this section (see p. 384 for details of whether you should or should not be registered). If you are registered for VAT, you will only expect to receive cash from the VAT system if for some reason your purchases, on which you can claim back VAT, are greater than your sales on which you have charged VAT.

This might happen as a rare occurrence if you have spent a lot of money while starting up, before your sales have got going. Another possible reason for this could occur if your sales are seasonal but your purchases are not. It could also happen if your sales are zero-rated, in which case you do not have to charge VAT on your sales, but you can claim it back on your purchases (p. 389).

You make your returns for VAT on a quarterly basis, so allow for this in your cash flow.

## 5. *Other receipts*

Put here any miscellaneous receipts of income which you expect to occur.

## 6. *Sale of assets*

This section is for you to record the proceeds you expect to get from selling any assets, for example, a car or office equipment, rather than any sales of your products.

## 7. *Capital*

Put the amount of money you are going to invest and make sure you put it in the month you expect to invest it. If anyone else is expected to invest or to lend you money (not including an overdraft with the bank), slot it in here.

## 8. *Payment to suppliers*

Put in here when you expect you will have to pay suppliers for their services or materials (p. 313). The longer you delay paying suppliers' invoices, the better it can be for your cash flow. This beneficial effect has to be balanced by any ill-will created by late payment. A realistic assumption for your cash flow forecast will be that you will not have to pay your suppliers' invoices until one month after you receive them.

Whether you are registered for VAT or not, enter the amount including any VAT you will be paying to your suppliers.

## 9. *Cash purchases*

If you may have to pay cash on the spot for purchases from suppliers, estimate the amount (including any VAT) and time in this section.

## 10. *Wages/drawings*

Put here the amount after deducting tax and national insurance contributions under the PAYE system for wages.

## 11. *PAYE/NIC*

Total the amount of tax under the PAYE system and the amount of national insurance contributions you will deduct from your employees each month, as well as the amount of the employer's contribution. You have to send this money into the tax collector within two weeks of the end of the month. So your payments of these amounts will be in the month after you have deducted them. If your business is a limited company and you pay yourself a salary as a director, your personal tax and national insurance contributions will also be collected in the way described above. If you are a sole trader or partner, your personal tax on what you pay yourself will not be collected in this way. Instead, you will pay tax, and Class 4 national insurance contributions if you pay them, in two lumps – on 1 January and 1 July. Enter the amount in the section TAX PAYMENTS.

However, your Class 2 national insurance contributions will be collected each month, and you should reflect the amount here under PAYE/ NIC. For more about your personal tax and national insurance contributions as a sole trade or partner, see p. 344 and p. 356.

### 12. *VAT (net payments)*
If you are not registered for VAT, do not enter anything here. If you are registered for VAT, you should estimate the amount of tax you will be paying over to the VAT collector each quarter (p. 394).

### 13. *Tax payments*
If you run a limited company, enter the amount of tax you estimate you will pay on your company's profits and when you will pay it. Corporation tax, that is, tax on your company's profits, is payable nine months after the end of your accounting year (p. 374).

   If you are a sole trader or partner, your tax and any Class 4 national insurance contributions payable will be paid in two lumps – on 1 January and 1 July. For how to work out the amount of tax you will be paying, see Chapters 28. and 29.

### 14. *Rent*
Enter the amount of rent you will pay in the months you will have to pay it.

### 15. *Rates*
Enter the amount of rates and when you will have to pay it. Do not forget you can opt to pay your rates monthly over a ten-month period. This can improve your cash flow.

### 16. *Heating/lighting*
These bills will be paid each quarter in arrears. Once you have received the bill, you will be able to delay payment by up to one month.

### 17. *Telephone*
The phone bill will be paid quarterly in arrears and you can probably take a further month's delay before you pay, although this is a delay which cannot be increased beyond the month.

### 18. *Professional fees*
Payment of these bills will be fairly erratic and you must make your best guess.

### 19. *General expenses*
Enter an estimate for those continuing and recurring, but small, expenses. These could include postage, fares, newspapers, or whatever is required in your business. Of course, if your business is a mailing service, for example, you should have a separate heading for postage. What exactly goes in here will have to be decided by you.

20. *Capital expenditure*
If you are going to buy any pieces of equipment, such as a car, typewriter, computer or machinery, enter the amount, including VAT, and when you estimate you will have to pay for it. If you are paying cash, put in the full amount. If you are going to buy on hire purchase or using a loan, you will enter the amount of the deposit and the monthly payments separately and in the correct months. Leasing payments will be monthly.

21. *Bank interest and charges*
If you have an overdraft or bank loan, estimate the amount and frequency of the interest charged. Get a quote from the bank manager.

22. *Other payments*
What goes in here depends on the nature of your business. It could include insurance, but if this is of a reasonable size, you should have a separate entry.

23. *Closing bank balance*
Work out the closing bank balance for the period by adding the opening bank balance to the total receipts and taking away the figure for total payments. The closing bank balance becomes the opening bank balance at the start of the next period.

## PROFIT AND LOSS FORECAST

A profit forecast should show what level of profit you expect your business to produce at the end of the period, according to the accounting records you keep. Your accounts will not be drawn up on a cash basis, so many of the figures in your profit forecast will be different from those in the cash flow forecast. In the guide to filling in the profit forecast, there is an explanation of how and why the figures will differ.

### DETAILED CALCULATIONS FOR PROFIT AND LOSS FORECAST

1. *Sales*
The figure you put in here is the sum of the invoices you expect to send out during the accounting period. It is not necessarily the sum of the cash you receive during the period (unless your business is a shop which makes only cash sales, for example). You could also describe the sales figure as the cash you receive during the period plus what you are owed at the end of the period less what you were owed at the end of the previous period.

If you are registered for VAT, you do not include the amount of VAT you charge on your sales.

If your business is likely to be seasonal, or if you know of events coming up which might temporarily increase or decrease your sales figures, show this monthly effect. A reader of your business plan will not be impressed by a monthly figure which is level or shows a very steady rate of increase, unless, of course, you can demonstrate that this is a realistic assumption.

When forecasting sales you need to consider two factors:

- the number of units you can sell

- the price you can get for these units.

MONTHLY PROFIT AND LOSS FORECAST (for the period 1 January 198x to 31 December 198x)

|  | JAN. | FEB. | – | NOV. | DEC. | TOTAL |
|---|---|---|---|---|---|---|
| SALES (A) | ... | ... | – | ... | ... | ... |
| less Cost of sales | | | | | | |
| Purchases | ... | ... | – | ... | ... | ... |
| Labour | ... | ... | – | ... | ... | ... |
| Other direct costs | ... | ... | – | ... | ... | ... |
| TOTAL (B) | ... | ... | – | ... | ... | ... |
| GROSS PROFIT (C) | | | | | | |
| Take (B) from (A) | ... | ... | – | ... | ... | ... |
| Less Overheads | | | | | | |
| Rent and rates | ... | ... | – | ... | ... | ... |
| Heating/lighting | ... | ... | – | ... | ... | ... |
| Telephone | ... | ... | – | ... | ... | ... |
| Professional fees | ... | ... | – | ... | ... | ... |
| Depreciation | ... | ... | – | ... | ... | ... |
| Employee costs | ... | ... | – | ... | ... | ... |
| Other overhead expenses | ... | ... | – | ... | ... | ... |
| Drawings | ... | ... | – | ... | ... | ... |
| Interest | ... | ... | – | ... | ... | ... |
| TOTAL (D) | ... | ... | – | ... | ... | ... |
| plus | | | | | | |
| Miscellaneous income (E) | ... | ... | – | ... | ... | ... |
| NET PROFIT (F) = (C) + (E) − (D) | ... | ... | – | ... | ... | ... |

## 2. *Cost of sales: Purchases*

You are estimating for this section those costs which you would expect to vary with the level of your sales; if your sales go up, the level of direct costs goes up and vice versa. In real life, things are not quite so cut-and-dried and often the distinction between direct costs and overheads is blurred. The important point is for you to have a clear idea about which costs in your business you are going to regard as direct and which you are going to regard as overheads.

Purchases could be the raw materials you buy from your suppliers to manufacture your products. Or, if you are not a manufacturing business, they would be the items which you purchase to sell on to your customers, having added on your profit margin.

The figure you put in your profit and loss account will be different from the cash flow figures, payment to suppliers and cash purchases. For the profit calculation you need the sum of the invoices you receive in the period for materials.

Another way of working out the purchase figure for this forecast is to say it is what you pay for supplies in the period plus what you owe at the end of the period less what you owed at the start of the period.

If you are registered for VAT, you do not include the figure for VAT which you are charged by your supplier for your profit forecast. If you are not registered for VAT, you do include the figure for VAT.

Points to look out for when you are forecasting costs include:

• make sure that the level of costs corresponds to the amount of sales you expect to make

• allow for any changes in the prices of raw materials which you can reasonably expect to occur in the period.

## 3. *Cost of sales: Labour*

Here include the cost of your employees who are directly involved with manufacturing your product. As with purchases, the distinction between staff who are directly involved with production and those who count as overheads can be blurred. On the whole, if you do not think that employees' wages are directly related to the amount of work you have, it may be more satisfactory to include employee costs in overheads.

Remember to include all your employee costs; this implies gross salary, your national insurance contributions as an employer plus any other costs.

The figures may diverge slightly from those in the cash flow forecast, as

PAYE and NI contributions are due the following month. Differences will only show up when you first take on an employee or if the employee's salary rises.

### 4. *Cost of sales: Other direct costs*
Estimate here any other direct costs which you foresee.

### 5. *Overheads: Rent and rates*
In the profit forecast, the total for rates should be spread evenly over the whole year. With rent, you should enter the cost for each period, which may not coincide with the timing of the payments.

### 6. *Overheads: Heating/lighting*
You need an estimate for the cost of heating and lighting which you will use in each period. As you will receive bills quarterly in arrears, you may need to estimate the cost in advance of each bill.

### 7. *Overheads: Telephone*
The treatment of the phone is similar to that for heating and lighting.

### 8. *Overheads: Professional fees*
The figure to include here is what it costs you in legal or accounting fees. You should include the cost in the period in which the work is done for you, even if you do not receive the bill until the next period.

### 9. *Overheads: Depreciation*
Depreciation is what you deduct from the value of an asset to reflect the fact that it is wearing out. This is an item which does not appear in the cash flow forecast. You work it out for each period by taking the value of capital equipment at the start of each period and estimating a figure for its depreciation during the period. Typically, cars and office equipment are written off over three, four or five years.

Note that you do not put in the profit forecast what you pay for capital equipment, which does appear in the cash flow forecast.

### 10. *Overheads: Labour*
This should be your estimate of employee costs which are not directly related to the volume of your sales, see above.

### 11. *Overheads: Other overhead expenses*
Include overhead expenses not slotted in elsewhere.

### 12. *Overheads: Drawings*
What you pay yourself.

### 13. *Overheads: Interest*
Estimate the interest on loans and overdrafts during the year and allocate an equal amount to each month.

### 14. *Miscellaneous income*
Put here an estimate of the other income you might receive, not as a result of the sales of your products. For example, if you have money invested, it might include interest.

### 15. *Working out the net profit figure*
You can work out a gross profit figure (C) by deducting the figure for direct costs (B) from the sales figure (A). On p. 299 you will see how you can use the gross profit figure to work out a gross profit margin for your products and to calculate the break-even point for your business.

Once you have arrived at an estimate for gross profit, deduct the figure for overheads (D) and add on the amount of any miscellaneous income (E) to give your forecast net profit level (F).

## BALANCE SHEET FORECAST

A balance sheet for your business will show what you owe and what you own on one particular day. A forecast one will show your estimate of that picture at the end of the period.

There is more about accounting records needed to produce the right information for a balance sheet once you are in business in Chapter 27. 'Keeping the record straight' (p. 331). Of course, your accountant should be willing to help if you find it difficult to produce a balance sheet yourself. If your business is likely to be fairly small-scale and you are only approaching your bank manager, and for a fairly modest sum, a forecast balance sheet may not be necessary.

In this section there are brief guidelines on how to work out what the balance sheet might be at the end of the period, once the forecast cash flow and profit and loss account are drawn up. And on p. 276 there is a blank balance sheet forecast for you to complete.

### DETAILED CALCULATION FOR BALANCE SHEET FORECAST

One important check on your balance sheet figures is to note that the figure for total assets should equal the figure for capital and liabilities together.

## 1. *Fixed Assets*

These figures are fairly straightforward to work out. You know from your cash flow forecast when you plan to buy particular bits of equipment. Include all equipment which you have received before the end of the period, even if you have not paid for it. A fixed asset is something of a permanent nature, likely to remain in use in your business for some time.

The value you put in here is not just what you paid for the equipment; you also have to allow for the fact that it will have depreciated since the period started. You can obtain the figure for depreciation from your profit forecast. Deduct these figures from the appropriate cost of each piece of equipment, or written-down value at the start of the period, and enter the figures here.

### *Example*

Richard Petworth is working out the depreciation for the office furniture he has bought for his business. There are a number of different ways of calculating this, but for office furniture he thinks he will write off the value in equal lumps over five years; this is called straight-line depreciation.

The furniture cost Richard £2,000. This means he writes off £400 from the value of it each accounting year. The written-down value at the end of the first accounting year is £1,600.

## 2. *Current Assets*

The main current assets you are likely to have in your business are:

● cash

● debtors (that is, what your customers owe you)

● stock (that is, products you have in store, either raw materials to make your product, half-finished products or your finished products which are not yet sold).

The figure for cash you will be able to take straight from your cash flow forecast.

You can derive the figure for debtors from the cash flow and profit forecasts. You will have made some assumption about number of units sold in each month and how quickly you will be paid your cash. From this you can calculate how much you would be owed for sales by your customers at the end of each period. Remember to include VAT in your figure if you are registered for VAT.

BALANCE SHEET FORECAST (on 31 December 198x)

---

ASSETS:

*Fixed Assets*
Freehold property £. . .
Leasehold property £. . .
Office equipment £. . .
Vehicles £. . .
Plant/machinery £. . .
Other equipment £. . .
TOTAL FIXED ASSETS (A) £. . .

*Current Assets*
Cash in hand and at bank £. . .
Stock £. . .
Debtors £. . .
TOTAL CURRENT ASSETS (B) £. . .
TOTAL ASSETS (A) + (B) £. . .

CAPITAL AND LIABILITIES:

*Capital*
Shareholders'/proprietor's capital £. . .
Profit and loss £. . .
TOTAL CAPITAL (C) £. . .

*Medium-term Liabilities*
Loans £. . .

*Current Liabilities*
Overdraft £. . .
Tax payable £. . .
Creditors £. . .
TOTAL LIABILITIES (D) £. . .

TOTAL CAPITAL AND LIABILITIES (C) + (D) £. . .

---

The figure for stock can also be derived from the other two forecasts. Count as stock all goods received from your suppliers to be used in your product but not yet used in products sold, even if you have not yet paid your suppliers' bills.

PROFIT AND LOSS FORECAST (for 1 January 198x to 31 December 198x)

|  | JAN. | FEB. | MAR. | APR. | MAY | JUN. |
|---|---|---|---|---|---|---|
| Sales | 950 | 950 | 675 | 675 | 275 | 275 |
| less *Direct costs* | | | | | | |
| Raw materials | 190 | 135 | 135 | 55 | 380 | 380 |
| Labour | 175 | 175 | 125 | 125 | 50 | 350 |
| Total direct costs | 365 | 310 | 260 | 180 | 430 | 730 |
| GROSS PROFIT | 585 | 640 | 415 | 495 | (155) | (455) |
| less *Overheads* | | | | | | |
| Rent and rates | – | – | – | – | – | 300 |
| Heating/lighting | 28 | 28 | 28 | 28 | 28 | 28 |
| Telephone | 100 | 100 | 100 | 100 | 100 | 100 |
| Stationery/labels | 50 | 50 | 50 | 50 | 50 | 50 |
| Administrative staff | – | – | – | – | – | 400 |
| Depreciation | 68 | 68 | 68 | 68 | 68 | 73 |
| Car expenses | 78 | 78 | 78 | 78 | 78 | 78 |
| Total overheads | 324 | 324 | 324 | 324 | 324 | 1,029 |
| NET PROFIT | 261 | 316 | 91 | 171 | (479) | (1,484) |

|  | JUL. | AUG. | SEP. | OCT. | NOV. | DEC. | TOTALS |
|---|---|---|---|---|---|---|---|
| Sales | 275 | 275 | 3,250 | 3,675 | 3,675 | 2,700 | 17,650 |
| less *Direct costs* | | | | | | | |
| Raw materials | 380 | 435 | 435 | 435 | 380 | 470 | 3,810 |
| Labour | 350 | 350 | 400 | 400 | 400 | 350 | 3,250 |
| Total direct costs | 730 | 785 | 835 | 835 | 780 | 820 | 7,060 |
| GROSS PROFIT | (455) | (510) | 2,415 | 2,840 | 2,895 | 1,880 | 10,590 |
| less *Overheads* | | | | | | | |
| Rent and rates | 300 | 300 | 300 | 300 | 300 | 300 | 2,100 |
| Heating/lighting | 67 | 67 | 67 | 67 | 67 | 67 | 570 |
| Telephone | 100 | 100 | 100 | 100 | 100 | 100 | 1,200 |
| Stationery/labels | 50 | 50 | 50 | 50 | 50 | 50 | 600 |
| Administrative staff | 400 | 400 | 400 | 400 | 400 | 400 | 2,800 |
| Depreciation | 73 | 73 | 73 | 73 | 73 | 73 | 851 |
| Car expenses | 78 | 78 | 78 | 78 | 78 | 78 | 936 |
| Total overheads | 1,068 | 1,068 | 1,068 | 1,068 | 1,068 | 1,068 | 9,057 |
| NET PROFIT | (1,523) | (1,578) | 1,347 | 1,772 | 1,827 | 812 | 1,533 |

At first they will work from home, but later in the year would like 500-sq-ft offices – they hope to get light industrial premises at £5 a sq ft on the outskirts of London. When they have premises they would like to employ someone for clerical work and organizing the outworkers, leaving themselves free to design and sell.

They produce cash flow and profit and loss forecasts to see how the business will shape up.

## CONCLUSIONS

Betty and Roger would be well advised to take advice before going ahead with their business; their idea is not viable as it is currently presented, especially with the increase in overheads (rent for premises and assistant's wages) in the second half of the year. They would certainly need to put in more money, but even then, unless they can increase their sales figures, the long-term prospects must be fairly negative.

## SU' MARY

1. : orecasts are very important if you make commitments on the basis that the figures are reasonably accurate.

2. Make the forecasts conservative.

3. A cash flow forecast is not the same as a profit and loss forecast; the figures will be different. In the cash flow, show what cash payments you expect to make and receive and when that will be.

4. If you find it difficult to produce the forecasts, ask for help from an enterprise agency or an accountant.

5. The treatment of VAT payments and receipts and depreciation need special attention.

6. Once you have the forecasts, use them to assess how viable your business will be and whether you will be able to make a living from it.

OTHER CHAPTERS TO READ

# 23. RAISING THE MONEY

Raising money needs careful planning, like a military campaign. You should regard it as the biggest sale you are ever likely to make. You need to get your act together to present your case. You need to know how much money you want. You need to know who to approach. You need to know how long you want the money for. You need to know what security you can offer backers. You need to know the business plan, the financial figures and the market place, inside out.

But that is not all. You should expect indifference, lack of interest, disbelief and doubt. *You* have to convince, persuade and excite sober, serious business people about the prospects for your business. This cannot be achieved by overstatement or rash predictions about success. Demonstrations of competence and skill are what is required.

Of course, a few strike lucky. There may be the odd story about bank managers agreeing overdrafts over the phone, or someone being able to pick and choose from a variety of backers who all want to put up the funds. But for most it is a hard, hard job.

WHAT IS IN THIS CHAPTER?

This chapter looks at:

● Money: it explains how much you should consider raising (see below), what it is for (p. 284) and what type you want, for example, loans or shares or both (p. 285)

● Lenders and investors: it considers how much you and your family can provide (p. 287), what the government, local authorities, charities and so on can do (p. 289), what banks offer (p. 290), what can be obtained from private individuals or companies (p. 291) and what venture capital funds do (p. 294) including details of the Business Expansion Scheme.

● The presentation: how to do it (p. 295).

## THE MONEY

HOW MUCH MONEY? WHAT YOU SHOULD ASK FOR?

Only when you have drawn up your business plan and done your cash flow and profit forecasts will you know how much money you need to raise, if at all. Take a few deep breaths before you rush round to make an appointment with your bank manager to see if you can get the overdraft you need. First, your bank is not always your first port of call, as you can see from later pages in this chapter. Second, you should take a second, closer, more critical look at the amount of money you think you will need.

Being optimistic, as anyone starting a business must be, you naturally believe you are going to make the sales you have projected on the timescale you estimated and keep the costs down to your forecast figures. But supposing things do not work out quite as you hope. Going back to your lender and asking for more money within a short space of time does not inspire confidence, and you may find your second request rejected, if it is not part of your plan. And there you are with a new business to which you have committed time and money, which is now short of cash, and you are unlikely to find any way of raising more.

There is a body of opinion which says when you first approach your lender or investor, ask for twice as much money as you think you will need. At any rate, be very conservative and go for more money than you think you are going to use. Obviously, the business plans which you present need to tie up with your request for cash, so adjust them if need be, incorporating more conservative figures.

There are drawbacks. First, if your figures are too conservative, it may make your business proposition unviable altogether; if this happens, you do not need to worry about being forced to go back for more, your business will not even get off the ground in the first place, because you will not get the initial backing. The second obstacle to this approach is that it is the natural inclination of any investor to try to make you manage with less money than you say you need.

The sensible advice is steer a middle course: be pessimistic, while remaining a sensible business proposal.

At this stage you know more than ever before about your proposed business and are likely to be very committed to it. But if the business does not look right – if you do not believe in it wholeheartedly – do not be afraid of ditching this plan and looking for a better alternative. You probably have only one chance of raising money for a business proposal, so do not choose a failure because it was your first idea.

For many people, this is the first point at which you are really learning what makes a business tick. One sign of a successful entrepreneur is that you can learn from your information and experience and can adapt. You

RAISING THE MONEY

want to go for calculated, but good risks. Of course, if you have already started trading, your business course is set.

*How much money? £50,000 or more?*

There is another odd fact about raising money: different sums of money can be harder or easier to find, depending simply on their size. Surprisingly, it is sometimes said to be much easier to find very large sums of money for your business (£100,000 plus) than sums in the £20,000 to £100,000 range (these figures are an indication only; there are always exceptions). This quirk of business funding is of no interest to the vast bulk of people who want to become self-employed or start a business in a small way, but if your plans are on a larger scale, think about being bigger still.

This oddity occurs because there appear to be more people around willing to invest in *either* small businesses which are past the start-up stage (that is, not brand new) and into a big expansion phase *or* in new businesses which look capable of very fast growth in profits. To achieve either of these objectives, the amount of money invested needs to be substantial to stand any chance of success. Other pre-conditions of success, apart from large funds, are a very strong management team and a fast growing market. If you cannot demonstrate that both of these apply to you and your business, your chances of raising very large sums of money are virtually nil.

### THE MONEY: WHAT IS IT FOR?

From your forecasts, you should have an indication of when your need for extra cash arises, how long it lasts for and when you would be able to pay it back or give a good return on it.

If you are starting a new business, you need money for:

● the 'once-in-a-business-lifetimes' expenses of setting up. These include what you have to spend on your premises, on equipment and furniture, on legal and professional costs, on initial marketing expenditure

● working capital. This is what you need to keep yourself going in the time gap between paying out cash for raw materials or stocks and getting in cash from the people you sell to. All businesses need working capital; the amount varies depending on the type of business, the credit terms you can negotiate from your suppliers and the amount of credit you extend to your customers.

The longer you can get your suppliers to wait for their payment and the shorter the period you allow to your customers to pay, the less working capital you need. Your working capital requirements will also be less if you do not need to hold big stocks of goods.

In practice, all these things are easier said than done and you need to work out a strategy for controlling your business which meets your need to keep down the money tied up with working capital, coupled with keeping your suppliers and customers happy. This is covered in more detail in Chapter 24. 'Staying afloat' (p. 298).

If your business is up and running, you may need funds simply because it is growing and hence the amount of working capital necessary has gone up. Or you may have some specific expansion in mind.

## THE MONEY: WHAT TYPE DO YOU WANT?

### Overdrafts

If your need for the money is likely to be fairly short-term, an overdraft or some sort of short-term loan is your likeliest bet. Your need for finance in the short-term could be to cover a temporary shortage of cash, or it could cover your start-up requirements if these are fairly small.

An overdraft is quick to arrange and fairly cheap, but there will be an upper limit above which you are not to go without permission of the bank manager. The serious drawback with an overdraft is that the bank can demand instant repayment. While this does not happen very often, you can bet that if the bank does demand repayment or reduction of the overdraft, this will occur when you cannot do so.

If there are no assets, such as debtors, to be taken as a security for the overdraft, it is more than likely that your bank manager will require that you give a personal guarantee even if you have formed a limited company. One benefit of getting substantial funding is that as a result of the strong balance sheet, personal guarantees, although asked for, can be avoided.

As a self-employed person you are personally liable anyway, so no further guarantees are needed. In the extreme, this means if you cannot repay an overdraft, your assets, including your house, could be seized to cover the debt.

Note that banks may be wary of taking stocks as a security for overdraft. The manager may insist on property or debtors as the only acceptable security. Always negotiate about the level of security needed; it is in your interests to give up as little as possible for security.

## Longer-term loans

If you know at the outset that you are unlikely to be able to repay the money you want to raise in the short-term, a longer-term source of finance might be the answer. You can get loans of between two and thirty years, often secured on your house. The repayment of the loan and the interest payments will be arranged at the start. The interest could be a fixed rate or it could be a certain percentage point above a bank's base rate. You may have the option to alter from one basis to another after a number of years.

## Selling shares

If you have formed a limited company, you may be willing to sell some of the shares in return for an investment in the business. If you do this, it means you will lose some of the potential capital gains you might get as a result of the shares increasing in value as the profits of the business grow. This is what an outside investor is looking for. The aim is to get a good return on the money invested through the shares increasing in value, rather than a stream of income from the business in the form of dividends.

An outside investor, such as a venture capital fund, will at some stage want to sell the shares to realize the profits. If you are hoping to raise money in this way, put in your plan that you intend to have your company floated on the stockmarket (the Unlisted Securities Market, probably) in five years' time.

The value you can obtain for your shares, if you are a new company, is a very vexed question. Frankly, they are not worth very much yet, so you might find that you are having to sell a bigger proportion of the shares than you would like to raise the money you need. This can lead to problems about voting control. What the value of the shares is can lead to a lot of haggling.

Opting for this route to raise money needs professional help; you will need to call in, perhaps, accountants, solicitors and corporate finance specialists. Ask for references from these professionals; this should help you steer clear of the rank unprofessionals.

## Taking partners

If you have started out as a sole trader but need to raise additional capital, you could do this by taking a partner. What share of the profits each partner gets in return for the capital put in is a subject to be negotiated. There also needs to be clarity about the management role each partner will have. For your own sake, you should do this before you form the partnership. A written partnership agreement is a must (p. 61).

# LENDERS AND INVESTORS

## YOU AND YOUR FAMILY

### *What proportion should come from you?*
The first fact you must come to terms with is that if *you* do not invest in your business idea, you cannot expect anyone else to do so. As a rough rule of thumb, the absolute most you will probably be able to raise from outsiders is five times as much money as you are putting in yourself, but, needless to say there are always exceptions. Normally, you can expect that someone will match your own investment, or if the idea is very sound a lender may put up two to three times as much as you do. But in the worst case, it could be nothing.

### *Example*

> Winston Carpenter has £10,000 to invest in his business. He works out from his forecasts and his business plan that he needs to raise more money. He is unlikely to be able to raise an extra £50,000 or more, but with a good presentation of his idea, he may persuade someone to lend or invest £20,000, say.

The rationale behind this insistence of how much you must invest yourself is that lenders, such as banks, and investors, such as venture capital funds, want you to be committed to your business, to make you work very hard and with great determination to be successful. If you have not risked the proportion of capital they would like, they may doubt your commitment. Of course, if you can point to the fact that, even though it is a low proportion of the total invested in your business, the sum of money you are investing is still a sizeable proportion of your own personal assets, you could be convincing.

### *Where are you going to get your share of the money?*
If you have money tucked away somewhere, or if you have a lump sum as a result of being made redundant, this is a relatively easy question to answer. Another common source of the money for your stake is to be given or lent it by someone in your family. But being financed by your family can lead to heartache if things start going wrong. So do not enter on this course lightheartedly. Conversely, you are more likely to convince your family than anyone else.

Another possible way of raising your share of the funds is to use your personal assets to act as security (for example, a second mortgage on your home) or by giving a personal guarantee. The drawback with this is that if your business fails, you have to find the money to carry on making your repayments, or you have to sell your home. You must give careful consideration before giving personal guarantees or using your home to raise money in this way for your business.

It would make sense to have some sort of agreed family plan for what would happen if your business failed. For example, you should discuss openly whether you are ready to sell your house and move to a smaller one should the security be called upon to repay your loan. If you cannot have some sort of strategy in your domestic life which is acceptable in return for the prospect of going it alone, you are likely to have family problems when the inevitable pressures mount on the business.

You can get tax relief on these loans. If you are a sole trader or partner, any interest you pay on a loan for business purposes is allowable as a deduction against tax in working out your taxable profits. If you take on a loan to invest or lend money to a close company (see p. 375, but most family companies are) you can get tax relief at your highest rate of tax on the interest you pay. To be eligible for this tax relief, you must either own more than 5 per cent of the shares or own some shares and work for the greater part of your time for the company.

### When should you put in your money?

The best advice is not necessarily to start your business straightaway, investing your money and then to approach other lenders or investors later when you need it. The wisest course may be to prepare your forecasts and your business plans and to approach possible sources of finance before you start your business and before you actually need the extra money. To plan ahead and get a commitment in advance can be crucial.

The reason why this could be the best approach is that lenders have a couple of infuriating habits. The first is to ask what money you are going to put in when they put in their share. You may be able to point out that you invested £3,000, say, six months ago and since then have worked without drawing any salary, but lenders are likely to be unimpressed. That is water under the bridge and may count for nothing as far as they are concerned. The second is for them to adopt an attitude of 'wait and see' how the business develops, while the cash is running out and you are under great pressure to raise more. In this way better deals can be struck for the investor or lender. So do not rush out and use up your money, if you know you will need extra funds in due course; get your financial backing in advance.

## GOVERNMENT, LOCAL AUTHORITIES, CHARITIES AND OTHER SOURCES

You may be able to get grants, allowances, cheap loans or prizes from a variety of sources.

### Government, local authorities

The best known source of funds from the non-commercial world is the government's Enterprise Allowance scheme. You have to meet various conditions to be accepted on this scheme:

- you must be at least eighteen and below state pension age

- you must be receiving unemployment benefit or supplementary benefit when you apply

- you must have been unemployed for at least thirteen weeks before you apply

- you must be able to show you have at least £1,000 to invest in your business in the first year

- you must agree to work full-time in the business

- the business should not have started trading when you apply for the scheme

- the business must be independent, that is, not part of or supported by another business.

If you meet all these conditions you will receive an allowance of £40 a week for the first year to supplement the income from your business while it is being established.

Do not claim the Enterprise Allowance the minute you begin work on setting up your business; wait until just before you start trading. In this way you will be able to receive benefits for longer than you otherwise would: unemployment or supplementary benefit while setting up, followed by the allowance for the first year of trading.

The other main government help available includes the Loan Guarantee Scheme. This is operated by the banks and there are more details on p. 291.

Local authorities can provide help to new businesses. This may range from grants and premises to advice and loans. The schemes are individual to the local authority and you will have to find out from yours locally what is available. Your local advice agency should know.

*Charities and other sources*
There are grants and cheap loans available to young people, aged under twenty-five, from the Prince's Youth Business Trust (p. 48). There are competitions run for young people, such as Livewire (p. 48). But there are also competitions run by accountants, banks and others for business ideas. Details of these are often published in newspapers (p. 46)

BANKS

*Which bank?*
Your bank manager is an obvious port of call, but not always the best nor the one you should make first of all. The advantages of going straight there is that if you have been a good creditworthy customer with a good record, your manager should favour your application. And this is what should happen to the vast bulk of people with a good business proposition which is well presented and well researched.

But there are a couple of reasons why you should not head straight here or why you might expect not to secure the money you want. In the first place, your presentation of your plan will improve with the number of times you give it. If your bank manager really is your best possibility and you have not practised your presentation, you might blow the opportunity. It could pay you to approach another bank, simply to practise what you are going to say and be prepared for the questions which will be asked.

The second disadvantage may occur if you are looking to your bank to provide substantial funds. Each branch bank manager has a different discretionary lending limit; above the limit your application may need to be processed elsewhere and so you may lose part of the personal touch on which you were relying for a sympathetic hearing of your case.

The moral is shop around. Do not be put off by being turned down, try another bank or another branch which you think may be more used to business deals. Remember to ask what rate you will be charged; compare this with what other banks would charge.

*What sort of money?*
Banks can offer money in two ways:

• overdrafts (p. 285)

● loans.

Loans can be very flexible and the exact terms vary from bank to bank. You can borrow money for periods of up to thirty years. The rate of interest can be fixed or variable, a number of percentage points over the bank base rate. Sometimes you can negotiate a repayment holiday from repaying the capital you borrow. So for, say, one or two years, you pay only interest. You may also be able to arrange stepped repayments. The amount you can borrow can vary from £1,000 to £1 million. The type of loan you can get depends on the viability of the plan.

There is also a government scheme called the Loan Guarantee Scheme, although not all businesses will qualify. A loan under this scheme can be for up to £75,000 and last for five to seven years. There can be a holiday for two years before you have to start repaying the capital. The Department of Industry guarantees 70 per cent of any shortfall on recovery of the loan by the bank. You have to pay the rate set by the bank plus the guarantee premium demanded by the government, currently 2.5 per cent on the part guaranteed. The scheme is intended to provide loans for businesses where there is not enough security for the bank from other sources (for example, your personal assets). The bank will take a floating charge on the business assets (that is, the loan is secured on assets in general rather than one or two specific named ones). Note that personal assets must be charged before the loan guarantee is considered.

The practice varies from bank to bank about the cost of setting up the loan. There could be an arrangement fee of 1 or 1½ per cent of the loan; check before you arrange the loan and try to negotiate on this point. You may be required to take out life insurance for the amount of the loan.

Apart from the standard requirements, such as soundness of your business plan and amount of money you have invested yourself, the banks will also look at the size of loans you have already.

PRIVATE INVESTORS (including Business Expansion Scheme)

It may be possible to raise money from individuals who wish to invest or lend money to small businesses. Since the advent of the Business Expansion Scheme (BES) more individuals are prepared to invest money in return for shares in your company.

*Taking advantage of the BES scheme*
Small businesses can raise money from individuals under this scheme as the tax relief for investors is very generous. It allows investors to get tax

relief on what they invest in the shares of new or small companies at their highest rate of tax, that is, up to 60 per cent. Each taxpayer (a married couple counts as one) can invest up to £40,000 in any tax year and get the full tax relief. Shares issued after 18 March 1986 are free of capital gains tax when you dispose of them after the required five-year period (if you sell before five years are up you are not eligible for tax relief against income).

Only outside investors get the tax relief. So you are not eligible if you put your own money in, nor are any paid directors or employees of your company.

To qualify under the scheme your business must be a company and must, among other things:

● be unquoted, that is, your shares cannot be bought or sold on the Stock Exchange or Unlisted Securities Market

● carry on business mainly in the UK, although you can export all your output.

You will not qualify if your business is banking, farming, insurance, leasing or hiring, share-dealing, accountancy or legal services or property development.

You may find that, because this tax relief is available, you can sell the shares in your company at a higher price than you would otherwise be able to do.

There are various categories of businesses who will not be able to use the scheme:

● you can only use the scheme if you are a limited company, so if you are a sole trader or partner wanting to raise funds, you cannot do so. You may still be able to find people willing to put up funds, by referring to the small ad section or through organizations which operate as brokers

● the scheme will not be much use to you if you want to raise money in a rush. Negotiations can take months – as many as nine in the extreme

● the tax relief is only for ordinary shares, so if you need to raise money through a mixture of ways, such as shares, preference shares or loans, a BES approach will not be suitable.

## BES funds

These are funds set up which attract individual investors who want to take advantage of investing under the BES scheme, but would rather not do it directly, perhaps because they do not have the necessary business expertise to assess new businesses. So the fund gathers in the money from investors and invests on their behalf in companies looking to raise money.

On the whole, this can prove an expensive way of raising money. The managers of the fund often want some shares in the company, for example, an option on 2 per cent of the shares, in addition to those for the people putting up the money. They may also demand expensive arrangement fees and require to have a non-executive director on your board whose yearly fee, between £4,000 and £10,000, you will have to pay.

*How to find individual investors*
There are several ways this can be done:

*LINC (Local Investment Networking Company)* (p. 408): these are run by several enterprise agencies (London, Leeds, Manchester, Bristol and Cardiff & Vale). They try to put companies wanting funds (less than £100,000) in touch with people who have funds to invest. They do this by sending out a regular bulletin listing the companies who hope to raise finance. You may be offered the opportunity to present your case at an investors' meeting, but this is not guaranteed. It would cost you £30 to be included in the bulletin and the agency would want to investigate you to check that your business idea could work.

*Venture Capital Report:* this works in much the same way as the LINC above (see p. 408 for the address and phone number).

*Small ad sections:* there are often ads in newspapers with Business to Business sections, such as the *Guardian*, *The Times*, the *Financial Times* and the *Sunday Times*, from people wanting to invest in new enterprises. Alternatively, you could advertise for funds in the same way, although you have to watch out for various legal restrictions.

*Advertising direct:* if you are looking to raise substantial funds, you could cut out the fund manager stage and advertise direct to the investing public by issuing a prospectus. You would need to employ an adviser to do this, for example, a stockbroker, and the administrative expenses would be high. You would have to publish and print the prospectus to make it available to members of the public and advertise in major national newspapers. To be able to do this your company must be in the public limited company (plc) category.

## VENTURE CAPITAL FUNDS

There are around ninety venture capital funds in the UK, with the money put up by pension funds, insurance companies, banks, investment trusts, industrial corporations, regional development agencies and private individuals through the BES Scheme. Not all of the ninety funds will provide money for people who are starting up; some may only provide funds for businesses which are expanding.

Venture capital funds are looking for companies with very good management, operating in a market which is either very large or is growing fast. The funds want to invest in companies which could reach profits of £300,000 or more within three to four years. Many, but not all, want to be able to sell their investment in five to ten years and hope that the company will have grown enough in that time to be floated on the Unlisted Securities Market. This would allow the funds to sell their shares and turn their gains into cash.

If you approach a venture capital fund, these are the things to look out for:

● *amount of shares:* the fund will normally want ordinary shares in return for the investment, as well as loan capital or preference shares, though there are exceptions. The percentage of shares varies from fund to fund; a few may want over 50 per cent. It is unusual for a fund to want a majority stake in the company. The percentage of shares is not always affected by the amount of money you want to raise nor by the voting structure

● *board director:* the fund will usually want to have one or two directors on your board and you will have to bear the cost of this. You will normally be able to approve the choice of director. The fees for a non-executive director can be in the £5,000 to £10,000 range

● *due diligence:* this is the term for the investigation which a venture capital fund will want to undertake before investing in your company. This can include visiting your offices and other work location, taking up references from customers, potential customers and past employers, studying your accounts and selling systems, having your product checked technically and so on. The fund will want you to pay for this investigation; you can negotiate on this. How successful your negotiation will be depends on the level of interest shown by other funds

● *legal and professional fees:* there are yours and theirs. You will have to pay the legal costs for the funds on top of all your costs for raising finance. You will have legal and accounting fees, running into several thousands, plus the fee paid to a corporate finance adviser, usually based on a percentage of the money raised. In total, your share of the costs could run up to 5 to 10 per cent of the money you raise

- *syndication:* if you are trying to raise a very large sum of money, a venture capital fund may want a partner or two to provide the funds you wish. This may be because providing the amount of money you want could take up a fairly hefty chunk of the total money they have to invest or they may just want to spread the risk. You may have to do a lot of the work yourself to bring together funds into a consortium to provide the money. This can prove very tricky and adds considerably to the amount of time it can take you to raise the money.

### Finding a fund

Funds come in all shapes and sizes. At any one time, you will find that some funds are rolling in money, while others have none to invest just then. They also have different monetary limits on the investments they will consider. Some funds specialize in a region or an industry; others are quite catholic in what they are looking for.

There are two quite different approaches to finding a fund. One approach is called the scattergun; you send off your proposal to as many funds as you can. This is often criticized on the grounds that funds do not want to compete against each other for good prospects, and so will not be interested if they know they will be competing against too many others.

The other approach is to select two or three funds, who have money at that time and are interested in your sort of business. If these do not work out, you can send your plan to a second tier of funds and so on. This approach can equally be criticized on the grounds that if the funds are not in competition with each other, you will not get the best possible financing terms that you could and the whole process could take longer.

There are several sources to find the details of venture capital funds (p. 408). Your advisers will also have suggestions on who you should approach, see Chapter 18.

## THE PRESENTATION: HOW TO DO IT

There are a lot of useful tips on how to present your plan scattered through this chapter and Chapter 6. The step-by-step guide overleaf draws all these tips together.

**1.** First impressions are all important. The first thing prospective lenders and investors will see is your business plan. It must be typed, clean, neatly arranged in a folder. It should look comprehensive without being over-detailed, not more than ten or twenty pages, but, if necessary, information can be put in appendices.

**2.** Practice your presentation of your plan. Do this by getting a colleague or friend to role-play or see if a counsellor at an enterprise agency will take you through it. If necessary, approach a source of finance which you regard as very low chance and use it to perfect your technique for those opportunities of which you are very hopeful.

**3.** Will be a face-to-face encounter. Look conventional; the people who have money to lend are middle-of-the-road types, so do not endanger your chances of getting the money by dressing in an odd way.

**4.** Get the facts at your fingertips. Your plan may look good, but if you sound unsure or muddled about the details, doubts about your management ability may be raised.

**5.** Be clear in your own mind what is interesting or exciting about your proposal. Do not get so bogged down by the details that you cannot bring out the really important points of your business idea.

**6.** Find out the names and positions of those who can lend. Try to get the real decision-makers, not their advisers or subordinates.

**7.** Listen carefully to the questions and make sure you answer what you have been asked.

**8.** If you are asked for any further information, make sure it is as well-researched and well-presented as the rest of your plan and provide it quickly.

**9.** Do not be too defensive about your idea; assume beforehand that it will be critically assessed.

# SUMMARY

1. Treat negotiating for money with the same planning and thought as making a sale.

2. Be very certain that you ask for the right amount of money; it is very difficult to go round a second time to ask for more.

3. It can be difficult to raise less than £100,000 for shares.

4. Overdrafts are for the shorter-term; long-term finance is provided by loans or selling shares, if you have a company.

5. As a rule of thumb, you will need to invest as much as an outside investor or perhaps half as much. Rare exceptions have managed to put in a much smaller proportion than an outside investor and still retain control.

6. Securing loans on your house or giving personal guarantees is a major step. Do not take it lightly or without discussing with your family.

7. Money can be raised from banks, private individuals and companies, venture capital funds, charities or local authorities.

8. Make your presentation carefully. Follow the tips on p. 296.

OTHER CHAPTERS TO READ
  6. 'The business plan' (p. 76)
22. 'Forecasting' (p. 264)

# 24. STAYING AFLOAT

You are launched. You have premises, even if it is your own home. You have started selling and now must produce the goods. You may have raised money to help finance the business. So what next? Staying afloat is the name of the game. Learning to live within the income your sales bring is a hard task, but one that has to be learnt.

For some, it is easy: this could apply to you if your sort of business is consultancy, or design, or some other type of work where the overheads can be contained, at least until the time comes for expansion. For others, there is this point to strive towards before your business is truly afloat. This is known as break-even point, and is the point at which the contribution your sales bring is large enough to cover the overheads of your business, for example, rent, rates, telephone, some employee costs.

When you see explanations of break-even point in textbooks, it seems straightforward. Your business struggles towards the level of sales you find from the laid-down formula and once you have reached there, your business is ticking along nicely. In reality break-even point is not like that at all. It has a most disconcerting habit of moving; as sales increase, so inevitably do the pressures on the business to get the job done. One way to ease the pressure is to increase the overheads and so the cycle continues. Trying to hit a moving target is notoriously difficult; and so is struggling to break-even.

To stay afloat in the longer term requires more than being permanently at break-even; you need profits. These can be used to develop new products and markets as existing ones mature and decline.

These are the problems. What about the solution? Clearly increasing the amount and value of the sales are top priorities, as well as containing costs. But these take time. The business needs a breathing space to allow sales to develop. To allow yourself that leeway, you must control the business. And cash control assumes the major role in this. Your business will stay afloat (in the short term) if the money goes round; you hope you can keep it going long enough for sales to reach that moving target and get to break-even. You cannot do it for ever; at some stage, it will be clear that your business must raise more money or it will fail. If you are unable to get more funds, you do not want to reach the point of trading illegally and you do not want your crash to take other small businesses with you. You have to recognize the warning signs (p. 327).

Of course, any well-run business should be interested in cash control, whether struggling for break-even or already well into profit. Making the cash go round more efficiently helps increase your profits. Controlling cash is essentially a question of controlling debtors (that is, people who owe you money), creditors (that is, people to whom you owe money) and stock (including work-in-progress).

WHAT IS IN THIS CHAPTER?

- Break-even point (see below)
- The business plan to control the business (p. 302)
- Cash (p. 304)
- Your customers (p. 308)
- Your suppliers (p. 313)

## BREAK-EVEN POINT

One management technique you should get to grips with is break-even point. This assumes extreme importance for the sort of business which makes losses initially; possibly, you may raise money to cover that loss-making period or you find it yourself. What you are working towards is the point at which the contribution (strictly, gross margin), which you make from sales, is sufficient to cover the overheads (also called indirect or fixed costs).

Overheads are the cost of setting up the structure of your business. For example, the cost of your premises does not rise and fall with the amount of sales you are making. In the long run, you could move to cheaper premises, but this is a major upheaval. In the meantime, this overhead cost is fixed. The value of your sales needs to be built up to the level which contributes to the expense of the premises.

Other examples of overheads are insurance, the cost of equipment – such as cars and typewriters – heating and lighting, the telephone and so on. One vexed problem is whether employees are a fixed cost or not. For most businesses, they will be, certainly for a few months (see p. 230 for more about the cost effect of employing people).

## HOW TO WORK OUT YOUR BREAK-EVEN POINT

To do this you need to know:

- gross profit margin
- total cost of overheads.

If your product or service is uniform, you can work out the gross profit (or contribution) on each item sold. The gross profit on each item is the selling price less the direct cost of each item. Direct costs are those items which you only have to pay for because you make a product or provide a service, for example, raw materials.

However, if the product can vary, work out the gross profit for one month's sales, say, and use this to find your gross profit margin.

The formula for break-even point of sales is:

$$\frac{\text{Overheads}}{\text{Price of product} - \text{direct cost of product}}$$

This gives you the number of items you must sell to cover the overhead costs, see Example 1 below.

*or* $$\frac{\text{Overheads}}{\text{Gross profit margin}} \times 100$$

Gross profit margin is the gross profit divided by the value of sales times 100. This formula gives you the value of sales you must make to cover the overhead costs, see Example 2 opposite.

*Example 1*

Robert Atherton sells quantities of paper cleaning cloths. He buys them in large rolls, cuts them and distributes them as duster-size (twelve to each packet). He has worked out the direct cost of each packet of twelve as 10p and sells them for 26p. Thus, gross profit on each packet of twelve is 16p. His overheads are £6,000 in the year, £500 a month. His break-even sales each month are:

$$\frac{\text{£500}}{\text{£0.16}} = 3,125 \text{ packets of twelve}$$

*Example 2*

Jane Edwardes runs a company which sells computer systems to the accounting profession. The prices of the system vary depending on the size of the computer, the exact form of the software and how many screens are run off the computer. The cheapest starts at £5,000 and the most expensive system is £15,000. For her business plan for the next twelve months, Jane has worked out the likely number of systems of each size she forecasts she will sell. For the year, sales are estimated at £300,000 and the direct costs, that is, the computers, screens and other parts, and the software, are forecast to be £120,000.

$$\text{Gross profit margin is } \frac{£300,000 - £120,000}{£300,000} \times 100 = 60\%$$

The overheads of the business are estimated at £108,000 for the next year, that is, £9,000 a month.

The break-even sales for each month are:

$$\frac{£9,000}{60} \times 100 = £15,000$$

This applies as long as the level of fixed costs remains unchanged and either the gross profit margin is the same on each product or the pattern of sales mirrors the forecast for the year.

The diagrams overleaf may help you to gain a better understanding of what break-even is all about. The level line shows the estimated level of overheads for different level of sales. The sloping line which starts at point A shows the amount of the direct costs for each level of sales. Total costs are the sum of the direct costs and the overheads.

The dotted line which starts at point O shows the value of sales at different levels of units sold. Point X is the break-even point. To the left of point X, your business is making a loss; to the right of it, your business is making a profit.

Diagram 1 on p. 302 assumes that the level of overheads stays the same no matter what the level of sales you can make. Frankly, this is difficult to achieve in practice. Once you start doing more business, you may well find that your overheads will go up too. For example, you may find you need more secretarial help, given the increased amount of sales you are

**Diagram 1: Finding the break-even point of your business**

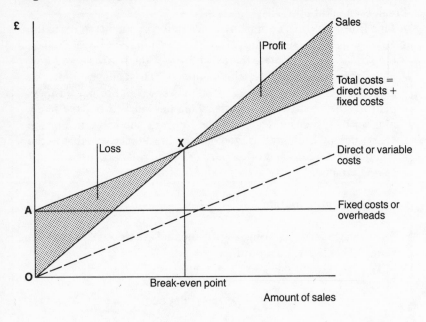

making. In Diagram 2 on the right, you can see the effect of break-even point, if there is an increase in overheads for the same business as above. The break-even sales figure is now much higher.

## THE BUSINESS PLAN TO CONTROL THE BUSINESS

When you produced your business plan before you started your business (p. 76), you incorporated some forecasts: profit and loss and cash flow. These could form the basis for your plan (or budget), which you need to control the business, although probably with some adjustments.

What you need for a budget which you use to control your business, but also which is to give you (and any employees) something to aim for, is a plan which incorporates figures which you believe you may be able to achieve. Be wary of including figures which are too easy for the business, in case meeting the budget turns into the objective, rather than striving for the biggest profit possible.

As you are going to use the budget to control the business, you need to have the next year's budget prepared before the previous year has ended, otherwise there is a time gap in which the business will drift. If you

**Diagram 2: How an increase in fixed costs moves the break-even point upwards**

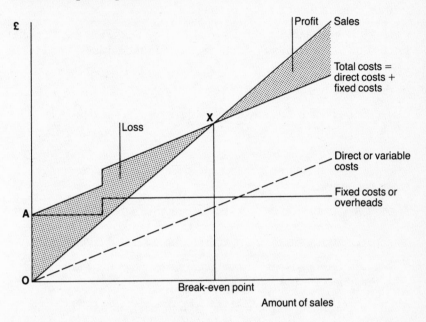

employ others in the business, they should be involved in drawing up the forecasts for their particular area of the business.

HOW TO USE THE BUDGET

Every month, as soon as possible after the end of it and not later than a fortnight after, you should have the actual profit, cost and cash figures to compare with the budget. Your comparison should be for two reasons:

● to identify what has gone wrong, and right, and to derive lessons for the future

● to identify problem areas for the future, which may only emerge as your actual performance fails to keep up with budgeted performance, for example.

KEEPING IN TOUCH WITH THE BUSINESS

Once you start employing others, you will no longer be dealing with every single aspect of the business yourself. Once others have areas of responsibility, you will need to devise a system of management reporting. There is no one system which is perfect for a particular business, but it should include some of the following elements:

*weekly reports:* these could be verbal, for example, a meeting. It needs to be sufficiently detailed, so that everyone in the business knows as a result of the report:

● their objectives for the next week

● what is on the critical path to allow sales to be made and products to be produced or made ready for sale.

*monthly reports:* these should be written by the person responsible, for example, salesperson or manager, production staff. The report should cover two aspects:

● what has been achieved in the past month, how it compares with budgeted figures and objectives set in the weekly reports and any explanation or lessons to be drawn from successes and failures

● what the outlook is for the next month, what should be achieved and what the objectives are.

While management reports allow you to keep informed about the business, they have an important side-effect. It forces your employees to concentrate on:

● the objectives of the business

● their own performance against budgeted performance

● their own priorities for action in the week and month ahead.

## CASH

If your cash runs out, your business will fail. It is as simple as that. Why your cash can run out is due to several possible reasons:

● you do not sell enough

● your costs are too high for the sales you make

● your sales and costs are rising nicely according to plan, but you do not have enough cash to fund the increased amount of debtors and stocks, which the extra business brings.

HOW TO CONSERVE CASH

There are three important steps in conserving cash:

- knowing how much cash you have and how much you will need

- speeding up the cash inflow from your customers (p. 309)

- slowing down the cash outflow to your suppliers (p. 313).

THE CASH BUDGET

Preparing your business plan (p. 76) will have taken you some way towards knowing how much cash you will need in the business; indeed, the most important purpose of preparing the business plan may have been to raise the cash your forecasts show will be required. Once the business is trading, the cash flow forecasts need to be turned into monthly cash flow budgets.

You can help to conserve cash by paying by instalments as much as possible. For example, consider leasing cars or furniture, rather than buying outright (p. 202).

Your aim should be not just to match your budget, but to do better than it says. Never despise a penny or a pound which can be saved; very small savings build up over time to very large savings. This penny-pinching attitude applies just as strongly if you have raised money.

Comparing the actual cash performance with the cash budget is an important tool in controlling your cash. It enables you to learn from mistakes and plan your cash requirements in the future.

WHAT ELSE CONTROLS CASH?

When cash is tight, you will take much more stringent measures than when you are cash rich. For example, you could consider instituting the following control system:

- daily cash balance

- weekly or daily bank statement

- weekly forecast of each individual cash payment in (from customers) and planned cash payment out (to suppliers). This could be set up as a sheet with each named customer and supplier. Each day check what money you have received and tick off on your forecast sheet. Do not pay any cheques until you have received the money you need.

Obviously, when cash is short, you need to put your cash receipts in the bank as quickly as possible; and when you pay people, send the cheque by second-class post. You will be able to say honestly that the cheque has been sent.

Clearly, the system does not work for every business; it is a good control tool for businesses which have a number of large receipts and payments. A retail business would not be able to operate in this way. However, a control sheet for a shop could consist of a weekly forecast of daily takings plus a list of those suppliers you intend to pay that week. Again the suppliers will not be paid until the forecast cash comes in. For what happens when things are out of control, see p. 326.

A cash system like this is a nuisance to operate, and so if cash is not particularly short, you could use a variant of:

- weekly cash balance

- weekly bank statement

- monthly payment cycle, that is, set aside one day in each month on which you pay the bills you plan for that month. This means that there is only one day in each month devoted to writing cheques. If a bill is not paid on that day, it does not get paid until a month later.

*Important note:* No cash control system can operate if you do not keep proper cash records, for example, a cash book. This is explained on p. 333.

### MAKING CASH WORK FOR YOU

Your problem may not be shortage of cash; on the contrary, you may have extra cash sitting around. In this case, do not leave it all in the current account. Instead, have sufficient handy to keep the business ticking over and put what you can in a seven-day notice or call account which earns interest. Remember to give the required notice so that you can transfer what you need to cover your payments in your once-a-month cheque cycle. There are also a few of the high-interest cheque accounts which can be used by small businesses.

### OPERATING YOUR BANK ACCOUNT

What your bank account will cost you as a small business used to be one of the more closely held secrets – and still is with some banks. It can be very difficult to get concrete information on what each payment into the account and each payment out will cost you. Recently, Lloyds Bank has introduced a Standard Business Tariff, which can be used by most small businesses: this gives you a clear idea of what each entry to the account costs. However, it is probably only economic for those businesses which make a few, but larger payments in and out. If your normal business style is to pay in a lot of cash or a large number of cheques, you can negotiate separate arrangements with your bank manager. A couple of the other clearing banks have now introduced similar accounts.

Here are a few ways bank accounts should be cheaper to run:

● use direct debits rather than standing orders (if this is relevant)

● it is cheaper to withdraw small amounts of cash using an automated machine rather than a cheque book

● using a credit or charge card for business expenses, as this is paid with a single payment, instead of lots of little ones.

However, it needs careful consideration before a card is given to an employee. Additionally, in the case of companies, use of a credit or charge card is a fringe benefit for employees, which would include you as a director; check how it would affect your individual tax bill.

If your business is on a very small scale, you should consider whether it is possible to run it using a building society account, rather than a bank account, bearing in mind there are limitations, such as no overdraft facility or business advice.

## GOING INTO OVERDRAFT

The time to ask for an overdraft is not the day you realize that you will not be able to cover the bills of suppliers who are really pressing you for payment. The bank manager simply will not like it. It is much better for you to present a well-argued case one or two months before you think you will need the facility. This means planning ahead, by using your forecasts or budgets as a proper control tool.

There is more detail on overdrafts on p. 285.

## OTHER WAYS OF RAISING CASH

Consider:

● using your pension scheme, if applicable, for a loan from a bank or from the insurance company (p. 398)

● factoring or invoice discounting (p. 312).

# YOUR CUSTOMERS

Selling is not the end of the story. Any old customer will not do. Making a sale to someone who does not pay their bill at all is worse than no sale at all. The ideal customer is one who pays their bill as soon as your product or service is handed over. Very few businesses are lucky enough to have that type of client. But there are steps you can take to try to ensure that you do get the cash in. First, you can check them out before you hand over the goods to them. Second, you can do everything you can to make them pay up as quickly as possible.

Giving credit to customers, that is, allowing them to become debtors and pay some time after they have received your service or product, costs you money. For example, if a bank charges 10 per cent on an overdraft, an oustanding bill of £1,000 costs you £100 if it is still unpaid after one year. Or, if it is unpaid after three months, the cost to you is £25. The more efficient you are at reducing the amount of time before you receive your payments, the lower the costs.

## INVESTIGATING POTENTIAL CUSTOMERS (CREDIT CONTROL)

Few businesses can confine their sales to completely 'safe' customers; there is usually an element of risk-taking with sales, which is needed to meet your business objectives. But the riskiness or otherwise of customers needs to be assessed, so that the risk is known and calculated. Assessment needs information, control and monitoring.

The extent of the investigation must also depend on the amount of the projected sale relative to your total sales. If it is a fairly small sale, the investigation alone may cost as much as the profit from the sale; you should establish a policy of rejecting or accepting such risks as a matter of course. But if the sale would be a significant order for you, further information is needed.

Consider the following steps:

• ask the prospective customer for a bank reference (but this will be based only on the bank's experience, so may indicate relatively little, but help in building a general picture)

• ask for a couple of trade references. Put a specific question such as 'Up to what level of trade credit is the customer considered a good risk?'

• ask a credit reporting agency to report (p. 312)

• ask the customer for the latest report and accounts or a balance sheet and profit and loss account. Ask your accountant to analyse them for you

• if you have not already done so, visit the business with a view to meeting the principals or directors. Put any questions which remain unanswered and use the visit to fill in the general picture.

Using the information you have garnered from all these sources, assess how risky you think this customer is and establish a credit limit. A common system is to have five categories of risk, ranging from the top category, who would be considered good for anything, to the bottom category, who you would sell to only on cash terms. You would draw up certain credit limits to apply to each category, for example, allowed £1,000 on thirty days' credit. The actual amounts would depend on the size of debts relative to your sales and what is considered normal practice in that industry.

THE PAYMENT TERMS YOU OFFER (CREDIT TERMS)

There is quite a variety of expressions applying to possible credit terms you could offer customers. Some of these include:

• cash with order (CWO)

• cash on delivery (COD)

• payment seven days after delivery (net 7)

• payment for goods supplied in one week by a certain day in the next week (weekly credit)

• payment for goods supplied in one month by a certain day in the next month (monthly credit)

• payment due thirty days after delivery (thirty days' credit).

And so on. You have to choose the best terms you can. This means you extend credit for as short a time as possible, but obviously industry and competitive practice may to some extent put you in a strait-jacket.

There are a couple of ways you can try to encourage early payment of your bills. First, you can offer a cash discount for early payment, for example, payment within seven days of the invoice means the customer can claim a discount of 1 per cent. The problem with this sort of discount is that customers tend to take it (and, if your debtor control is a little sloppy, are allowed the discount) whenever they pay. Introducing a cash discount of this type needs to be accompanied by close monitoring to make it clear to customers that they are entitled to the discount *only* if they meet the conditions offered.

Second, you can make a charge for late payment. This has to be established in advance, for example, printed on the invoice. This idea does not always work, as it may imply to the customers that you do not mind if they pay late as long as they pay the extra charge levied. Hence a late payment charge may have the opposite effect to that desired; in other words, your bill is put to the back of the queue by the debtor, instead of leaping to the head. The only way out of this dilemma is to make the charge a fairly penal one, which might simply have the effect of deterring people from buying from you again. All in all, a policy of charging for late payment needs careful consideration and implementation.

### SENDING OUT INVOICES

Be very prompt in sending out invoices. This is crucial to any policy of keeping tight credit control. Failure to do this will give the impression to debtors that you do not mind how long you wait for your money, and as we have seen, giving credit costs you money. No matter how busy you are keeping up with the work you do, sending out invoices, as soon as goods are delivered or services supplied, must take precedence.

### THE RECORDS YOU NEED FOR CONTROL

There is more detail on how to set up the records you need on p. 335, but the records need to provide you with the following information:

• say how much you are owed in total at any time

• say how long you have been owed the money and by whom; this information is known as an aged analysis of debts

• a record of sales and payments including the date made for each customer. This allows you to build up your own picture of the credit-worthiness of individual debtors.

## HOW TO CHASE MONEY YOU ARE OWED: A STEP-BY-STEP GUIDE

1. Make sure your credit terms are known to your customer. The best way is to print them clearly on the invoice.

2. As soon as your customer has overstepped the mark and the bill is overdue, ask for the money you are owed. This should be done politely in writing.

**3.** If there is no reply within seven days, check that the details of the invoice are correct and that you have quoted all the information the customer needs to identify it, for example, the customer's own reference.

**4.** Send another letter by recorded delivery.

**5.** No reply within seven days? Make a phone call to find out what the problem is. Do not assume that the customer has no money; there may be queries on the account or other problems. Find out the apparent reason for the non-payment.

**6.** Use the phone call to find out if the customer has a weekly or monthly cheque run (p. 306) and find out the day this is done.

**7.** Still no payment? Keep ringing and especially two or three days before the cheque run. Try to extract a promise of payment.

**8.** Keep the pressure up. Do not pester and then drop for a few weeks; all your previous chasing is undone. Keep up a steady and persistent guerrilla warfare.

**9.** If the customer is always out or in a meeting when you telephone, and you suspect this is due to a desire not to speak to you, try pretending to be someone else who you are sure your customer *will* want to speak to. If you deal with an accountant or book-keeper, try speaking to the managing director of the customer's business.

**10.** Try different times of the day and the week: lunchtime is not usually a good time, but first thing Monday morning can be effective.

**11.** When you eventually manage to speak to the person you want, if he or she says 'I'll chase it up and see what has happened', say you will keep holding until they do.

**12.** If the customer says 'The cheque has been posted', ask for the date this was done, whether it went first- or second-class, how much the cheque was for and what the cheque number is.

**13.** If the cheque does not arrive, go to collect the money in person; this is what the Inland Revenue and the Customs and Excise people do. Get the cheque cashed as soon as possible, so that it cannot be stopped.

**14.** Check all the details of the cheque: your name, the amount, the date, the signature.

**15.** If all the previous steps have failed, send a formal letter, preferably from your solicitor, either threatening to take legal action to recover the debt or to start bankruptcy or winding-up proceedings (p. 328) or threatening to use a debt-collection agency. Keep the threat.

**16.** Consider using an agency (p. 408).

**17.** Consider issuing a writ for the debt or consider starting bankruptcy proceedings against an individual or winding-up proceedings against a company. Consider using the small claims court. Ask your solicitor's advice.

## USING AN AGENCY

Once the money has been overdue for two to three months, you could hand it over to an agency. They will write and phone and eventually either collect the money or report that it will only be collected by legal action. The usual charge for an agency is some percentage of the money recovered. There is a list of a few of the agencies on p. 408.

A half-way house to an agency is an organization like the Credit Protection Association. In this case, a letter is sent pointing out that non-payment will be reported to credit-reporting agencies – and CPA is one itself – which may harm the customer's credit rating. As this is very important to a business, this often has the desired effect. However, payment is actually made to you, not the agency, and so as long as this is done, the information is not entered on the customer's file at the reporting agency.

## SELLING YOUR DEBTS TO RAISE CASH (FACTORING)

Essentially, a factor buys your debts in return for an immediate cash payment. In a full service, the factor takes over your records for debtors and collects the debts. In return, you could receive a payment of up to 80 per cent of the face value of the invoices. The balance of the money will be paid when the debts are collected. Factoring occurs on a continuing basis, not for one individual set of debtors. The factor will often offer insurance against bad debts.

There are less complete services, for example:

*Example*

---

Jason Bottomley has a small shop selling jumpers, tops, shirts and so on. He is currently making profits of £15,000, but he does not regard this as sufficient to give him a comfortable living. He wants to increase his profits. His forecast sales and costs look like this:

| | |
|---|---|
| Sales | £120,000 |
| less Direct costs | 60,000 |
| Gross margin | £60,000 |
| less Overheads | 45,000 |
| Net profit | £15,000 |

Jason wants to look at how his profit would be affected if he could cut either his direct costs by 10 per cent or his indirect costs (or overheads) by the same amount. It would look like this:

| | Cut direct costs by 10 per cent | Cut indirect costs by 10 per cent |
|---|---|---|
| Sales | £120,000 | £120,000 |
| less Direct costs | 54,000 | 60,000 |
| Gross margin | £66,000 | £60,000 |
| less Overheads | 45,000 | 40,500 |
| Net profit | £21,000 | £19,500 |

This shows that if Jason could cut direct costs by 10 per cent, his profit would increase by 40 per cent, if he could cut overheads by 10 per cent, profit would increase by 30 per cent. In fact, he estimates that every time he manages to cut both direct and indirect costs by only 1 per cent he would have more than £1,000 extra income. Quite small cuts can lead to a big jump in Jason's income.

---

## COSTS: AUDIT CHECKLIST

- *raw materials:* are there any alternative suppliers who are cheaper for the same quality and delivery? Can you renegotiate your existing terms from your present supplier? Everything is negotiable and is worth trying

- *stocks:* this ties up cash which means bigger interest charges at the bank. Can you keep lower stocks by organizing yourself more efficiently?

- *efficient systems:* are all repeated jobs standardized in your business? For example, if you have to do a lot of quotes is there a standard form which simply needs filling in? Or are you drawing up a fresh form each time you quote? Does this apply in all business areas, financial, production and personnel, as well as selling?

● *the range of products:* is the gross margin you get on each product satisfactory? Does one product require a much greater share of overheads than others? If you stopped selling or manufacturing one of your products, what effect would it have on costs and profit?

● *customers and suppliers:* are your customers taking too long to pay? And are you paying your suppliers too promptly? If you're doing either of these you are using up cash you do not need to. This means either extra interest charges on your overdraft or less interest because you have less on deposit

● *numbers of employees:* your payroll has the extraordinary ability to mushroom with sales; this includes not only staff directly involved in production or manufacture, but also administrative staff, the so-called overheads. The trick is to keep the same number of employees, while achieving higher sales. Have you closely examined the work done by employees? Can you improve their productivity?

● *the right person for the job:* a lot of time and money is wasted recruiting, training and subsequently dismissing unsuitable staff. Putting a lot of effort into finding the right people in the first place, and not just grabbing what pops up, can be cost-saving

● *your own time:* managing your own time better can save money, too. Try to sort out some system of priorities in jobs to be done. There are quite a range of time-planning systems available, often based on diaries. See if you can find one that suits you.

## INCREASING PRICES

There is no automatic link between prices and costs. This means you do not need to feel uncomfortable about raising your prices, even if you have not had an increase in costs. And quite small increases in price can lead to a big jump in profits. There is an example in the box on p. 321 which demonstrates how effective a price rise can be.

Real life is not as simple as this. Increasing your prices could lead to a fall in sales volume if you are operating in a price conscious market. This is one of the reasons why you should think carefully about creating some sort of image or impression for your product, such as high quality or good

*Example*

Jason looks at the effect of increasing his prices by 5 per cent all round. His new forecast looks like this:

| | |
|---|---|
| Sales | £126,000 |
| less Direct costs | 60,000 |
| Gross margin | £66,000 |
| less Overheads | 45,000 |
| Net profit | £21,000 |

Jason can get an increase of 40 per cent in his profits for a 5 per cent price increase.

service, so that the sales of your product are not so price sensitive. To sell on the basis of price alone is a dangerous strategy. Read Chapter 11. 'The right name' (p. 134) for some guidance on image and Chapter 15. 'How to set a price' (p. 175) for more about prices.

PRICES: AUDIT CHECKLIST

• *discounts:* try to avoid giving discounts, or if you are giving quantity discounts, make sure you stick to the quantity set. It can be very tempting if you are competing head-on with a competitor to try to win the sale by offering a discount. Keep your nerve and try to emphasize the benefits of your product or service

• *payment discounts:* do you give a discount for your customers paying by a certain date? Have your customers started to take the discount whether paying by that date or not? Is the discount too big? Do you need it at all, or could you achieve the same effect by better chasing?

• *better quality product:* is there scope to upgrade your product with some improvements? Can you charge a higher price to give a better margin?

• *inflation:* if you can, adjust your prices to allow for the effects of inflation

• *contracts:* try including price escalation clauses in your terms and conditions for any product you are selling

• *minimum order:* if you sell your product in large numbers, have you set a minimum order? Is it too low? Small orders can take as much time to administer and carry out as large ones, so see if you can set your minimum order at a level which ensures it is at least making a contribution.

## SELLING MORE

The third way in which you can increase your profits is to sell more of your products or service – see the example in the box on p. 323. This is the most difficult to achieve and the results will not show up in the short-term; however, potentially increasing your sales gives the greatest increase in profits of the three. You are unlikely to be able to double your prices or halve your costs, but you might be able to double the amount you sell.

Your first approach should be to try and sell more of the same products to the same market. You will already have invested time and money in researching this market and refining your product to meet customer needs, so the extra investment needed may be minimal.

You can increase your sales by more effective promotion or better selling. The one method of trying to increase your sales which you should avoid like the plague is cutting your prices. This achieves little except:

● starting a price war because your competitors feel forced to follow suit

● putting pressure on your profit margins and your own profit level.

Cutting prices can only increase your profits if the increase in volume generated is enough to offset the smaller profit you make on each item sold. This could only apply in markets which are very price sensitive; and in this sort of market, cutting prices is most likely to lead to severe price competition. Think twice before you act.

### SALES: AUDIT CHECKLIST FOR SHORT-TERM IMPROVEMENT

● *image:* have you thought clearly about how your product is positioned? Can it be differentiated more from your competitors' products?

● *advertising:* are you aiming your message in the right place? Are you getting as much press coverage as you could? Is your advertising consistent with the style of your product?

● *selling:* have you clearly articulated your benefits? Have you prepared a detailed analysis of how your product compares with competitors? Have you developed proper scripts, either for person-to-person selling or telephone selling? Are you following up all leads, pursuing leads to turn

*Example*

---

Jason looks at the figures on the assumption that he could increase
the amount he sells by 5 per cent, while keeping prices and
overheads the same:

| | |
|---|---|
| Sales | £126,000 |
| less Direct costs | 63,000 |
| Gross margin | £63,000 |
| less Overheads | 45,000 |
| Net profit | £18,000 |

Jason finds that a 5 per cent increase in the volume of the sales
means a 20 per cent increase in his profits.

---

them into quotes and converting quotes to orders? Prepare a breakdown
of sales statistics, of conversion from leads to quotes to orders and analyse
where you are going wrong

● *remember:* increasing sales means increasing working capital, so your
business may need more finance.

NEW MARKETS AND NEW PRODUCTS

At some stage in your business, you may feel you have exhausted the
potential from your existing products or markets. This may occur because
the product or market has now become mature. At this point (ideally
before you have reached it, but not until your business is profitable), you
may start examining new markets for your existing product or new
products.

To achieve this, you need to undertake very similar steps to those you
followed in the first two chapters of the book when you were starting out:

● develop a shortlist of ideas/markets to try

● carry out market research to find sectors or niches to exploit

● remodel product ideas to take advantage of gaps and to meet customer
needs.

## DOING ALL THREE

In practice, you will try to do all three at the same time: cut costs, increase

324 · HOW TO INCREASE PROFITS

prices and sell more. It is astonishing the effect very small across-the-board improvements can have on your profit.

*Example*

> Jason thinks realistically that he could manage small improvements in all areas:
>
> - cut costs by 1 per cent
> - increase prices by 1 per cent
> - increase amount of sales by 1 per cent.
>
> Doing all three would have this impact on profits:
>
> | | |
> |---|---|
> | Sales | £122,412 |
> | less Direct costs | 59,994 |
> | Gross margin | £62,418 |
> | less Overheads | 44,550 |
> | Net profit | £17,868 |
>
> This means an increase in profits of 19 per cent; and gives Jason an extra income of £2,868.

The moral is never despise small improvements in costs, prices and sales. They can transform your profit figures.

## IMPROVING PROFITS THROUGH YOUR EMPLOYEES

If you have people working for you in your business, you may find it difficult to generate in them the same interest in profits as you have. The result could be that your attempts to improve profits are dissipated because employees do not have the same drive to save money or increase sales.

One way you may be able to improve their appreciation of profits is to make their income partly dependent on this. For example, with sales people their commission could be related to the gross margin on each sale, rather than the total value of the sale. This could make them less likely to give away discounts which are not essential. With other staff, you could consider introducing a profit-sharing scheme, although this obviously requires careful thought.

The government has proposed introducing tax relief for part of the pay which is linked to profits.

## SUMMARY

1. There are three ways you can increase profits; you can cut costs, increase prices or sell more.

2. The quickest way of boosting profits is to cut costs and increase prices; but the greatest long-term potential comes from increasing the amount you sell.

3. Use the audit checklists to pinpoint areas for action; remember to look at each area with an open mind.

4. Avoid cutting prices either to increase the amount you sell or to keep level with competitors; it could ruin your business.

5. Do not dismiss any improvement which can be made because it is too insignificant. A series of tiny changes in the right direction can lead to much bigger profits.

6. Try to involve your employees in the need to increase profits.

**OTHER CHAPTERS TO READ**

# 26. NOT WAVING BUT DROWNING

If you put this book's guidelines into operation at the right time, fewer of you should need this chapter than the average small business might do. Nevertheless, there are those who will. Some businesses will go to the wall.

Few people can appreciate before the event how traumatic the slide into failure can be. Gradually hemmed in with fewer and fewer avenues of escape, you have to come to terms with the crushing of your hopes and expectations. For natural optimists, such as entrepreneurs, it is appallingly difficult to do. At what point do you realize that your business is not going to survive? When do you accept that to carry on is to put other businesses into jeopardy and to impose the same pressures on them as on you? At what point does it become illegal to carry on?

That point may be easy to recognize for an outsider, who is calm and rational. But it is incredibly difficult to recognize, when you have been fighting for weeks, or even months, to avoid it. You may find that you slid past the point so gradually that you did not have time to notice. Sometimes, of course, matters are taken out of your hands by an outsider, such as a creditor or a bank, beginning the steps to close your business.

The problem of acceptance is made worse by the usual existence of somewhat schizophrenic behaviour. To avoid rumours and doubts emerging about the future of your business, you may well be putting on a brave face to the outside world. And you are doing this while knowing within yourself that it does not ring true. The title of this chapter is from a poem by Stevie Smith. Two lines from this poem are: 'I was much further out than you thought / And not waving but drowning.' This aptly summarizes the dilemma for someone whose business is in financial difficulties.

Further emotional difficulties are caused by society's attitudes towards the failure. Often the assumption is that failed businesses are run by crooks. Sometimes they are, but they are also run by people who tried hard but had bad luck or made too many mistakes. This chapter tries to help you recognize the point at which you have to say: 'Enough is enough'.

WHAT IS IN THIS CHAPTER?

The warning signs of failure (see below)

The final process:

## THE WARNING SIGNS OF FAILURE

Chapter 24. 'Staying afloat' (p. 298) describes how to control your cash to help avoid an ignominious end to your business. At some point, you may unfortunately find the following signs:

- you only pay a supplier when a writ is issued and your suppliers are refusing to sell you any more goods

- you are near or above your overdraft limit at the bank

- you are unable to raise any more money

- your liabilities are greater than your assets.

Once your business has reached the point that liabilities (what you owe) are more than assets (what you own), the business is insolvent. It may become insolvent at an earlier stage, when current liabilities are greater than current assets: in other words, when the amount you have in cash and debtors is less than the amount you owe to creditors. This may occur even though you have sufficient fixed assets to cover what you owe. These fixed assets may take too long to sell, particularly at other than a knock-down price, to satisfy your creditors.

As well as insolvency occurring as a result of sales being too low or costs too high, outside events can force it on you. For example, you may be owed a large sum of money by a customer who is slow in paying and may even be unable to pay. A common complaint for small businesses is that some large companies are prone to do just that – be very slow payers – and this can start the vicious cycle ending in failure.

Earlier warning signs can be detected which identify businesses which are at a high risk of failure. Studies (p. 409) pinpoint, among other things, these faults – not all of them relevant for the self-employed and small businesses:

- the boss takes no advice
- the managing director and chairman (for limited companies) is the same person
- the board of directors do not take an active interest
- the skills of the business are unbalanced
- there is no strong financial person
- there is no budget, cash flow plan or costing system
- the business is failing to respond to change.

If your business displays some of these characteristics, while not yet being in the advanced stage of failure, get advice now, either from your professional advisers (p. 205) or an enterprise or other agency (p. 49).


## THE FINAL PROCESS

There is one constructive step you can take: consider whether you could negotiate with creditors to pay off what you owe in instalments or to pay a smaller sum which they will accept in full settlement. Of course, once you have floated this idea your problems may well be out in the open and, if your creditors do not agree, you are left only with one possibility, liquidation or bankruptcy. Agreement is more likely where there are a small number of creditors; if there are lots, there is bound to be at least one who will not agree.

### LIMITED COMPANY

You can seek to wind-up your company on a voluntary basis or have it imposed on you by the court or under the supervision of the court. And under the 1986 Insolvency Act there are the options of administration and voluntary arrangements.

Voluntary winding-up can occur if 75 per cent of the members vote for it. The resolution for voluntary winding-up must be published in the *London Gazette*. If the directors make a statutory declaration, having investigated the company's affairs, that in their opinion the company will be able to pay its debts within twelve months, the winding-up carries on as a members' voluntary winding-up. However, if the company is not solvent, the winding-up is a creditors' voluntary winding-up. The difference between the two is that if it is a members' voluntary winding-up, the members appoint the liquidator. Otherwise, the creditors will hold a meeting at which the liquidator is appointed by them.

The liquidators will normally pay what debts can be covered in the following order:

• loans and debts which have been secured on a fixed asset (p. 285)

• the costs of the winding-up

• local authority and water rates, income tax, wages and salaries

• loans and debts which have been secured with a floating charge on the assets, that is, secured on assets in general, not one specific named asset

• ordinary trade creditors

• shareholders.

If you do not start proceedings to wind-up the company on a voluntary basis, you may find it forced on you if a creditor, for example, a supplier or your bank, applies to the court for a compulsory winding-up because you cannot pay your debts. In this case, the court will appoint a liquidator, who is usually the Official Receiver. The Official Receiver is an officer of the Department of Trade and Industry.

The secretary or director of the company must provide the Official Receiver with a statement, verified by affidavit, listing the assets or liabilities of the company. The Official Receiver will call a creditors' meeting to decide whether to appoint a liquidator or whether the Official Receiver will carry on in that role. The liquidator will pay off the company's debts in the same order as that outlined for the voluntary winding-up.

The 1986 Insolvency Act has strengthened the responsibilities of directors. One of the provisions could mean that a director may be made personally liable for a company's creditors. This could occur if the director has allowed the company to go on trading even though there is no way it can avoid insolvent liquidation (that is, the assets of the business cannot be sold to provide a sufficient sum of money to pay all the creditors).

## SOLE TRADER

A creditor may force bankruptcy on you by beginning proceedings for payment of a debt. Once proceedings have begun, being able to pay the specific debt which started the proceedings will not do. It becomes a case of paying all the debts at once. Even if you can show that you have the assets to pay all your debts in time, you are still likely to be made bankrupt so that your creditors can be paid at once.

## PARTNERSHIP

With a partnership you have an added problem to that of being a sole trader. Each partner is responsible for all the liabilities of the partnership, regardless of what the profit-sharing arrangements are in your partnership agreement. If you have more personal assets than your partner, it is you and your family who will suffer the most.

## WHAT HAPPENS AFTERWARDS?

There is reading suggested in 'Reference' (p. 409) for what happens when you have been made bankrupt and gives the name of an association you can join. If you have been made bankrupt the chances of you being able to start another business are remote indeed.

However, if you are the director of a company which is wound-up you may be able to make one more attempt, although under the terms of the Insolvency Act you may be disqualified from being a director after one insolvency, if you are deemed unfit to be so. It is not an automatic disqualification, so if you do get a second chance learn from your mistakes this time around.

## SUMMARY

1. Watch out for the warning signs.

2. See if your creditors will agree to you paying off what you owe by instalments or see if they will accept smaller payments in settlement.

OTHER CHAPTERS TO READ

24. 'Staying afloat' (p. 298)

# 27. KEEPING THE RECORD STRAIGHT

Fate decrees that one of the least interesting business activities is also one of the most crucial for its continued success. Keeping records must rank fairly low in an entrepreneur's satisfaction rating. It is much more gripping to go chasing sales or to carry out a negotiation with a supplier, which will lower your costs. But a complete 'seat-of-the-pants' approach to business will only keep you afloat in the short term.

If you hope to avert the dangers of sliding into failure, one thing you should try to achieve is *not* to allow yourself to be buried in a quagmire of bills, invoices and tax demands. Failure to organize your records from Day One may mean just that. However, it is never too late to start; so if you have been pushing aside that task, now is the time to tackle it.

Allowing yourself to drift into paper chaos is understandable. Discovering a system for organizing records which is suitable for your business can be difficult. Too simple a system for your particular business may mean that you cannot derive the information from it that you need. Too complicated a system may mean that you have to spend too much time keeping it up-to-date. There is no one system which will apply to all businesses. You may find that you need to adjust yours with the benefit of experience, until you have developed one that fits what you want.

WHAT IS IN THIS CHAPTER?

- Why you need records (see below)
- Which records? (p. 332)
- A very simple system (p. 333)
- When the business is more complicated (p. 339)
- Using ready-made systems (p. 342)

## WHY YOU NEED RECORDS

Good accurate records are needed for two extremely important reasons. First, records are needed to substantiate what is in the accounts.

One of the advantages of choosing to be self-employed or in a partnership is that your accounts do not have to be audited (p. 53). But they must convince your tax inspector. If the accounts cannot be backed by written documentation, you may find yourself paying a higher tax bill than otherwise. Or, just as bad, your tax inspector may launch an investigation into your business affairs. If you have a company, your accounts must be audited and so you need the back-up records to satisfy the auditor.

Accounts have to be prepared for every accounting period and sent to your taxman. The accounts for the self-employed should consist of details of sales and expenses. A balance sheet is helpful, but not essential (it is essential for a company).

Second, accurate records are needed to help you know what is going on in your business. This, in turn, means you can keep better control and you can plan for the future. It is impossible to make realistic estimates and projections if the basic data is patchy and inaccurate.

## WHICH RECORDS?

The first and most important record you need is for cash. You need some way of keeping information about payments into and out of your bank account and also any petty cash which you keep on the premises. The aim of your cash records should be to enable you to know at any moment how much cash you have.

For those businesses which do not sell all their goods for cash, your records will need to cope with keeping tabs on what people owe you and how long they have owed it. This allows you to forecast what money you will be getting in during the months ahead and enable you to chase debts which are overdue.

Most businesses will buy goods, services and raw materials from others. Unless you are forced to pay cash for all your supplies, you will need to organize the bills which you have to pay. Following on from this, if you keep stocks of raw materials or stocks of finished goods, you need to have a tally of what there is: what has come in the business, what is presently held by the business and what has gone out.

Once you start employing people, your employee records need to be meticulously kept; in particular, the records which relate to your role as tax collector for the government (p. 244) need to be very well organized and kept up-to-date.

Finally, information about fixed assets, such as cars, equipment or property, needs to be recorded.

## A VERY SIMPLE SYSTEM

If your business has only a few transactions, for example:

- it is very small, or
- you sell only large items, or
- you sell your time, for example, as a consultant

the system you introduce can really be very simple. It would indeed be a mistake to get bogged down in very complicated record-keeping, because it would take up a lot of time without improving the accuracy of your system. Complexities such as double-entry book-keeping can be put aside. A couple of simple accounts books may well be sufficient. Being methodical is far more important than sophistication.

### CASH

You will need a cash book. This should show the cash payments you receive and the cash payments you make. It gives a way of recording what you have paid into the bank and what you take out of it. The same cash book can also record your petty cash position.

Diagram 3 overleaf gives an example of a way of setting up the cash book. As you can see there are two sections: one for recording cash receipts and one for recording cash payments. The cash receipts section has five columns and the cash payment section, six columns.

For cash receipts, the columns are from left to right:

- the date you received the payment
- the invoice number which has been paid
- the name of the person who made the payment
- the amount of the payment
- the value of what you have paid into the bank.

If you offer discounts for prompt settlement, you will need to have an additional column to show the amount which was taken.

For cash payments, the columns are from left to right:

- the date you made the payment
- the cheque number
- the reference number you will have put on the supplier's invoice when it was received (p. 337)
- the name of the person or business who has been paid
- what you have cashed from the bank for petty cash purposes
- the amount of the payment.

If it is normal business practice to be offered a discount, you need another column to record the amount taken. When you start paying wages, you will need a further column to record what you have cashed from the bank for this purpose.

**Diagram 3. Cash**

Cash receipts

| Date received | Invoice number | Customer | Amount £ | Paid into bank £ |
|---|---|---|---|---|
| | | | | |

Cash payments

| Date paid | Cheque number | Reference number | Supplier/ Payee | Petty cash £ | Amount of payment £ |
|---|---|---|---|---|---|
| | | | | | |

Using the cash book, you should be able to work out how much cash you have and whether cash receipts are exceeding cash payments or vice versa. When you get a bank statement, which should be monthly (and when your business gets more complicated ask for a statement more than once a month), you can check that the two cash balances agree. If they do not, you should be able to identify why, that is, cheques you have sent which have not yet been cashed or cheques you have paid in which have not yet been cleared. This is called a bank reconciliation. It is useful to write your reconciliation down.

All cheque books, paying-in books and bank statements should be carefully kept.

### PETTY CASH

You can deal with petty cash items in a number of ways. You could write a voucher or piece of paper each time you use petty cash and keep the voucher in the petty cash box. If you get a receipt for money you spend, staple this to the back of the voucher. Once a month, you could tot these up and put them in your purchases record (p. 336).

Another approach is to carry a little notebook with you and jot down the expenses as they occur. A further alternative is to keep a sheet of paper in your office and write down the amounts spent at the end of each day, again stapling any receipts to it.

Finally, you could set up a recording system in your cash book, using perhaps the back half of the book.

Whichever way you record petty cash items, you need the following information:

- the date the cash was spent

- how much it was

- what it was for.

If you are registered for VAT, when you make an entry in your purchases record, you will need to know which items include the standard rate of VAT (p. 388) and to work out the amount of VAT you will be claiming.

### SALES

Every time you make a sale, you should produce an invoice (or, if you are selling for cash, a receipt). The invoices should be numbered and filed in numerical order. If there is a fair number of invoices, it might be sensible to have one file for unpaid invoices and another for paid invoices. As every invoice is paid, any documentation which comes with the payment should be stapled to it. It should then be transferred to the paid file. A separate file should be kept for every accounting period to avoid confusion.

The next step is to write down in your accounts or analysis book a record of every sale. For every sale there should be four columns, six if you are registered for VAT. The diagram below gives you an idea of what it will look like.

The columns reading from left to right are:

- the date of the invoice

- the name of the customer

- the number of the invoice

- the amount of the sale, including VAT.

If you are registered for VAT, there should be two further columns:

- the amount of the VAT

- the amount of the sale, excluding VAT.

**Diagram 4. Sales**

| Date of invoice | Description: Name of customer | Number of invoice | Amount of sale (incl. VAT) | VAT | Amount of sale (excl. VAT) |
|---|---|---|---|---|---|
| 12.6.87 | Arnold Warehouses | 344 | 1,725.00 | 225.00 | 1,500.00 |

*Example 1*

Peter Brown is entering the details of one of his invoices. The invoice number is 344 and the invoice is to Arnold Warehouses. Peter has charged £1,500, but VAT has to be charged. This comes to £225 and the total, including VAT, is £1,725. When the invoice is paid, Peter will enter the details in the cash book.

PURCHASES

If your business is simple, you can record the details of purchases in the same accounts or analysis book as your sales, perhaps using the second half of it. As every invoice comes in for goods or services which you have bought (or a receipt for items which you pay cash for), it should be numbered and filed in numerical order.

When it comes to recording purchases, a more detailed analysis than for sales can be useful for producing the accounts which you need for tax purposes. If your business is simple, your records may need to be updated only once a month.

You will probably find you use all the columns of your analysis book. The columns should read from left to right (see Diagram 5 below):

- the date the invoice is received

- the name of the supplier

- whether the invoice is paid or not, for example, a tick if paid

- the number you put on the invoice

- the amount of the invoice, including VAT.

If you are registered for VAT, you will need two further columns:

- the amount of the VAT

- the amount of the invoice, excluding VAT.

**Diagram 5. Purchases**

| Date invoice received | Name of supplier | Paid | Number of invoice | Amount (incl. V.A.T.) | V.A.T. |
|---|---|---|---|---|---|
| 12.6.87 | British Telecom | | 222 | 257.83 | 33.63 |

| Amount (excl. VAT) | Supplies | Car expenses | Station-ery | Postage | Telephone | Heating/ lighting |
|---|---|---|---|---|---|---|
| 224.20 | | | | | 224.20 | |

The remaining columns of the book should be devoted to showing the nature of the items purchased. The exact headings you put on the columns will depend on the type of the business. Some examples could be stationery, fares, petrol, postage, heating and lighting. The amount of every invoice, excluding VAT if you are registered, should be entered in the appropriate column. Diagram 5 on the previous page (p. 337) can give you some idea of how to set it out.

*Example 2*

Peter Brown has received an invoice for the telephone. He numbers the invoice 222 and enters the details in the analysis book – see Diagram 5. He puts the date he received it, the supplier and the amount of the invoice including VAT, £257.83.

As he is registered for VAT, he now works out the amount of VAT, that is £257.83 less £257.83 divided by 1.15. This gives £257.83 − 224.20 = £33.63. He enters this in the VAT column and puts £224.20 in the column for the amount, excluding VAT. He puts the amount of the invoice without VAT in the analysis column.

When he pays the invoice he ticks the appropriate column and also enters details in the cash book.

FIXED ASSETS

If your business is a limited company, you are obliged by law to keep a record of fixed assets. If your business is fairly simple, a list in a notebook will suffice. But this should show the cost of the asset and the amount of the depreciation.

VAT

You are required to keep separate VAT accounts if you are registered for VAT (p. 392). You can put these in your analysis book, if there is sufficient room. This should show for each month:

• the amount of the sales, including VAT

• the amount of VAT charged

• the amount of the purchases, including VAT

• the amount of the VAT paid.

# WHEN THE BUSINESS IS MORE COMPLICATED

There will be many businesses for whom the simple system described above will not be sufficient. This will apply to you if you make many sales or purchases each month and keep a lot of stock on the premises. There will be an increasing number of documents and records needed. Your business may need to set up a system for recording information which includes some or all of the following records.

### PURCHASE ORDERS

This could be a formal document which has the name and address of supplier plus the goods ordered and the details necessary for that. A copy of your letter may suffice, as long as they are numbered and kept in a file. This document will be needed to ensure that what the supplier sends you is actually what you ordered.

### A RECORD OF WHAT GOODS ARE RECEIVED IN THE BUSINESS

As your business grows, you will no longer know yourself exactly what has come in; there may well be employees who do this for you. The only way to keep track of what has been received is to have a formal way of recording this. This could be a specially prepared form to fill in and match against the purchase order. Or it could be a book in which you write down the details. Whichever it is, the details are needed before a supplier invoice is passed for payment.

### WHAT HAVE YOU GOT IN STOCK?

You need to know at any time what raw materials or finished goods you have got in stock. Going to have a look is not the best way of doing this. Written records are the answer because:

- they are the best way to control and plan your business
- they will protect against staff pilfering.

If you have lots of different items which you keep in stock, stock cards may be the most suitable way of recording what there is. With fewer items, a stock book may suffice.

### SALES INVOICES

This could be a printed form or it could be typed on business stationery and a copy kept.

EMPLOYEE TIME SHEETS

For certain sorts of businesses, for example, manufacturing or assembly, records of how many hours employees work are important and are the basis for paying wages. You could keep a time book with a simple record of when the employee started work and when the employee finished for the day.

PETTY CASH VOUCHERS

As the business gets bigger with more employees, a proper petty cash voucher will become a necessity. This should show the date, the employee who received the petty cash and what it was for. Any voucher should be signed by an appropriate responsible person with the authority to do so.

RECORD OF PURCHASES (OR PURCHASES DAY BOOK)

This has already been described under the very simple system. The difference will be how often it is filled in once your business grows. Initially, when there are only a few items purchased, filling it in once a month may be sufficient; as there is more business activity, once a week or even once a day may be necessary.

RECORD OF SALES (SALES DAY BOOK)

This has also been described under the simple system. As your business develops with particular customers, you will find that you need to keep a record of sales per customer, so you have a record of what each person or business has bought from you.

CASH BOOK

The cash book which you developed at the start of your business (p. 333) will suffice as it grows.

WAGES RECORD

You have certain legal duties towards your employees (Chapter 20. 'Your rights and duties as an employer' (p. 234)). These include giving an itemized pay statement (p. 241) and deducting tax and national insurance contributions from salaries and wages. Proper records need to be kept.

You must keep the following information for all employees:

• name and address
• national insurance number

- income tax number
- pay
- pension deductions
- any other deductions authorized by the employee.

The actual wages record needs to show the payments made:

- gross pay, with a breakdown of how this is made up, for example, bonuses and commission, as well as basic wage
- pension contributions
- total pay this period
- total pay to date
- tax-free pay to date (see tables from Inland Revenue)
- taxable pay to date
- tax due to date (see tables from Inland Revenue)
- tax paid to date
- tax due on earnings for this period
- national insurance contributions this period
- other deductions
- net pay
- employer's national insurance contribution.

This is also information which needs to be put on an employee's pay slip.

### THE JOURNAL

This summarizes what has happened in the sales and purchases records, for example. It is also where information about fixed assets, and their depreciation, is entered. On the whole, unless you know something about accounting, this is probably something which your accountant or book-keeper will keep up-to-date. It does not need to be maintained on a daily basis.

## USING READY-MADE SYSTEMS

There are a number of accounting systems for sale; these include manual ones as well as computing ones. The details of a couple of the better manual systems are given on p. 409. To choose a computerized system, see HOW TO PROTECT YOURSELF AGAINST THE COMPUTER WOLVES in Chapter 17. 'Getting equipped' (p. 198).

## SUMMARY

1.  You need records to back up what is in your accounts for tax purposes or for auditors if you have a limited company.

2.  Planning the business and controlling it cannot be achieved if records are inadequate.

3.  Keeping your records in a methodical way is more important than installing very sophisticated systems.

OTHER CHAPTERS TO READ

# 28. TAX AND THE SOLE TRADER

There is nothing more likely to turn your stomach to stone than a letter dropping through the letter-box from the Inland Revenue. Sometimes, the envelope can contain nasty shocks, too; it is not unknown for estimated assessments to be way above a realistic figure for your profits. This may occur despite your tax inspector having evidence to the contrary.

The arrival of this sort of letter can create havoc in your day ahead, causing you to drop everything you planned to do, while you scurry about trying to check that the figures in the assessment are not correct. Even if you have an accountant to sort out your tax affairs, this sort of letter will still be sent direct to you, causing you the same worry.

It is in your own interest to have some understanding of the way your tax bill as a sole trader will be worked out, even if you have someone else to do the actual sums and presentation. Knowing how the tax system works, and what sort of allowances you can set against your income, can be very helpful. You will need to keep your accounting records so that you can back up your tax calculations and these records will need to be devised to help you keep your tax bill to a minimum. Additionally, some of the tax allowances you can get may be influential in some of your financial decisions, such as whether you should buy or lease capital equipment.

Using a professional tax adviser, such as your accountant or your bank, to help you present your accounts and tax calculations can be helpful. They should know how to put down the figures on paper in a way which your tax inspector will be used to; it also gives your figures some sort of credibility. Unfortunately, you cannot always rely on the advisers; there are lots of good ones, but there can be poor ones, too.

### WHAT IS IN THIS CHAPTER?

This chapter will not answer every question you may have about how your income tax bill is calculated. But you should be able to elicit a working knowledge of the system so you know the key moves to make in your dealings with your tax inspector. It will help you to answer these questions:

- how can I estimate and plan for my tax bills?
- what must I do to keep my tax bill to a minimum?
- what information must I send my tax inspector and when?

The answers to these questions are included in:

- When you pay income tax (see below)
- Working out your income tax bill (p. 347)
- Business expenses (p. 348)
- Capital allowances (p. 351)
- What happens if you make losses (p. 354)
- National insurance contributions (p. 356)
- Capital gains tax (p. 356)
- You and your tax inspector (p. 357)

## WHEN YOU PAY INCOME TAX

Self-employed people normally pay their income tax bills in two chunks; the first part on 1 January and the second on 1 July. This can be quite a change for former employees used to paying their income tax monthly, or weekly, through the PAYE system.

A puzzling aspect of tax for the self-employed is that often you are paying tax bills of income earned over one, or two or even three years before. This happens because tax is normally charged on a preceding year basis. Herein lies one possible advantage of being taxed as a self-employed person; quite a number of months can pass between earning the profits and paying the tax. If the profits from your business are rising year by year, this can have a beneficial effect on your cash flow. The rules are different for the first couple of years or so when you start your business and also for the last couple of years, if you close it.

Another possible source of confusion occurs when you have set up your business as a limited company. In this case, you do not count as self-employed for tax purposes. Instead, you are an employee of the company and pay income tax through the PAYE system in the usual way. The tax on profits from your company is corporation tax and is dealt with in Chapter 30. 'Tax and the limited company' (p. 370).

## WHICH PROFITS ARE TAXED

Once your business has been in existence for two or three years, your tax bill will be sorted out on a preceding year basis. You will pay tax in any tax year on the profits from your accounting year ending in the preceding tax year. For example, if your accounting year ends on 31 December, your tax bill in the 1987–8 tax year will be based on the profits you earned during the accounting year from 1 January 1986 until 31 December 1986.

## CHOOSING WHEN TO END YOUR ACCOUNTING YEAR

This rather odd method of calculating tax can be used to your advantage by maximizing the gap between earning the profits and paying the tax. The greatest gap is if your year-end is just after 5 April. Example 1 in the box on p. 346 shows why this is.

You can change your accounting year-end at a later date, but it can be complicated so you should only consider doing so for a compelling purpose.

## HOW YOUR PROFITS ARE TAXED WHEN YOU FIRST
## START IN BUSINESS

You can really get in a muddle here. In the first couple of years of your business, the preceding year basis will not work. The rules your tax inspector will follow are:

● *first tax year:* the profit you made (see p. 346) during the first tax year

● *second tax year:* you can choose *either* the profit you made during the second tax year *or* the profit you made during your first twelve months of business

● *third tax year:* if you choose the profit you made during the second tax year, actual profit for the third year too. If you do not choose this, you are taxed on the profit you made in your accounting year ending in the previous tax year. If your first accounting period has not finished, you will normally be taxed on the profit you make during your first twelve months.

*Example 1*

---

Jonathan Smith starts his business on 1 November 1986 and looks at when he should end his accounting year. He examines several possibilities:
1. 31 October
2. 31 December
3. 30 April.

After the first few years, this is when his tax would be due on the profits he earns:

1. If his year-end was 31 October 1989, he would pay half the tax on 1 January 1991 (fourteen months after he earned the profits) and the second half on 1 July 1991 (a delay of twenty months).

2. If his year-end was 31 December 1989, he would pay half the tax on 1 January 1991 (twelve months after he earned the profits) and the second half on 1 July 1991 (a delay of eighteen months).

3. If his year-end was 30 April 1989, he would pay half the tax on 1 January 1991 (twenty months after he earned the profits) and the second half on 1 July 1991 (a delay of twenty-six months).

He believes his taxable profits, after deductions such as capital allowances, will be rising over the years. It makes sense for him to go for the greatest delay which is given by choosing a 30 April year-end.

---

Which part of your profits falls into one tax year and which part into the next year is apportioned on a time basis, strictly by day but by month will probably be accepted by your tax inspector. The profits you made will be:

$$\frac{\text{number of months of accounting period in tax year}}{\text{number of months in accounting period}}$$

$\times$ profits in accounting period.

When you start your business and your first accounting period is more than a year, you will have to work out the profits actually made in each tax year for the third and fourth years as well (see Example 2.).

You should choose to be taxed on your actual profit in the second and third tax year, if this makes your tax bills, for the two years together, less than it would otherwise be. If you wish to make the choice about actual profit for years two and three, you must do so within six years after the end of the third year of assessment.

*Example 2: Working out profit to be taxed at the start of the business*

The profits in Simon Wilson's first accounting period, from 1 January 1987 to 30 April 1988, are £12,000. Profits for the next period ending on 30 April 1989 are £11,000. His assessments of taxable profits are likely to be:

Tax year 1986–7     3/16 × £12,000 =    £2,250
        1987–8     12/16 × £12,000 =   £9,000
        1988–9     12/16 × £12,000 =   £9,000
        1989–90    12/16 × £12,000 =   £9,000
        1990–91                     £11,000

So while Simon is earning profits of £11,000 in his accounting period 1988–9, he is paying tax on profits of £9,000.

## WORKING OUT YOUR INCOME TAX BILL

First, turn your profits from your accounts into taxable profits:

**1.** If you have taken any items out of stock for your own use, include these in your sales figure at the normal selling price.

**2.** Deduct from your profits any business expenses which are normally allowable against tax, but which you have not included (p. 348).

**3.** Add back to your profits any business expenses which are not allowable for tax purposes (p. 351).

**4.** Deduct any income which is not part of your trading income and on which tax is paid separately, for example, bank interest.

**5.** Deduct any items which are allowable for tax purposes; these are capital allowances (p. 351), loss relief (p. 354), half of any Class 4 national insurance contributions you pay (p. 356).

**6.** Add back any balancing charges from the sale of assets (p. 353).

*Example: Working out taxable profits*

Patty Woodward adjusts the profits from her accounts to provide a figure on which her tax inspector can base the tax calculations, if agreed. Her profits according to the accounts are £7,500.

**1.** She has not used any stock for her own use, so no adjustment needed here.

**2.** She checks carefully against the list of business expenses which are normally allowed for tax purposes (see below). She realizes she has forgotten to include bank charges, which for the year total £48. The adjusted profit figure is now £7,452.

**3.** However, her accounting profit includes a figure for depreciation of her computer, £200. She adds this back; her adjusted profits are now £7,652. This is the figure for business profits.

**4.** She has no business investment income.

**5.** Patty now claims the allowances she can. She takes the full writing-down allowance on her computer. For this year, it comes to £150.

She has no losses to use for relief, but she can claim relief on half her Class 4 national insurance contributions. For 1987–8, these are payable at 6.3 per cent on earnings over £4,590. For Patty this means 6.3 per cent of £7,502 − £4,590 = £183.46. She deducts half this amount (rounding upwards to the nearest whole £), which comes to £92. This leaves a figure of £7,652 − £150 − £92 = £7,400.

**6.** She has not sold any assets this year. Her tax bill is calculated on £7,400.

## BUSINESS EXPENSES

### WHAT BUSINESS EXPENSES ARE ALLOWED

You can claim, and be allowed, an item as a business expense for tax purposes if it is incurred 'wholly and exclusively' for the business. The golden rule with expenses is that if you are in any doubt as to whether an expense is allowable, claim it.

Allowable business expenses are not confined to those items used only in your business, as long as they are sometimes used wholly for the business. For example, you may be able to claim some of the expenses of running your home if you run your business from there. Similarly, a car can be used privately, as well as in your business, as long as on some occasions your car is used wholly for your business. Negotiate with your tax inspector the proportion of car and home expenses which will be allowable for tax relief. Typical home expenses which will be allowable are part of the costs of heating, lighting, telephone, insurance and security.

An expense incurred partly for business and partly for private reasons, for example, a trip in your car to a customer, could strictly not be allowed if you dropped in to see a friend on the way.

Be careful of claiming expenses for part of your home used exclusively for your business, as it may mean capital gains tax to pay when you sell your home. Instead, phrase it as a claim for 'non-exclusive use of a room at home'.

CHECKLIST OF EXPENSES YOU CAN NORMALLY CLAIM

1. *General expenses*

Claim the expenses of making your product and running your premises:

● cost of goods you sell or use in your product

● selling costs, such as advertising, sales discounts, gifts costing up to £10 a year (if gift advertises your business or product), reasonable entertainment of overseas trade customers

● office/factory expenses, such as heating, lighting, cleaning, rates, rent, telephone, postage, stationery, normal repairs and maintenance

● proportion of home expenses, if used for work (see above)

● other expenses, such as relevant books and magazines, professional fees, subscriptions to professional and trade organizations, replacing small tools, travel expenses (but not between home and work, or, usually, meals), running costs of car (see above), delivery charges, charge for hiring capital equipment, such as cars.

If you are not registered for VAT, include the cost of VAT in what you claim, as it is a business expense which you cannot get back through the VAT system. If you are registered for VAT, do not include it, unless it is impossible for you to claim it back from the VAT man, because, for example, it is included in what you have purchased for part of your business which is exempt for VAT purposes.

## 2. *Staff costs*

Claim the normal costs of employing people:

- wages, salaries, bonuses, redundancy and leaving payments, pensions to former employees and dependants (but not your salary or your partner's salary)

- cost of employing your wife (if you can show that the work is actually done, and that her wage the going market rate). If your wife does not earn anything else, you can pay up to the amount of wife's earned income allowance before having to pay any tax (but the best saving is paying her just below the national insurance exemption limit, see p. 244). There is no additional tax benefit if the wife has the business and employs the husband. If your income is high, husband and wife should consider forming a partnership, as long as it is genuine. You could choose separate taxation of the wife's earnings if it is worthwhile

- employer's national insurance contributions (but not all your own, see p. 356)

- entertaining staff

- gifts to staff

- subscriptions and contributions for benefits for staff.

## 3. *Financial expenses*

- bank charges on business accounts

- interest on loans and overdrafts for your business, and cost of arranging them (but not interest paid to a partner for capital put in the business, or interest on overdue tax)

- charge part of hire purchase payments (that is, the interest plus additional costs)

- business insurance (but not your own life insurance, accident insurance, sickness insurance)

- bad debts which you specifically claim (but not a general reserve for bad or doubtful debts)

- incidental cost of obtaining loan finance, but not stamp duty, foreign exchange losses, issue discounts or repayment premiums.

4. *Legal and other expenses*

- legal charges such as debt collection, preparing trading contracts, employee service contracts, settling trading disputes and renewing a short lease (that is, fifty years or less)

- premium for grant of lease, but limited to the amount assessed on the landlord as extra rent spread over the term as the lease is paid

- fees paid to register trade mark or design, or to obtain a patent.

## WHAT IS NOT NORMALLY ALLOWED AS A BUSINESS EXPENSE

1. Your own income and living expenses, most of your national insurance contributions (p. 356), income tax, capital gains tax, capital transfer tax, fines and other penalties for breaking the law.

2. Depreciation or initial costs of capital equipment, buying a patent, vehicles, permanent advertising signs, buildings and the cost of additions or improvements to these (but could be a capital allowance to claim).

3. Legal expenses on forming a company, drawing up a partnership agreement, acquiring assets such as leases.

4. Business entertaining expenses (except overseas customers), gifts to customers (but see p. 349), normally charitable subscriptions and donations, donations to political parties.

5. Reserves or provisions for expected payments, such as repairs, general reserve for bad and doubtful debts (but see p. 350).

## CAPITAL ALLOWANCES

### WHAT CAPITAL ALLOWANCES CAN BE CLAIMED

Depreciation on capital equipment and its initial cost are not allowable business expenses (see above), but you can get tax relief on capital expenditure. You do this by claiming capital allowances, known as writing-down allowances.

The way in which you pay for equipment does not affect the capital allowance, which can still be claimed on the cost of the item. But you do not claim a capital allowance for the interest on a loan or overdraft to buy equipment; this is an allowable expense, not part of the cost of the asset.

If you are buying on hire purchase, the charge is also a business expense. With leased equipment, you can claim the rent as an expense, not a capital allowance.

To qualify for a capital allowance, expenditure must be 'wholly and exclusively' for the business. But this does not mean you cannot claim a capital allowance for some item which you use in your private life as well as in your business. For example, if you use a car half in your business and half for private purposes, you work out the capital allowance on the cost of the car and claim half the allowance.

When you first start your business, if you use anything in it which you already owned and used privately, you can claim a capital allowance on the market value at the time you start your business.

The capital allowance is claimed each year, usually on the value of the item or items at the end of the previous accounting year.

## THE MAXIMUM WRITING-DOWN ALLOWANCES IN 1987–8

These are the maximum allowances you can claim for what you spend:

| | |
|---|---|
| *plant and machinery* | 25 per cent |
| *cars* | 25 per cent |
| *industrial buildings* | 4 per cent of original cost |
| *agricultural buildings* | 4 per cent of original cost |
| *hotels with ten plus bedrooms* | 4 per cent of original cost |
| *buildings in enterprise zones* | 25 per cent of original cost (but not if you claim full first-year allowance – see p. 190) |
| *buying a patent* | 25 per cent |
| *know-how* | 25 per cent |
| *scientific research* | nil (but can claim first-year allowance) |

## WORKING OUT THE ALLOWANCE FOR PLANT AND MACHINERY

If you only have one piece of capital equipment, the allowance for the first year you claim is worked out on its cost (or its market value, if taken into the business). In the second year, the allowance is claimed on its value at the end of the previous accounting year, that is, the cost less the amount of the allowances previously claimed.

With several items, you form a pool of expenditure from the values (the cost if you have just bought an item). The writing-down allowance is claimed on the value of the pool at the end of each accounting year. The amount of the allowance claimed is deducted from the value of the pool at the end of each year to form the new value for the next year. The cost of any new equipment bought during the next accounting year is added to the value of the pool. Work out the writing-down allowance on the value of the pool at the end of that accounting year and so on. The example below shows you how to do it.

*Example: What capital allowance can be claimed*

---

Adam Horsfield buys a desk for his business; the cost of the desk is £100. At the end of the accounting year, Adam claims a writing-down allowance of 25 per cent of £100, that is, £25. He deducts this from the value of the desk, giving a value of £75 at the end of the accounting year.

In the next accounting year, Adam buys a filing cabinet costing £150. He adds this to the value of the desk, giving the value of his pool of expenditure of £150 + £75 = £225. At the end of this year, he claims a writing-down allowance of 25 per cent of £225, that is, £56.25. He deducts this from the value of the pool, giving a value for the next year of £225 − £56.25 = £168.75.

---

If you already have sufficient deductions to reduce your taxable profits to zero or to the level of your personal allowances, it will not save you tax if you claim your full writing-down allowance. Instead, claim none or less than the full allowance. This will mean a bigger allowance can be claimed next year than would otherwise be the case.

When it comes to selling an asset on which you have claimed capital allowances, you have to reduce the value of your pool by the lower of the sale proceeds or the original cost. Do this before working out the amount of the writing-down allowance you can claim for the accounting year in which you sell the asset. If the sale proceeds are more than the value of the pool, add the difference (the *balancing charge*) to your figure for profit for the year. Note that this also applies to an asset which has formed its own separate pool, see below.

### WHAT IS NOT INCLUDED IN THE POOL

These have separate pools of expenditure:

- cars (but not lorries or vans). If the car costs more than £8,000, it must form its own separate pool

354 · TAX AND THE SOLE TRADER

- anything used partly in your business, partly in your private life

- if you choose, any piece of plant and machinery (but not cars) which you expect to sell or scrap within five years of buying. These are known as short-life assets.

With a short-life asset, for example, tools, you have to choose to put it in a separate pool within two years of buying it. If, when you sell the equipment, you sell it for less than its value after deducting the capital allowances you have claimed on it, you will be able to write off the difference in that year. (This does not happen under the normal tax treatment.) If you sell it for more than the value, the difference will be added to your profit. If you do not sell it in five years, its value will be added to your main pool as if it had never been treated separately.

## WHAT HAPPENS IF YOU MAKE LOSSES

If you have made a loss in your business, what can you do with it to cut your tax bills? If you have been going a number of years, you can:

- set off the loss against other income

- carry the loss forward and set it off against future trading profits from your business.

### SETTING THE LOSS AGAINST OTHER INCOME

You have two choices open to you. Firstly, you can set the loss against any other income you have in the current tax year or you can choose to set the loss against other income you have in the next tax year. If you choose to use the loss in the current tax year, you have to use the loss as a deduction for tax before you can use any other outgoings or allowances you may have. So don't make this choice if you have other deductions to reduce your taxable income to nil or these will be wasted. Instead you can choose to set the loss against other income in the next tax year or against future trading profits.

If you cannot set off all your loss in the current tax year, you can carry forward what's left of the loss and set it against other income in the next tax year.

Your second choice is to set off the loss against other income in the next tax year, skipping the current one. You can do this as long as your business is still going in the next tax year. Whether you make the first or the second choice, if you have any losses which you have not been able to

WHAT HAPPENS IF YOU MAKE LOSSES · 355

use in the next tax year, you can use them against future trading profits from the same business (see below).

Other income could be dividends from shares, earnings from employment, any income of your husband or wife, or profits from your business made in the preceding accounting year (this only applies if you are using the loss in the current tax year). This loss would be set off against your earned income first, unearned (or investment) income second. If your wife or husband has income in the year as well as other income you may have, you can choose to use the loss only against your income and use other outgoings and allowances you may have against the second income.

If you want to use the loss to set against other income, you have to make the choice within two years after the end of the year when the loss occurred.

## SETTING THE LOSS AGAINST FUTURE TRADING PROFITS

If you make this choice, you carry forward the loss and set it against future profits from the same trade. If you have any losses left over, you carry them forward against future profits *ad infinitum*, until they are used up. If you are going to use your loss in this way, you have to use the whole of the loss before you can use any other deductions, such as outgoings or allowances, which you may have. The main disadvantage of making this choice to use your loss relief up is that it takes quite a while to turn it into cash.

If you want to make this choice, you need to do so within six years after the end of the year in which you want the relief.

## IF YOU ARE STARTING A NEW BUSINESS

If you spend money before your business actually starts, it may count as pre-trading expenditure. It will be treated as a loss in your first year of trading, and you can get loss relief.

There is special tax treatment for a loss you make in the first four tax years of a new business (as long as your inspector believes it was reasonable to plan for profits during that period). You can get a tax refund by setting the loss against any other income (for example, wages from a job) which you had in the three years before the loss. Set the loss off against the earliest year of income first, then the next earliest and so on.

If you want to set off your loss in this way, you need to do so within two years after the year when the loss occurred.

## NATIONAL INSURANCE CONTRIBUTIONS

If you are self-employed, you will have to pay Class 2 national insurance contributions (but if your earnings from self-employment are less than a certain amount, £2,125 in 1987–8 you can claim exemption from payment). This is a flat rate contribution of £3.85 a week in 1987–8. You can pay it either by buying a special stamp each week from the Post Office and sticking it on to a contribution card or you can pay by direct debit.

Paying Class 2 contributions entitles you to most contributory benefits, but not unemployment benefit, invalidity pension or widow's benefit.

If your earnings from your business are above a certain amount, £4,590 in 1987–8, you will have to pay Class 4 contributions. These are earnings-related and collected along with your income tax. For example, in 1987–8 you pay 6.3 per cent of the amount by which your profit exceeds the limit, up to £15,340, giving a maximum contribution of £677.25. You get tax relief on half the Class 4 national insurance contributions you pay.

## CAPITAL GAINS TAX

You do not normally pay capital gains tax (CGT) on stock you sell, but you may have to pay it when you dispose of land and buildings, plant and machinery or goodwill. Disposing includes selling, giving away, exchanging or losing. For where to find out more about capital gains tax, see 'Reference' (p. 410).

In general, you pay no CGT on your home if you claim some of the costs of running your home as a business expense because you work from home. But if you use part of your home *only* for business purposes, you pay tax on any gain from that part.

### REPLACING BUSINESS ASSETS

If you sell or otherwise dispose of assets from your business, and make a gain, you could pay capital gains tax on the gain. But if you replace the assets in the three years after the sale or one year before the sale of the old one, you can claim *roll-over relief* and defer paying capital gains tax. You can also claim relief if you do not replace, but use the proceeds to buy another qualifying business asset. You usually get the relief by deducting the gain from the old asset from the acquisition cost for the new one. So, when you sell the new one, the gain on it has been increased by the size of the gain on the old one. However, if you replace again, you can claim further roll-over relief. And so on. Capital gains tax will not have to be paid (under current legislation) until you fail to replace the business asset.

Not every business asset qualifies for the relief. But if it is land or building used by the business, goodwill, fixed plant or machinery, for example, it will qualify for roll-over relief.

## RETIREMENT RELIEF

There are more details of this in Chapter 33. 'Planning for retirement' (p. 396).

## YOU AND YOUR TAX INSPECTOR

### WHEN YOU FIRST START IN BUSINESS

When you start working on your own, tell your local tax office. Look in the telephone directory for Inland Revenue and get the address from there. You will be sent Form 41G to fill in, which asks for things like what is your business name, your business and private address, the nature of your business, the date to which you will be making up your accounts and so on.

If you have finished a job as an employee, you will have Form P45, which should be sent to your tax inspector, so that the amount of your personal allowances and the amount of tax to be paid for that tax year can be sorted out. If you start self-employment part way through the tax year, having been an employee before, you can ask for a refund of part or all of the tax paid under PAYE. This can help with cash flow problems of starting the business.

You also need to contact the Department of Health and Social Security to tell them you have started a business as a self-employed person.

### ONCE YOU HAVE STARTED IN BUSINESS

Once you have been going nearly a year, your tax inspector will ask you for your accounts for your first accounting period. If you can do so, you should send these in. If you have decided that your accounting year end is not going to coincide with the anniversary of starting in business, you will not be able to produce accounts for your first trading period. In this case, your tax inspector will have to assess you and produce a figure for estimated profits. On the assessment form, there will be an 'E' beside the figure for profits.

You will receive two assessments at the end of the first year of trading, one for each of the first two tax years. If you do not agree with the assessments, you should appeal against them and apply to postpone payment (p. 360).

## LINES OF COMMUNICATION WITH YOUR TAX INSPECTOR

You are required by law to make a true return of your income, including profits from your business, each year. There are several formal and informal lines of communication with your tax inspector (and there is an example at the end of the section on p. 362). These are:

### Assessments

After the first year, you will receive an assessment for each tax year, which will arrive through your letter-box normally in the autumn. Even if your tax inspector knows the level of profits you have earned, this assessment may still be estimated.

You may receive a further estimated assessment for that tax year at a later stage, especially if your tax inspector does not think you have given the information needed to produce an accurate final assessment.

After the end of the tax year, you will receive a final assessment. Any further and final assessments are made on a slightly different form from the first assessment for that tax year. The example in the box on the right explains the entries.

### Your tax return

You will receive a tax return to fill in at the start of the tax year in April. Part of the tax return (income and outgoings) refers to the last tax year and part refers to the current tax year (allowances). The tax return to be filled in by men and single women who are self-employed is Form 11.

In the return, you enter the figure for income which will be assessed for the last tax year (it can sometimes be tricky to sort out which this refers to, see p. 344). You also put the figure for deductions and outgoings which you are claiming in that tax year. Depending on the accounting year-end you have chosen, these allowances and deductions may be for a different accounting period than the income you are going to be assessed on – see the example on p. 361.

Be careful not to miss out simple figures, like National Savings interest, from your tax return. It is this sort of omission which can prompt your tax inspector to launch an investigation into your affairs.

If you are a self-employed married woman, communication with your tax inspector is considerably hampered by the fact that you do not personally have to fill in a tax return, that all assessments of profits are made in your husband's name and very often correspondence is in your

*Example: A Notice of Assessment*

Peter Farrow checks his Schedule D assessment for 1987–8.

1. Part 1 shows the amount of tax payable according to this assessment. It gives the payments due in each instalment. In a note below, Peter can see when he is supposed to pay each instalment.

Under Part 1 is a calculation to show how the Class 4 NIC is worked out.

2. Part 2 shows the calculations made by Peter's tax inspector to arrive at a figure for tax and Class 4 contribution payable.

First, the assessment gives where the profits come from which are included in this assessment. In Peter's case, from his business as a taxi service. The amount of profits is included in the column. In Peter's case, there is an 'E' before it. This means the inspector has estimated the amount, because the information needed from Peter has not yet been sent.

Under Deductions, there are the figures for Peter's personal pension payments, capital allowances and half the amount of Class 4 contributions due.

Under Allowances, the personal allowances to which Peter is entitled are included, in this case, married man's allowance.

The heading, NET AMOUNT CHARGEABLE TO TAX, shows the amount which tax will be calculated on. In Peter's case, this is at the basic rate only.

3. Part 3 would show what rates of tax would have been charged on the income.

husband's name, too. An additional problem is caused by the fact that tax on your business, even though in your husband's name, will be dealt with by a different tax office from your husband's income. If you have opted to be taxed separately (you and your husband need to be earning jointly at least £26,870 in the 1987–8 tax year before you should consider this), information on your husband's tax return does not normally filter through to your tax inspector.

Nevertheless, it is your responsibility to make sure that your tax inspector has the correct information to produce a correct tax bill. If you suspect that information from your husband's tax return does not get through to the tax office dealing with your business' tax affairs, send in what you think the tax computations for the year should be. This should include a statement showing the income assessable, less deductions allowable and any personal allowances or outgoings you think should be deducted from your income. A list of fixed assets with an analysis of the capital allowances claimed during the year would also be advisable.

## Your accounts
At the end of each accounting period, once your accounts have been finalized, send in a copy to your tax inspector. Your accounts should consist of a profit and loss account, giving details of expenses deducted, and, preferably, a balance sheet. You are not required by law to produce a balance sheet, nor do you have to have your accounts audited. However, both of these are helpful in your dealings with your tax inspector and should be considered.

You may need to back up your figures with your records if they are queried by your tax inspector, so keep your records well (p. 331).

## Other helpful communication
There are some steps you can take to mitigate the chance of misunderstanding between you and your tax inspector, which might lead to your business accounts being investigated (see p. 362 for what happens).

1. Your tax inspector will review all the business accounts sent in and one of the factors examined will be gross profit margin (see p. 299 for what this is). If your gross profit margin is very different from the typical one for your sort of business, your accounts may be chosen for investigation. If you know that your profit margin is lower than others, send in a note with your accounts explaining why this is so.

2. If the income you take out of the business is very low, because, for example, you are living on savings, explain this to your tax inspector.

3. If you have made a loss in your business, explain it.

## APPEALING AGAINST AN ASSESSMENT
You have thirty days from the date on an assessment to appeal against it. If you do not appeal, you cannot alter the assessment at a later date. You

*Example: Filling in a tax return*

---

Althea Adams is filling in her 1987–8 tax return. Despite its name, the tax return deals with two years. Althea has to put in her income, deductions, outgoings and capital gains for the 1986–7 tax year. She also has to put in the personal allowances she is claiming for the 1987–8 tax year.

Althea's business has been running a number of years and the accounting year end is 30 June. Her tax bill will be calculated on a preceding year basis (p. 345). This means she pays tax on the income she earns in the accounting year ending in the preceding tax year. For this tax return she is asked to put in the income to be assessed for the 1987–8 tax year. This is the income for the accounting year ending in the preceding tax year, 1986–7. This refers to the accounting year ending on 30 June 1986. So Althea enters the figure for income she earned in her accounting year running from 1 July 1985 until 30 June 1986.

Althea also has to enter the deductions she is claiming for the 1986–7 tax year. She enters the figure for capital allowances for equipment she bought during her accounting year ending 30 June 1986. When it comes to outgoings such as tax relief on mortgage interest and personal pension payments, she enters the figures for payments during the 1986–7 tax year.

---

must write to the Inspector saying why you are appealing (you may be sent a form with the assessment which you can use, which would be the best way, or you can simply write a letter).

If you cannot appeal within thirty days, because, for example, you are away on holiday, write as soon as you can explaining why you are late. If your appeal is not allowed you can ask to go before the General Commissioners to make a late appeal.

When you appeal you should also ask to postpone paying the tax on the assessment. If you do not, you still have to pay it by the normal due date, even if you are appealing against the size of it. Even if you apply for postponement, unless you apply for all of the tax, you will have to pay the amount you are not applying to postpone on the due date.

Once you have agreed with your inspector, any tax due is payable within thirty days of the date of the revised assessment, or the normal due date, if this is later. If you applied for postponement, and subsequently

*Example: Communication with the tax inspector*

William Jones has an accounting year which ends on 31 December. During 1987, he has the following communications with his tax inspector:

1. His accounts for the accounting period 1 January 1986 to 31 December 1986 are finalized in March 1987. He sends a copy of his accounts to his tax inspector.

2. He receives his 1987–8 tax return in April, which asks for information about his income in 1986–7. In William's case this refers to his income in his accounting period 1 January 1986 to 31 December 1986.

3. He returns his tax return in May.

4. His tax inspector works out a final assessment for the tax year 1986–7 and sends it to William in August (this is somewhat later than normal). He studies it carefully and agrees to it. If he did not he should appeal against it and apply to postpone payment within thirty days of receiving it. As William owes some extra tax, this is due within thirty days of receiving the assessment.

5. In September, he receives an assessment for the tax year 1987–8, based on the accounts he sent in during March 1987 and the 1987–8 tax return. He must appeal within thirty days if he wishes to do so. Otherwise, half the tax bill is due on 1 January 1988 and the other half on 1 July 1988.

agree that the tax should be paid, you can be charged *interest*. So do not make any frivolous appeals and applications for postponement.

If you cannot agree with your inspector, it is not necessarily the end of the matter – you can go to the Commissioners. But this is a big step to take and needs careful contemplation.

BEING INVESTIGATED

If you have been selected for investigation, probably the first thing that will happen is that your tax inspector will write to you asking some detailed questions about your accounts. The inspector may subsequently request an interview.

The purpose of the interview will probably be to establish:

- why your business, and hence profits, are different from other similar businesses

- whether you have correctly calculated adjustments for tax purposes

- if the amount shown for what you have taken out of the business seems adequate to support your lifestyle. You may need to work out an estimate for your living expenses, for example, general household expenses, as well as leisure expenditure and so on.

If the inspector is satisfied with your records and explanation, there will probably be a fairly minor adjustment to your accounts. However, if a more serious view is taken, you may find that your figures for profit for this and previous years are increased.

With small adjustments to your profit, you pay the extra to the tax collector as usual. In more serious cases, you may have to pay interest and even a penalty.

DO YOU COUNT AS SELF-EMPLOYED?

It may be obvious that you are self-employed, but sometimes it is not clear-cut. You cannot simply declare yourself self-employed; you will have to convince your tax inspector that you are. The sort of points which will help are:

1. working for more than one customer

2. showing that you control what you do, whether you do it, how you do it and when and where you do it

3. providing the major items of equipment you need to do your job

4. being free to hire other people, on terms of your own choice, to do the work that you have agreed to undertake

5. correcting unsatisfactory work in your own time and at your own expense.

If you do the above, there will probably be little difficulty in persuading an inspector that you are self-employed.

## SUMMARY

1. Choose an accounting year-end which will give the greatest delay between earning the profits and paying the tax, but only if you expect profits to rise year by year.

2. If you expect your first accounting period when you start business to have low profits, it could pay you to make your first accounting period longer than a year.

3. Remember to claim all your business expenses. Where possible get invoices and receipts to back-up your claims.

4. If you use your car partly for business, you can claim part of your car expenses (and capital allowances). If you work from home, you can claim part of the running expenses, but watch out for CGT.

5. Consider employing your wife in your business. You can pay up to the amount of the NI contribution limit without paying tax or contributions.

6. If you take assets into your business when you set up, don't forget you can claim capital allowances on them.

7. Try to cut down the risk of being investigated by your tax inspector. For example, do not omit items from your tax return, such as bank interest. If you know your profit margin is lower than others in the same business, or if you make a loss, explain why.

8. If you do not agree with your assessment, do not delay. Appeal against it and apply for postponement of the extra tax within thirty days of the date on the assessment.

# 29. TAX AND THE PARTNERSHIP

The partnership tax rules can lead to some very strange results; this arises because you and your tax inspector use different rules for dividing the profits between partners. However, you can help to mitigate its oddities by making clear agreement with your partner on how to divide up the tax bill. You should also plan ahead to allow for tax difficulties if the partnership changes.

WHAT IS IN THIS CHAPTER?

• How your partnership tax bill is worked out (see below)

• What happens when the partnership changes? (p. 367)

• What happens if the partnership makes a loss? (p. 369)

## HOW YOUR PARTNERSHIP TAX BILL IS WORKED OUT

WHAT IS THE TAXABLE INCOME?

The taxable income for your partnership is worked out in much the same way as if you were working on your own and taxed as a sole trader. From your sales figure, you can deduct business expenses which are allowable for tax purposes (p. 348). Your partnership can get tax relief on capital expenditure (capital allowances, see p. 351), tax relief on half the Class 4 national insurance contributions (p. 356) and tax relief for losses (p. 354).

Once your partnership has been in existence for two or three years, you pay tax for any tax year on profits earned in your accounting year ending in the preceding tax year. So, for example, if your partnership accounting year ends on 30 June 1987, your partnership will pay tax on the profits from that year in the tax year 1988–9. This is known as being taxed on a preceding year basis. The advantages of this are spelt out on p. 344.

The tax bill for the opening and closing years of business of your partnership is worked out in the same way as for a sole trader (p. 345).

If your partnership has any non-trading income, such as interest, this will not be included in the taxable profits of the partnership, but taxed as investment income. In practice, partnership investment income is normally allocated in the same ratio as the profit share and each individual partner is given a tax bill for the investment income. Any capital gains of the partnership will be subject to capital gains tax.

If a partner has other income or gains which do not come as a result of the partnership, the partner will be taxed on these as an individual in the normal way.

## WHO PAYS WHAT TAX?

This is where the tricky bit starts. It works like this:

● if your partner does not pay his or her share of the partnership tax bill as worked out by your tax inspector, you can be forced to pay it instead. This is because all partners are jointly and severally liable for all the tax on the profits from the partnership *but*

● this does not apply to a capital gains tax bill or tax bill for non-trading income for the partnership. For these each of you is responsible for your share of the bill. If your partner does not pay up, you do not have to stump up the extra money

● the size of the tax bill depends on the rates of tax each of the partners pays. If one of you has large income from some other source and pays tax at a higher rate, 50 per cent for example, part of the profits of your partnership will in all likelihood be taxed at that higher rate. So, if the partnership profits are £6,000 and you and your partner are sharing them in a 1:1 ratio, ignoring any outgoings or allowances which each partner may claim, your partnership tax bill will be £3,000 at 27 per cent plus £3,000 at 50 per cent. This comes to £810 plus £1,500 = £2,310

● your tax inspector will share out the profits (and tax) for the partnership in any tax year by finding out how you and your partner are sharing the profits for that same tax year. But you and your tax inspector are talking about a different set of profits, because your partnership will normally be taxed on a preceding year basis. This gives partnership tax its Alice in Wonderland appearance

● however, you and your partner can agree to pay your tax bill in any proportion you like. How your partnership tax bill is worked out by your tax inspector does not mean that this is what you each should pay, if you have agreed otherwise.

*Example*

Wayne and Sharon are partners. In the 1986–7 tax year, they agree to split the profits on a 1:1 basis. But the tax inspector is using the profits earned in the tax year before to work out the tax bill for 1986–7. And in the year before Wayne and Sharon had not shared the profits equally – Wayne had 25 per cent and Sharon 75 per cent of the £20,000 profits.

In the 1986–7 tax year, Sharon pays tax on the last part of her income at a rate of 40 per cent while Wayne pays it at 29 per cent (they both have other incomes). So the tax on the £20,000 profits is calculated as follows:

|  | WAYNE | SHARON |
|---|---|---|
| Profits received 1985–6 | £5,000 | £15,000 |
| Share of profits to be taxed in 1986–7 | 50% | 50% |
| For tax bill 1986–7, share of £20,000 profits | £10,000 | £10,000 |
| Tax rate | 29% | 40% |
| Tax | £2,900 | £4,000 |

This distribution of tax is obviously inequitable. Sharon would pay tax of £4,000, having had profits of £15,000 and Wayne would pay tax of £2,900 on profits of only £5,000. Wayne and Sharon may come to some other agreed distribution of the tax bill.

## WHAT HAPPENS WHEN THE PARTNERSHIP CHANGES?

If a partner leaves or joins, the partnership counts as automatically coming to an end unless:

● all of the partners before the change and all of the partners after the change agree that it should continue (known as continuation election) *and*

● at least one of the partners before the change continues to be a partner after the change

A continuation election needs to be made in writing to your tax inspector within two years of the change.

## IF A CONTINUATION ELECTION IS MADE

The tax bill is calculated in the same way as if there had been no change, that is, the tax bill is based on the preceding year basis (p. 345). This means that the tax bill will be shared out by your tax inspector between different people from those who actually got the profits. It is easiest to see using an example.

*Example*

In the 1986–7 tax year, Wayne and Sharon made profits of £24,000 which were split equally between them. They decide to take in a third partner, Jenny, and their agreed share of the profits in the next year will be 40 per cent Wayne, 40 per cent Sharon and 20 per cent Jenny. The tax inspector works out the tax bill for 1987–8 as follows:

|  | WAYNE | SHARON | JENNY |
|---|---|---|---|
| Share of 1986–7 profits | £12,000 | £12,000 | none |
| Share of 1987–8 profits to be | 40% | 40% | 20% |
| For tax bill 1987–8, share of £24,000 profits | £9,600 | £9,600 | £4,800 |
| Tax rate | 27% | 40% | 27% |
| Tax bill | £2,592 | £3,840 | £1,296 |

So the tax inspector hands Jenny a bill for £1,296 on profits she did not earn. Wayne, Sharon and Jenny could agree to a different division for paying the partnership tax bill, although Jenny is still responsible for paying it.

This example assumes that the partnership changes at the start of the tax year. If the partnership changes on another date the tax inspector would apportion the profits on a time basis.

## IF A PARTNERSHIP CEASES

If a partnership comes to an end, and no continuation election is signed, although it was possible for there to be one, this is what happens: broadly, in the year of the change and in the following three tax years, tax will be charged on a current year basis.

This means it is based on the actual profits earned each year. In years five and six, there is a choice of being taxed on an actual or preceding year basis; the partners can make the choice. With a partnership in which the profits are rising year by year, it would be an advantage to pay tax on a preceding year basis. If this is likely to happen, you should carefully consider making a continuation election, so that the partnership does not come to an end and the new partnership is not taxed on a current year basis.

However, the above rule does not apply if you were a sole trader before the change and partnership after; nor does it apply if you were a partnership before, but a sole trader after.

## WHAT HAPPENS IF THE PARTNERSHIP MAKES A LOSS?

Losses can be treated in much the same way as if you were a sole trader (p. 354). You and your partners share the losses on the same basis as you would share any profits; the losses are apportioned on the basis applying in the year in which they arise. You cannot carry back losses if the partnership continues.

You can each treat your losses as you want. One of you can set it off against other income, while the other can carry it forward and set it off against future partnership profits.

If you are a limited partner, the amount of loss you can set against other income will be limited broadly to the amount of capital you have contributed to the business.

## SUMMARY

1. The tax bill for your partnership is worked out in much the same way as if you were a sole trader.

2. The division of the tax bill can appear odd; it would be advisable to have a clear agreement on who pays what tax.

3. It might make sense for you and your partners to agree that if, in the future, one of you leaves or a new partner joins that you will sign a continuation election. This means for tax purposes the partnership continues. This would be an advantage if profits from your partnership are rising year by year.

4. If your partner does not pay his or her share of the partnership tax bill, you will have to dig deep into your pocket to fill the gap.

# 30. TAX AND THE LIMITED COMPANY

The first thing to note about the tax for a limited company is that it has a different name from the tax you pay as an individual or partner; it is called corporation tax. Corporation tax replaces both income tax and capital gains tax for a limited company. There are other differences; when you pay the tax and how you should pay yourself are not the same as if your business was organized as a sole trader or partnership. But there are some similarities, too. The way the amount of income and gains is worked out, but not taxed, is much the same, and money spent on capital equipment is dealt with in the same manner.

This chapter looks at how the taxable profits of a company are worked out, how the size of the tax bill is determined and what happens to losses. It gives brief details of a close company and some advice on how to pay yourself, if you are the owner.

The chapter can give only a very brief outline of corporation tax; further reading is given in 'Reference' (p. 410).

## HOW TAXABLE PROFITS ARE WORKED OUT

The taxable profits of a company include:

- trading income

- capital gains (called chargeable gains)

- some investment income, such as rents or interest (including the amount of any tax deducted before your company receives it)
*but not*
- dividends and distributions you get from UK companies.

Once you have arrived at a figure for taxable profits, there are some charges you can deduct before the tax bill is worked out; these do not apply in many cases and include things like royalty payments and some interest paid, on which you have already deducted income tax before paying them.

## HOW TRADING INCOME IS WORKED OUT

Trading income is worked out in the same way as if you were a sole trader. You take the figure for profit which you have derived from your normal accounting procedure and make several adjustments to arrive at a figure for taxable profits:

• add back any business expenses which are not allowable for tax and deduct any which are; see the list on p. 349

• add back the figure for depreciation and deduct the amount of capital allowances; see p. 351

• deduct what you can for loss relief; see p. 372.

## HOW CAPITAL GAINS ARE WORKED OUT

A company has to include in its taxable profits the figure for net taxable gains. You may have a gain if you dispose of something (a chargeable asset) for more than you originally paid for it. However, you may be able to deduct an indexation allowance, which allows for the effect of inflation.

The amount of the gain is worked out in the same way as an individual. You take the cost and anything you have spent on it, either buying it, improving it or disposing of it, and deduct this from what you have sold it for, or its market value. If this leaves you with a gain, you can deduct what you are allowed to by the tax laws to compensate for the effect of inflation. Finally, you can set off any gain you are still left with against any losses of the same period or prior periods which you have incurred.

You have to add the figure for net taxable gains (that is, after the deductions you can make) to your taxable profits. There is no yearly amount allowed which is free of tax, as there would be if you were a sole trader (£6,600 in the 1987–8 tax year).

This is a very brief outline of how capital (or chargeable) gains are taxed. For further reading see 'Reference' (p. 410).

## HOW INVESTMENT INCOME IS WORKED OUT

If you receive interest or rents, which have already had basic rate tax, or its equivalent, deducted, the amount you include in taxable profits is the gross amount, that is, the amount of the interest plus the amount of basic rate tax.

The income tax which has already been paid will be used to reduce your corporation tax bill. If the amount of corporation tax to be paid is less than the income tax, the excess income tax paid will be reimbursed.

If you receive dividends from a UK-resident company, these will already have had corporation tax paid (called advance corporation tax or ACT (p. 374)). The dividends are paid along with a tax credit attached. This sort of investment income is called *franked investment income*; you do not have to include this when you work out taxable profits, because corporation tax is not due on it.

The tax credit you receive with franked investment income is not automatically repayable; but you can use it to offset advance corporation tax which is payable on dividends *your* company pays. This is called franking your dividend payments.

Note that the amount of franked investment income is the sum of the distributions or dividends you receive plus the tax credit.

### THE ACCOUNTING YEAR

Corporation tax is payable on the actual profits of an accounting period. If your company makes up its accounts every twelve months, the accounting period is a twelve month one. If your company makes up its accounts for less than twelve months, that period is still an accounting period. If your company makes up its accounts over a longer time – eighteen months, for example – the time will be split into two accounting periods, an accounting period of twelve months and one of six months.

## WHAT HAPPENS TO LOSSES

Trading losses are worked out in the same way as trading profits. You have several choices about what you can do with them:

- set the loss off against current profits
- carry the loss back against earlier profits
- carry forward the loss against future profits
- set the loss off against franked investment income.

### SETTING THE LOSS AGAINST CURRENT PROFITS

A trading loss, calculated after deducting any capital allowances, can be set against any profits of the same accounting period. Other profits include other income or chargeable gains. This relief only applies if the company is carrying on a commercial business intending to make profits.

WHAT HAPPENS TO LOSSES · 373

If you want to claim this loss relief it needs to be done within two years after the end of the accounting period of loss.

## CARRY BACK THE LOSSES AGAINST PREVIOUS PROFITS

After setting the loss against current profits, any left over can be carried back and set against profits for a previous period of the same length as the accounting period of the loss. This only applies if that particular trade was being carried on in the previous period, although the loss can be set off against any profits.

If you want to claim this loss relief it needs to be done within two years after the end of the accounting period of loss. You need to be carrying on your business in a commercial manner with a view to making profit.

If the loss includes first year allowances you have claimed, you can carry back that part of the loss for three years.

## CARRY FORWARD THE LOSS

Any loss still not set off can be carried forward and set against future trading profits of the same trade; there is no time limit for this relief. If you choose this relief, you have to do so within six years after the end of the accounting period in which you had the loss.

## SETTING THE LOSS OFF AGAINST FRANKED INVESTMENT INCOME

If you have exhausted other possibilities for setting off losses against current or past profits, you can set off losses against franked investment income, unless it has already been used to offset advanced corporation tax on dividends. If you have not, you can get a refund of basic rate tax on the franked investment income, rather than carry forward the loss to set against future trading profits.

If you choose this relief, you have to do so within two years after the end of the accounting period in which you make the loss.

## IF YOU CLOSE YOUR BUSINESS, WHAT CAN YOU DO WITH THE LOSSES?

If you cease trading because of losses, you can carry the loss sustained in the last twelve months back against trading profits for the preceding three years. You can only get this relief if the loss cannot be set off in any other way. The order in which you can set off losses for the final period of trading is:

1. against profits of current accounting period
2. against profits of the previous accounting period

3. if any of the loss has not been set off under 1. and 2., against the trading profits of the previous three years.

You have to choose this relief within six years of stopping that trade.

## THE TAX YOU PAY

The rate of corporation tax is fixed for each fiscal year, which runs from 1 April to 31 March the following calendar year. If your accounting year does not coincide with the tax year, profits will have to be apportioned on a time basis between the two tax years, if the rate of corporation tax changes from one tax year to the next.

For tax year 1987, if profits are £100,000 or less, the rate of corporation tax on trading income is 27 per cent. This is known as the small companies' rate. Firms with higher profits will pay a higher rate of tax.

### ADVANCE CORPORATION TAX

If your company pays dividends, you will discover that you have to pay some corporation tax at the same time. This is known as *advance corporation tax* (ACT). The current amount of ACT is as follows:

$$\text{dividend} \times 27/73.$$

So, for example, if the dividend is £500, the amount of ACT is £500 × 27/73 = £184.93. The dividend is paid with a tax credit for this amount, £184.93. The shareholders use this in their own income tax calculations, and no more basic rate is payable on the dividend. Higher rate tax will be due.

If your company receives franked investment income (p. 372), you can pay dividends out of this and no ACT will be payable, but your shareholders will still get the tax credit. If the dividend is paid partly out of other dividends received, the ACT is reduced in proportion.

When it comes to working out the full corporation tax bill, after the accounting period, you can set off the amount of ACT you have paid, subject to certain restrictions. If you cannot set it all off, because of the size of your corporation tax bill, any surplus ACT can be carried back and set off against the tax bills for the six previous accounting years. You start with the latest period first. Any excess remaining is then carried forward.

### WHEN ARE THE TAXES PAID

Tax is worked out on a current year basis and is payable nine months after the end of the accounting year or thirty days from the date on the Notice of Assessment, whichever is later. If you appeal against an assessment, but do not ask for a postponement of payment, tax is due at the normal times. If you have asked for a postponement, the amount postponed will be due as above or, if later, within thirty days of the date on the notice issued once the appeal and the amount of tax payable is settled.

If the tax payment is overdue, interest may be payable. The rate of interest is currently 9 per cent. If the amount of the interest is £30 or less, it will normally not be charged.

RATE OF TAX ON GAINS

The small companies rate is charged on the trading income, not the chargeable gains. These pay tax at the full corporation tax rate – currently 35 per cent. The amount of the gain, however, is adjusted to make sure the amount of tax paid on the gains is not more than 30 per cent. The gains are adjusted by what is known as the capital gains reducing fraction. For the tax year 1987, the fraction is 1/7.

*Example*

| | | |
|---|---|---|
| Millicent Mounts Ltd has trading income of £50,000 and a capital (or chargeable) gain of £10,000. Corporation tax payable is: | | |
| Trading income £50,000 at 27 per cent (small companies rate) | | £13,500 |
| Chargeable gain: | | |
| £10,000 | | |
| less 1/7     1,428 | | |
| £ 8,572     at 35 per cent | | 3,000 |
| In total | | £16,500 |

## CLOSE COMPANIES

If there are five (or fewer) people controlling a company or it is controlled by its directors, it is likely to be a close company. The definition of who controls a company broadly means its shareholders and their family, their partners and the like.

If you receive fringe benefits, like living accommodation, loans or entertainment, and you are one of the people controlling the company (but you are not a director paid under Schedule E as an employee), the benefit might count as a distribution of the company and be taxed.

One advantage of a close company is that if you borrow money to buy ordinary shares in the company or to make it a loan, your interest may be eligible for tax relief. To get the relief, the rules are broadly that you must either own more than 5 per cent of its shares, or own some shares and work for the greater part of your time for the company.

## PAYING YOURSELF (and your family)

SALARY

If you are trying to minimize the total tax bill which you and your company will face, the ideal salary to pay yourself is the amount at which the tax rate on your salary is equal to the tax rate on the company's profits. In the 1987–8 tax year, this means a taxable income of up to £17,900; the salary level will be somewhat higher as you will get tax relief through personal allowances and outgoings. Above that level of taxable income, the rate rises to 40 per cent, which is higher than the small companies' rate of corporation tax (27 per cent). Whether you will pay yourself this sort of salary depends on what you need to give yourself an adequate standard of living.

In general, your company is free to pay whatever wages you and the directors want. This includes wages paid to members of your family, if they work in your company. However, the wages paid may not be regarded as an allowable expense for tax purposes by your tax inspector, if he regards the wages or salary as excessive in relation to the value of the work done.

For tax purposes, your income during a tax year is what you have earned rather than what you have been paid. Once you become a director, you may find that your tax inspector will not finalize your tax bill for the year until a copy of the accounts for the accounting periods covered by the tax year has been presented. Because of this your tax bill may not be finally known to you until quite a long time after the end of the tax year.

The tax inspector wants to see the accounts to check what has been voted as payment to you, for example, bonuses or commission, as well as salary. In your first year as a director, you will be taxed on what you earned during the period; if necessary, your earnings will be apportioned to tax years. After that, you may choose to be taxed on what you earned during the accounting period ending in the tax year. This may be beneficial if your earnings are rising each year.

## FRINGE BENEFITS

Providing fringe benefits rather than salary can be very tax effective. The tax system treats some fringe benefits favourably compared with a rise in salary. Some fringe benefits are tax-free to you or your family if you are employees of the company. These include pension contributions paid by the company, life insurance, the cost of an insurance which would pay out an income if you could not work through illness, cheap or free drinks (tea or coffee, for example) and meals.

Some fringe benefits are taxed only if you are treated as higher-paid. This means for tax purposes earning at a rate of £8,500 or more a year, including any fringe benefits valued as though you were higher-paid. If you are a director, you normally count as higher-paid, no matter what you earn. If you are treated as higher-paid, you are normally taxed as an individual on the amount your fringe benefits cost your company to provide, less anything you pay as an employee towards the cost.

One exception to this way of valuing a fringe benefit is a company car. With a car, the taxable value is set each year. These taxable values are much less than the value of the benefit to you as an employee. For example, the taxable value of a new 1.3-litre car is £525 for the 1987–8 tax year. The value to you could be more like £2,500 to £3,000.

## DIVIDENDS

From a tax point of view, it makes no difference to you as owner of a company whether you receive income from the company as salary or as dividends. But:

• national insurance contributions, which both you and the company pay, are not affected by the amount of dividends you receive, whereas level of salary does affect them

• receiving dividends means paying higher-rate tax at a later date than the tax paid on a salary as a PAYE employee

• if both husband and wife are shareholders in the business, paying dividends could be a drawback. A wife's investment income is aggregated with her husband's, whereas earned income (that is, salary) can be taxed separately

• where there is no company scheme, the amount you can put into a pension is set by the level of what is called relevant earnings; dividends do not count for pension purposes

378 · TAX AND THE LIMITED COMPANY

• paying dividends should not be considered unless the company will be paying corporation tax at the level necessary to cover ACT (advanced corporation tax) payable on dividends. If there are no profits this year, there may have been some last year in which case ACT can be recovered against the corporation tax paid. ACT can be carried back six years.

## SUMMARY

1. Work out profits and losses in the same way as for a sole trader.

2. Corporation tax is payable on all profits, including capital gains, not just trading profits.

3. A company does not get the yearly tax-free limit on gains which an individual does.

4. Do not forget that fringe benefits are a tax-effective way of remunerating yourself as a director.

5. If both husband and wife are in the business, pay the wife a salary rather than dividends.

6. Do not pay yourself dividends unless the company is paying enough corporation tax in this or previous years to cover ACT on the dividends.

# 31. TAX ON SPARE-TIME EARNINGS

There is no quick answer to the question of how you will be taxed if you have spare-time earnings. It will depend mainly on whether your income counts as starting a business. You could find yourself in a dilemma as to how your spare-time earnings will be taxed, if:

• you are still employed but earning some extra money in your spare-time. You might be doing this either because you have started your business in a small way to see how it goes before you take the plunge and hand in your notice; or because you are doing the occasional bit of freelance work to boost your income

• you are not employed, but you are starting your business on a part-time basis. This could be the case if you are at home looking after young children, for example.

Some people who earn extra income in this way hope that they will be able to keep it out of the clutches of the taxman. Very often they ask for payment in cash. In the section THE BLACK ECONOMY (p. 383), you will see how the taxman can catch you and what the penalties are if he does.

## WHAT YOU MUST DO WHEN YOU GET SPARE-TIME EARNINGS

By law, you must notify your tax inspector when you get income from a new source. You must do this within twelve months of the end of the tax year in which the income first arose. The onus is on you to tell your tax inspector and you cannot plead as an excuse that you did not receive a tax return. Nor does it make any difference whether you are making a profit or a loss; what matters is that you are receiving payments from a new source which your inspector does not know about. If you do not tell your tax inspector about a new source of income, you can be charged a penalty of up to £100.

# IF YOU COUNT AS SELF-EMPLOYED

## WHY IT IS BETTER TO BE TAXED IN THIS WAY

It is definitely worth your while to spend a little time in planning how to convince your tax inspector that, for your spare-time earnings, you are self-employed and seriously starting a business, rather than earning the occasional bit of money. If he accepts that you have started a business, any earnings from your business will be taxed on a preceding year basis once your business has been going a couple of years or so, that is, your tax bill will be based on the profits you made in the accounting year ending in the preceding tax year. This is an advantage if the earnings from your business increase, as it means you will be paying tax based on the lower profits earned earlier.

For most people, there will be no difficulty in establishing that you are running a business. A problem may occur if your work is consultancy or writing, for example, but see below for the sort of evidence that will influence your tax inspector when he assesses whether you are self-employed.

## HOW YOU WILL BE TAXED

If your tax inspector accepts that you are self-employed, you will be taxed as described in Chapter 28. 'Tax and the sole trader' (p. 343) for the earnings which you get from your business.

## THINGS TO DO TO INFLUENCE THE TAXMAN'S DECISION

**1.** Describe your activities as a business or profession.

**2.** Do not describe your income as 'occasional' or 'casual'.

**3.** Let your tax inspector know that you believe your sales will repeat and grow.

**4.** Register for VAT, if you consider it appropriate (see Chapter 32. 'VAT' (p. 384) for more details).

**5.** Get headed notepaper for your correspondence.

**6.** Be careful if your business is writing or consultancy. Explain to your tax inspector why you regard it as a business, for example, because your work covers other aspects such as research and collation of information or because you carry out your profession or vocation on a regular basis.

**7.** Keep your accounting records carefully and on a business-like basis.

## IF YOUR INCOME COUNTS AS CASUAL

### WHY YOU DO NOT WANT TO BE TAXED IN THIS WAY

Try to dissuade your tax inspector from reaching the decision that your income is occasional or irregular and does not amount to a business or profession as this has some disadvantages.

First, you may find your income is taxed on a current year basis. This means that your tax bill for any tax year is based on the income due to you in that tax year (technically, the income is taxed under Schedule D Case VI).

The second disadvantage is that the treatment of losses is less favourable than if you are taxed as being self-employed. If you make a loss it can only be set against certain profits taxed in the same way, made either in the same tax year or in the future. It cannot be set against any other income you have, for example, from your job if you have one.

Finally, if your income is taxed in this way, it may be regarded as investment income. In theory, if you are a married woman, the income will count as your husband's for tax purposes and you may not be able to set the wife's earned income allowance against it. In practice, your tax inspector may let you do so.

### HOW YOU WILL BE TAXED

If your inspector decides your income is casual, you may find that your earnings are being taxed on a current year basis, which means you will be paying tax on the actual earnings you make in the tax year.

In practice, if you make the earnings on a regular basis, for example, letting furnished accommodation, your tax inspector will often work out your tax bill on what you earned in the last tax year.

If you have expenses which you necessarily incurred in getting the income, you can deduct them when working out your tax bill, which will be based on your profits or gains. The tax is due on 1 January of the tax year or thirty days after the assessment is received, if this is later.

## IF YOUR BUSINESS IS TO DO WITH PROPERTY

The tax treatment of this income is outside the scope of this book and only brief details can be given here. The Inland Revenue publish a leaflet IR27 *Notes on the taxation of income from real property* and you can get this from your local tax office.

IF YOU RUN A HOTEL OR GUEST HOUSE

Your income will normally count as earnings from self-employment and be taxed on a preceding year basis.

IF YOU LET FURNISHED PROPERTY

Your income is normally treated as investment income and taxed on a current year basis. But if the property (including caravans) is let as furnished holiday accommodation for part of the year the income will be treated as earned income. This means, for example, that you will be able to get tax relief on these earnings for pension payments (p. 398) and you can get capital allowances for what you spend on equipment you buy and use in your letting (p. 351).

To qualify to be treated as earned income the property must be available for letting to the general public at a commercial rent for at least 140 days in the tax year. It must also be let out as living accommodation for at least seventy of those days and not normally occupied by the same tenant for more than thirty-one days at a stretch during a seven-month period.

Your tax bill for earnings from holiday lettings will be worked out on a current year basis and be due in two lumps – on 1 January and 1 July.

If your business is letting furnished caravans for holidays, your earnings could be taxed on a preceding year basis, if your tax inspector accepts that you are operating a business.

IF YOU OWN LAND OR UNFURNISHED PROPERTY

The income from land or unfurnished property is normally treated as investment income and taxed on a current year basis. The income which is taxable is usually the income you are entitled to receive in a tax year, rather than what you actually do receive. You can deduct certain expenses, including rates, water rates, ground rent, normal repairs and decoration, insurance costs and so on. If you let only part of your home, or let it for only part of each year, you and the taxman will have to agree on the proportion you can claim. You cannot claim anything for your own time.

WHY YOU MIGHT NOT WANT TO BE TAXED AS A BUSINESS

If you are selling some piece of property, such as a house which is not your only or main residence, it would be preferable if it were taxed as a capital gain rather than as income because the tax bill will be lower. Whether any profit will be treated as a capital gain or as income from a trade will depend on several factors. These include how long you have owned the property, whether you have carried out similar deals, why you are selling it and if your motive is to make a profit.

## THE BLACK ECONOMY

It is illegal to try to conceal any earnings from your tax inspector. The taxman has various ways he can discover that you are earning money. Employers who make use of freelance staff, such as consultants, writers, caterers and so on, can be made to give details to the Inland Revenue of the payments made. There is also a department in the Inland Revenue which keeps an eye on advertisements in the press to make sure that any source of income has been declared. And if you annoy any neighbours, acquaintances or customers who suspect what you are doing, you also run the risk that they might inform on you to your tax inspector.

Once your tax inspector has started an inquiry into your affairs, you will find it very time-consuming. You may find you end up paying interest on unpaid tax from the day it was due until the date of payment; the current rate of interest is 9 per cent. On top of that, the taxman can slap on a penalty: up to £50 for each incorrect tax return. If your tax inspector thinks you have been negligent in giving the wrong information, you can also be charged a maximum penalty equal to the amount of overdue tax, in addition to paying the tax due. If your tax return is incorrect because of fraud, the penalty may increase to twice the amount of the unpaid tax, and the Inland Revenue can prosecute you as well.

## SUMMARY

1. Tell your tax inspector about any new source of earnings within twelve months of the end of the tax year in which the earnings first arose.

2. Try to convince the taxman that your earnings are not casual or occasional.

3. Even if your income is regarded as casual, remember to claim any expenses you met in getting the income.

4. If you get income from property it can be treated in a number of ways depending on what the property is and what you do with it.

# 32. VAT

One subject which is guaranteed to raise ire among small businesses is VAT. It is frequently referred to as a burden; there are mutterings of a VAT trap; there are moans about the red tape caused by the VAT system. Nevertheless, the drift in legislation has been towards more draconian measures. For example, severe surcharge penalties were introduced in late 1986 for those who submit late returns.

Essentially, the VAT system is operated by businesses acting as tax collectors for the government. As far as the consumer is concerned, it is what is called an indirect tax. It is only paid by the consumer when something is bought, but the amount of the VAT cannot be claimed back by a consumer. As far as you the business person is concerned, you pay tax when you buy goods from someone else, and charge the tax when you sell them on. Broadly speaking, you hand over to the Customs and Excise the difference between the amount of tax you charge your customers and the amount of tax you have paid your suppliers.

## WHAT IS IN THIS CHAPTER?

- How the VAT system works (p. 385)
- Who has to register? (p. 386)
- What rate of tax? (p. 388)
- Applying to register when you do not have to (p. 389)
- How is the tax worked out? (p. 390)
- The records you need (p. 392)
- Paying the tax (p. 394)

VAT seems a very mysterious tax and this chapter can only outline the principles. The examples given are deliberately simplifed. You may be well advised to ask for professional help with VAT if your affairs are at all complicated.

# HOW THE VAT SYSTEM WORKS

The principle of the system is that tax is paid on the value added at each stage of the business process.

*Example*

> Jason King grows timber. He sells £1,000 of oak to A.J. Furniture, who will turn the oak into hand-crafted timber. He charges £1,000 for the timber and adds on 15 per cent to the invoice for VAT. The total A. J. Furniture pays to him is £1,000 plus £150 VAT, £1,150 in all. Jason pays the £150 tax collected (called output tax) to Customs and Excise.
>
> A.J. Furniture makes the oak into ten tables. These are sold on to a furniture shop run by Doris Bates. Doris is charged £250 for each table plus VAT. On the invoice, this is shown as £2,500 plus £375 VAT. A.J. Furniture claims back the VAT charged by Jason King (called input tax), that is, £150, and hands over the VAT Doris pays to them, £375 (called output tax). This means a net payment of £375 − £150 = £225 to the Customs and Excise.
>
> Doris sells the tables in her shop at a price of £500 plus VAT. She receives in total for the tables, £5,000 plus VAT of £750. When she makes her VAT return, she claims back the £375 VAT (called input tax) she paid to A.J. Furniture, while handing over the £750 VAT paid by the customers (called output tax), a net payment of £750 − £375 = £375.
>
> The customers cannot claim back the VAT they have paid on the tables, but all the businesses are registered for VAT and can do so.

VAT is charged on what is called taxable supplies. In the example above, Jason King makes taxable supplies (the timber) of £1,000, A.J. Furniture makes taxable supplies (the tables) of £2,500 and Doris makes taxable supplies of £5,000 (the tables). Not all goods supplied to businesses are taxable; some are known as exempt and VAT is not charged on those (p. 387).

In VAT jargon if you sell something to a business which is a taxable supply, the VAT you charge on it is known as output tax. The business you sell to, if it is registered for VAT, when it makes its return to Customs and Excise it claims back the VAT paid to you, which is known as input tax paid by that business. More illustrations of what is meant by input tax and what is meant by output tax are in the example above.

# WHO HAS TO REGISTER?

It is the person, not the business, who is registered for VAT. Each registration covers all the business activities of the registered person. For VAT purposes, a company is treated as a person. There are a number of reasons why you might not have to register. These include:

• your sales (strictly, the amount of your taxable supplies, see below and p. 387) are too low, but you might wish still to register for VAT purposes and charge it on your sales (p. 389)

• your business operates outside the VAT area (p. 387)

• you make only exempt supplies (p. 387)

• you carry out non-business activities (but you would still charge VAT on what counts as your business activities) (p. 388).

If you fail to register when you should do so, Customs and Excise can impose financial penalties. This is equal to the amount of VAT evaded, as well as the tax due, but can be reduced by up to 50 per cent if you are very cooperative during the investigations. During 1987, the period in which you must register has been increased from ten to thirty days.

## YOUR LEVEL OF SALES

You must register your business for VAT if your sales are likely to be above a certain limit (strictly, the limit is for the value of your taxable supplies, see right, rather than sales). The limit increases each year in line with the rate of inflation and there is a limit for the year, as well as for a quarter. For the year 1987–8, you must register if:

• your sales for the year are likely to be above £21,300

• your sales for the quarter just ended were £7,250 or more or were £21,300 for that and the previous three quarters. However, you may not have to register if you can satisfy Customs and Excise that the quarter just ended and the next three will not be above the yearly limit or that the value for the next four quarters will not be more than £20,300.

Should your sales fall below the limit above, you can ask to have your registration cancelled. You would have to establish that your sales, including VAT, will be £20,300 or less for the next twelve months.

On the whole, requesting cancellation when your sales are on the border of registration seems likely to plunge you into an administrative nightmare and great uncertainty. If you get it wrong and you should have been registered, you may have to pay a financial penalty (see p. 386). Learning to live with VAT seems a better option.

## THE AREA FOR VAT

VAT applies to England, Scotland, Wales, Northern Ireland and the Isle of Man. It does not include the Channel Islands. If you have customers or suppliers there, the goods you buy or sell will be treated as imports or exports (p. 389).

## WHAT ARE TAXABLE SUPPLIES AND WHAT ARE EXEMPT?

Broadly speaking, if you supply goods and services in your business (including anything you take for your own use or sell to your staff), these will be taxable, unless the government has specifically laid down that they are not. If they are not taxable, they are called exempt.

If all the goods or services which you supply are exempt, you cannot be registered for VAT. What this means for you is that you cannot claim back the VAT on any of the things you have bought for your business.

On the other hand, with a business composed of some taxable and some exempt supplies, you will still have to comply with the registration limits for the value of your taxable supplies. You will be able to claim back the VAT you have paid for the whole of your business if the value of your exempt supplies is always:

- less than £200 a month, or

- less than £8,000 a month *and* less than 50 per cent of the total value of your supplies, or

- less than £16,000 a month *and* less than 25 per cent of the total value of your supplies, or

- less than 5 per cent of the total value of your supplies.

The main items which are exempt as far as VAT is concerned are broadly speaking:

- most sales, leases and lettings of land and buildings (but *not* lettings of garages, parking spaces or hotel and holiday accommodation)

- financial services

- insurance

- certain education and training

- most health care

- postal services

- most betting, gaming and lotteries

- certain supplies by undertakers

- membership benefits provided by trade unions and professional bodies.

## WHAT IS BUSINESS AND WHAT IS NON-BUSINESS?

As far as the VAT system is concerned, business is supplying goods or services to someone else in return for something which could be regarded as payment; it does not need to be money. You must be supplying the goods on a continuing basis to be a business activity.

If you are carrying out only non-business activities, you cannot be registered for VAT; if you have some non-business activities, the VAT you can reclaim is reduced.

## WHEN IS YOUR REGISTRATION CANCELLED?

Apart from you requesting it to be cancelled, see p. 386, your registration will be cancelled if:

- the business is closed down

- the business is sold

- you take a partner or become a sole trader rather than a partner

- as a sole trader or partnership, you change the business into a company and vice versa.

## WHAT RATE OF TAX?

For taxable supplies there are at present two rates of tax:

- the standard rate is currently 15 per cent; and

- the zero rate.

The standard rate is charged unless the government specifies otherwise.
These are the main supplies which are zero-rated at present:

- most food and drink, but not if supplied for catering, or certain items like chocolate, crisps and so on which are regarded as 'non-essential', or 'hot food' to be taken away

- books and newspapers

- heating and lighting

- young children's clothing and footwear

- transport, but not taxis or hire cars

- exports

- sales of new buildings and construction of most new buildings

- dispensing prescriptions

- mobile homes and houseboats.

Do not confuse exempt and zero-rated. The effect of the two categories is quite different. Neither charges VAT on what they sell, but the exempt category cannot claim it back on what they have paid, while the zero-rated category can. Costs for the exempt category are likely to be 15 per cent higher than the costs for the zero-rated category.

## APPLYING TO REGISTER WHEN YOU DO NOT HAVE TO

You can apply to register even if the value of your taxable supplies is below the limit. You have to satisfy Customs and Excise that you have a compelling and business need for registration and that the income from your taxable supplies contributes substantially to your livelihood.

There are two reasons why you might apply to register even if your sales are likely to be below the yearly or quarterly limits (p. 386). In both cases, registering will mean lower costs.

The first instance would be if you sell to businesses which can claim back VAT, so charging the 15 per cent on your sales will not mean you lose business. If this is the case with you, consider applying to register. You may still decide not to, if the administrative set-up is too difficult, for example, if you sell a large number of low value items. But if you register, your costs are 15 per cent less than they otherwise would be. See Example 1 overleaf.

*Example 1*

> Susan Hammond runs a car hire service. Her main customers are businesses. She considers whether she should apply to register for VAT, although her sales at present are £17,000, below the limit. Her costs are £5,000 including VAT of £500 (she is not charged VAT on all the goods and services she purchases).
>
> If she registers she would have to charge VAT of £2,550 on her sales of £17,000, but her customers can claim this back. She can claim back the £500 of VAT (input tax) she has paid on her purchases. The net result is that she receives £17,000 from her sales, claims back £500 VAT and pays £5,000 to her suppliers. Her income goes up from £12,000, before registering, to £12,500, after registering.
>
> An alternative would be to lower her prices as her costs are now lower, but this does not seem necessary as she is not losing sales because of the price she charges.

The second instance when registering is beneficial is if your sales are zero-rated, but you are paying VAT on the goods you buy in.

*Example 2*

> Barbara Croft runs a business making bibs and similar items for babies. Consumers cannot claim VAT back, but clothing for children is zero-rated and so she does not charge VAT. Her sales are £12,000 and her costs are £3,500, including VAT of £300. If she did not register her income would be £12,000 − £3,500 = £8,500. This would be increased by £300 to £8,800 if she can voluntarily register.

## HOW IS THE TAX WORKED OUT?

### WHAT DO YOU CHARGE VAT ON?

You charge VAT on the taxable sales you make; this is known as output tax. The amount of VAT is worked out on the price for the goods or services you are supplying. Generally, secondhand goods are treated in the same way as new goods. There are some special schemes for secondhand goods.

You cannot escape charging VAT if you decide to take other goods, for example, rather than money in full payment or in part exchange. In this case, you have to work out the VAT to add on the basis of the open market value of the goods or services you are supplying.

With discounts, the treatment varies depending on the type of discount. If the discount is unconditional, the VAT is charged on the discounted amount. This is also what applies if the discount is for prompt payment. Whether the customer pays promptly or not, VAT is worked out on the discounted amount. If the discount you offer is dependent on something happening later, for example, the customer buying more, VAT is worked out on the full amount for the first payment. If the discount is subsequently taken, the VAT is adjusted at that time.

Packaging is treated as part of what you are selling, so there will normally be no extra VAT to pay; and if the thing you are selling is zero-rated, that also applies to the packaging. With delivery, if you charge extra for it, VAT is due on that extra amount. But, if the delivery is included in the selling price, no extra VAT is due.

Exports of goods are normally zero-rated and this also applies to many exports of services, although some are standard-rated.

WHAT YOU CLAIM VAT BACK ON

You can claim back VAT on the goods and services you use in your business; these include imports and goods you remove from bonded warehouses. However, there are some supplies on which you cannot usually claim back the VAT. These include:

- motor cars

- business entertainment expenses

- if you are a builder, on certain things you install in buildings

- on some imports if you do not wholly own them

- on assets of a business transferred to you as a going concern

- on goods which are zero-rated or are exempt supplies (because you have not been charged VAT).

WORKING OUT THE AMOUNT OF INPUT TAX YOU HAVE PAID

In Chapter 27. 'Keeping the record straight' (p. 331), you can see how to organize your records to obtain the information you need for VAT purposes. There are also guidelines below on some of the records you need. Basically, if your business is very simple, you can work out the input tax like this:

**1.** Get all your purchase invoices in date order.

**2.** In your records (p. 336), you will have some way of showing the VAT you have paid on each invoice.

**3.** You cannot claim back VAT on exempt or zero-rated supplies.

**4.** Some invoices show the amount of VAT you are charged, so these are quite straightforward. Enter the amount in the column marked VAT

**5.** Other invoices are not so detailed and you will have to work out the amount of VAT yourself. See example below for how to do this.

**6.** Remember you can only claim back the proportion of VAT for goods which you only use partially in your business. For example, if you use your car, half for business purposes and half for private, you can only claim back half the VAT paid on petrol or car repairs.

*Example*

> Peter Taylor is working out what VAT he can claim back on some stationery he has purchased for his business. The amount of the VAT is not shown on the receipt he has from the shop. The stationery cost him £4.75. He needs to know the amount of the VAT and the net cost of the stationery.
>
> He divides £4.75 by 1.15 *or*
>
> he does this sum £4.75 × $\frac{100}{115}$
>
> Both calculations give the same figure £4.13, which is the net cost; the amount of VAT he can claim back is £4.75 − £4.13 = £0.62.

## THE RECORDS YOU NEED

These are the main additional records you need for VAT purposes and these must be kept for six years:

- the tax invoice
- a VAT account showing the results for each tax period

• the returns to Customs and Excise showing the VAT payable or repayable.

If you fail to keep your records properly, you can be charged a financial penalty (p. 386). VAT inspectors will come to see you every so often to check that your records are satisfactory.

TAX INVOICE

When you supply goods, you should send a tax invoice (your ordinary invoice will do as long as it includes the following details) and keep a copy of it:

• invoice number

• tax point (see below)

• your name and address

• your VAT registration number

• your customer's name and address

• what it is you have supplied (for example, a description of the goods or services). For each item, the invoice should show the quantity, the rate of tax and the amount payable before VAT is charged

• the type of supply (for example, whether you have sold it, sold it on hire purchase or rented it)

• the total amount payable, excluding VAT

• any cash discount

• the total amount of VAT charged.

If you are supplying goods and services direct to the public, for example to a shop, you do not need to provide such detailed invoices for items which are £50 or less, including the VAT. Nor do you need to keep copies of these. There are a number of special schemes for retailers, as it would be very time-consuming to keep records of every single sale.

A tax point is nothing more than the date on which you are liable to account for the VAT to Customs and Excise; this is the date on which you provide the goods or services. However, if you invoice earlier, the tax point is the earlier date and if you invoice within fourteen days of supplying the goods, the later date is the tax point. Finally, if you want to invoice monthly, you can use a monthly tax point.

## VAT ACCOUNT

The results for each VAT period need to be summarized separately in your accounting records. This should show the totals of input tax and output tax and the difference between the two, either a repayment to you or the amount due to Customs and Excise.

## VAT RETURNS

This is the form which you need to fill in at the end of each VAT period, normally every three months, although if you constantly are claiming a repayment, for example, because you are zero-rated, you can arrange monthly returns. In the return, you show the information you put in your VAT account, see above, plus any under- or overpayment from the previous period. You also enter any bad debts you may have. As a check for Customs and Excise, you have to enter the figures for your total purchases and total sales for the period.

The VAT period can be arranged to coincide with your accounting year-end, which can make keeping your records much more convenient.

During 1988 a new optional system of annual accounting is being introduced. It is available for businesses with taxable supplies of £250,000 or less. It means making only one VAT return a year.

## PAYING THE TAX

Any VAT which is due to Customs and Excise is payable within one month of the end of the quarterly accounting period. This is regardless of whether you have actually yet received the money from your customers on which the VAT is due.

If you fail to send in the return on time, you are given a warning. If you have received two warnings within a period of one year, you are open to having a surcharge placed on you if you should be late again within the next twelve months from the date of the last warning. The surcharge is 5 per cent of the amount of VAT due. A second failure within the next year will mean a surcharge of 10 per cent and this carries on rising up to 30 per cent for the sixth and any further failures. To start again with a clean slate, you must make sure that you send in all your returns on time for a year.

Under the new annual accounting system being introduced in 1988 (see above) VAT would be paid in ten instalments. The first nine would be based on the likely tax due and the tenth would make up the difference between the estimated and actual tax due.

Also during 1987–8 a system of cash accounting for small businesses is being introduced. With this you would pay VAT due only when you had been paid by your customer; and claim it back only when you had paid your supplier. The change would mean you did not have to pay VAT on bad debts.

## SUMMARY

1. If your sales are approaching £21,300 for the 1987–8 year or £7,250 for a quarter, it is probably wiser to register; otherwise, it is a constant worry in case you have inadvertently failed to register when you should have done so.

2. You do not need to register if the value of your sales is too low, but it could still be worthwhile to apply to do so if you sell to businesses who can claim back the VAT or if you are zero-rated.

3. Do not confuse zero-rated with exempt supplies. If you supply only exempt goods, you cannot claim back VAT on goods you purchase.

4. If the level of your sales falls below a certain limit (£20,300 for 1987–8) you can ask to have the registration cancelled.

OTHER CHAPTERS TO READ

27. 'Keeping the record straight' (p. 331)

# 33. RETIREMENT

No doubt all your thoughts and energies are devoted to making your business successful, but spare a thought for what will happen when you retire. Your business may be the sort which you will be able to sell when it comes to retirement. This means you will have a lump sum which you can invest to give yourself an income to live on.

But with lots of self-employed people this is not so; if they retire, the business retires too, because their skills are essential to the success of their enterprise. Even if you hope that you will be able to sell your business on retirement, there is no certainty of this and you should show some caution in relying on it. You may be forced to retire earlier than you had intended because of ill health and this might coincide with a bad patch in your business fortunes. Or you may simply not be successful in building your business sufficiently to be able to sell for the sort of sum of money you need. The prudent course is to make separate arrangements to provide yourself with a pension.

This chapter looks at how to build up a pension during your working life. It also looks briefly at what happens from a tax point of view if you sell or give away your business on retirement under the current tax rules.

## BUILDING UP A PENSION

### WHAT YOU GET FROM THE STATE

If you are self-employed, you will pay Class 2 national insurance contributions. If you have set up a limited company and count as an employee of the company, you will pay Class 1 contributions (and the company will pay employer's contributions). Both these contributions will entitle you to the basic state pension retirement scheme, assuming you have paid sufficient contributions during your lifetime. The Class 4 contributions you make as a self-employed person do not increase your entitlement to a pension.

If you count as an employee of your company, for example, if you are a director, you will probably be building up an entitlement to an additional state pension scheme under current legislation by paying bigger national insurance contributions. This is known as being 'not contracted-out'. In this case, for example, if you are earning £100 a week or more, you pay 9 per cent on all earnings up to £295 a week in the 1987–8 year (which runs from October to October). Your company will be paying employer's contributions – 9 per cent on your earnings if you earn between £100 and £150 a week, 10.45 per cent if you earn £150 or more each week.

However, in 1988 a new pensions era begins. Benefits from the earnings-related bit of the state pension will be reduced (but not until the year 2000). There will be tax relief available for a new sort of pension if you contract out of the state earnings-related pension.

### HOW TO INCREASE YOUR PENSION IF YOU ARE SELF-EMPLOYED

The simplest way of doing this is to start paying money into a personal pension plan, which is organized and invested by an insurance company; and, because you can get tax relief on what you pay at your highest rate of tax and your money is put into a tax-free fund, doing this is also likely to be the best way of saving for retirement. Note that your tax inspector will refer to a personal pension plan as a self-employed retirement annuity.

A personal pension plan will pay out an income; the size depends on how long and how much you have saved, although there are limits imposed on how much you *can* save. It also depends on how well the investments in the pension fund have done. You can choose when you want to start receiving the benefits from the plan, but it will be somewhere between your sixtieth and seventy-fifth birthday. (As part of the new pensions arrangement starting in 1988, you will be able to draw benefits from your fiftieth birthday.) If you retire early because of illness, you can start taking the benefits before then, but the size of the pension you will be able to take will be less.

Personal pension schemes are very flexible. For example:

• you can invest a lump sum when you want or save on a regular basis

• you can alter the premium from time to time

• the pension you choose at the end does not have to be a level amount, you can choose an income which starts off lower, but increases each year to allow for inflation

• you can choose a joint-life pension, which will be paid as long as either of two people is alive; this will be lower than a pension on one life only

• most plans offer an 'open-market' option, which allows you to shop

around to see if you can use the sum of money you have built up with one
company to get a higher pension from another company

- you can normally choose to take a lower amount of pension and have a
tax-free lump sum as well, up to three times the size of the pension

- you can use your pension scheme to back up a mortgage, in much the
same way as an endowment mortgage

- most of the plans have loanback facilities, which allows you to use your
pension to get a loan.

### SETTING OFF WHAT YOU PAY AGAINST TAX

You can set off what you pay for a pension against your tax within certain
limits, at your highest rate. This means this sort of saving can be very
cheap, especially for higher-rate taxpayers.

*Example*

> Daniel Patten is considering putting money aside for retirement.
> His income for tax purposes for this year is £30,000, so he is paying
> tax at the rate of 50 per cent on the last slice of his income. If he
> invested £1,000 in a personal pension scheme, it would actually cost
> him only £500, because he would otherwise pay tax at 50 per cent on
> this £1,000.

There are limits on how much you can pay into a personal pension
scheme. The limit depends on your *net relevant earnings* for the tax year,
that is, your taxable profits which are being assessed in this year. If you
are being taxed on a preceding year basis (p. 345), this means your net
relevant earnings for the 1987–8 tax year, for example, are the taxable
profits for the accounting year ending in the 1986–7 tax year.

You get tax relief on premiums which come to $17\frac{1}{2}$ per cent or less of
your net relevant earnings for the tax year (more than this if you were
born before 1934 and the proposals for 1988 mean you will get tax relief
on a higher percentage if you are over a certain age). You can claim more
than this limit if you have not paid the maximum premiums allowed in any
one or more of the previous six tax years.

The premiums you pay reduce your tax bill for the tax year in which you
pay them, except if you ask to have the premiums treated for tax purposes
as if you had paid them in the previous tax year (as long as you have

sufficient unused relief for that year). If you did not have any net relevant earnings in the previous tax year, you will be able to get the premiums treated as if you had paid them in the year before that. This is useful if you paid tax at a higher rate in the previous year.

CHOOSING YOUR PERSONAL PENSION PLAN

There are many schemes available and it is very difficult to choose which is the right personal pension plan. An insurance broker (p. 257) can help, but they have differing levels of expertise, so you should shop around in the same way as you do for your business insurance. An insurance broker may not recommend an insurance company which does not sell through brokers and so does not pay commission to them; you will need to check these out direct.

There are four different types of personal pension plans:

● *non-proft:* from the outset, you know what your pension will be when you retire, and that is what it will be, no more and no less. This means the pension is likely to be low

● *with-profits:* the insurance company invests your money as it thinks fit, often in loans, British Government stocks, shares and property. The company will guarantee the minimum pension or lump of money you will get, but this will be lower than for a non-profit one (see above). However, you stand the prospect of receiving a much higher pension in the end, because the company adds bonuses to your pension, depending on the profits it makes on its investments

● *unit-linked:* with this type of policy you have some choice as to how your money is invested. Commonly, you can choose for the money to be invested in property, shares, fixed-interest investments such as British Government stocks, cash investments such as bank deposit accounts or you can choose to invest in a mixture of all these.

With a unit-linked plan, the value of your pension is directly linked to the value of the investments, so it can fluctuate. This could be a problem if values happen to be low when it comes to retirement

● *deposit-administration scheme:* like the non-profit policy, these give a safe, if unexciting, return.

If you are saving ten to twenty years before retirement, and the earlier the better, choose either a with-profits or unit-linked scheme. If you have less than five years to retirement, a choice of or a switch to a non-profit or deposit administration scheme could be safer.

### GETTING LIFE INSURANCE

Self-employed people can also get tax relief at their highest rate on life insurance policies, called Section 226A policies. These will provide your widow or widower with an income or a lump sum after your death. The premiums must be not more than 5 per cent of your net relevant earnings to obtain tax relief; what you spend on this cuts into your overall $17\frac{1}{2}$ per cent limit.

### HOW TO INCREASE YOUR PENSION IF YOU HAVE A LIMITED COMPANY

If you are a director of a small company which has not organized a pension scheme for employees, you could take out a personal pension plan in the same way as if you were self-employed. In 1988 you will be able to take out a new type of personal pension. The extra national insurance contributions paid for the earnings-related bit of the state pension can be paid into this new sort of pension and you will get tax relief on this rebate of contributions. Additionally, a further 2 per cent of earnings will be added by the state until 1993. The new type of pension can be sold by insurance companies, unit trusts, building societies and banks.

Alternatively, you could arrange a scheme through your own limited company. A scheme of this type has to be approved by the Inland Revenue if it is to qualify for the tax concessions. It can be arranged for you by an insurance company or you can choose to administer the investments yourself.

If you and your family own most of the shares in the company, and you are both employer and director, there are three possible advantages:

● the pension fund can provide the capital for buying company assets, such as business premises

● up to half the pension fund can be loaned back to the company, and

● with a self-employed pension scheme, there is a limit on contributions of $17\frac{1}{2}$ per cent of your net relevant earnings. With a company pension fund, yearly contributions can be much higher. This could be very useful if you are starting to save at a late age, for example, fifty.

SUMMARY · 401

This area of pensions is very specialized. If you do want to go ahead, consult an insurance broker with specialist knowledge, but don't be rushed into decisions by salespeople. Consider straightforward ideas too, like a personal pension plan.

## CAPITAL GAINS TAX WHEN YOU RETIRE

If you sell, give away or dispose of your business or shares in it you will be liable to capital gains tax. But this does not necessarily apply if you are aged sixty or over, or if you are retiring earlier than that due to ill-health.

Retirement relief is available, for example, when you sell the business, give it away or sell off assets after you have closed the business. You get the relief if:

- you have owned the business for a year or more
*or*

- you have owned shares in the business (either a family company or a holding company for the business you work for) for a year or more. You must own at least 25 per cent of the voting shares (or if your family has over half the voting shares, you must hold at least 5 per cent). You must also be a full-time working director.

The maximum relief you can have is £125,000; this would apply if you had owned your business or shares for ten years. There is a sliding scale of relief which reduces by £12,500 for each year, until the relief is £12,500 if you have owned the business or shares for one year.

The relief is only available for the fixed assets of the business, not stocks. If you are disposing of shares, the relief is only for what part of the value of the shares accounts for the fixed assets.

There is only one lot of retirement relief available to you, that is, up to a total of £125,000, but it can be made up of several disposals of assets.

## SUMMARY

1. Saving for retirement through a personal pension plan, or a pension scheme organized by your company, is very cost-effective. This is because you can get tax relief at your highest rate of tax.

2. There is a retirement relief available on capital gains tax if you dispose of your business or shares, as long as you meet certain conditions.

# REFERENCE

This section provides a handy list of further reading, names and addresses of organizations and other details which do not fit into the main text. Inclusion in this section of any organization which is run commercially is not to be taken as a recommendation. You must rely on the usual precautions, for example, taking up references etc. Nor should you interpret exclusion of a commercial enterprise from a list as indication of anything adverse.

## CHAPTER 1. YOU AND YOUR IDEAS

For further reading, try *The Small Business Guide* by Colin Barrow (BBC, 1984). Its main usefulness lies in the fact that it lists lots of organizations and references.

## CHAPTER 2. WHO WILL BUY?

*Introducing Marketing* by Gordon Wills, John Cheese, Sherrill Kennedy and Angela Rushton (Pan, 1984)
*Marketing for the Small Firm* by Rick Brown (Holt, Rinehart & Winston, 1985)

This book is specifically about market research:
*The Industrial Market Research Handbook* by Paul N. Hague (Kogan Page, 1987)

## CHAPTER 3. A SPOT OF COACHING

COURSES

Manpower Services Commission:
  *Head Office:* Moorfoot, Sheffield S1 4PQ (0742-753275)
  *Scotland:* 9 St Andrew Square, Edinburgh EH2 2QX (031-225 8500)
  *London:* 236 Gray's Inn Road, London WC1 8HN (01-278 0363)
  *East Midlands:* 2nd Floor, 2 Clinton Street East, Nottingham N61 3DQ
  *West Midlands:* Alpha Tower, Suffolk Street, Queensway, Birmingham B1 1UR (021-643 6338)
  *Northern:* Broadacre House, Market Street, Newcastle upon Tyne NE1 6HH (091-232 6181)
  *North West:* Washington House, The Capital Centre, New Bailey Street, Manchester M3 5ER (061-833 0251)
  *South East:* Telford House, Hamilton Close, Basingstoke, Hampshire RG21 2UZ (0256-29266)

*South West:* 4th Floor, The Pithay, Bristol BS1 2NQ (0272-273755)
*Wales:* 4th Floor, Companies House, Crown Way, Maindy, Cardiff CF4 3UZ
(0222-388588)
*Yorkshire & Humberside:* Jubilee House, 33–41 Park Place, Leeds LS1 2RL
(0532-446299)

Umbrella organization for enterprise agencies is: Business in the Community,
227a City Road, London EC1V 1LX (01-253 3716)

British Institute of Management, Management House, Cottingham Road,
Corby, Northants NN17 1TT (0536-204222)

Scottish Vocational Education Council (SCOTVEC), 38 Queen Street, Glasgow
G1 3DY (041-248 7900)


COUNSELLING

DTI's Small Firms Service: Dial 100 and ask for Freefone Enterprise

*Small Firms Centres:*
  *Birmingham:* 9th Floor, Alpha Tower, Suffolk Street, Queensway,
    Birmingham B1 1TT (021-643 3344)
  *Bristol:* 6th Floor, The Pithay, Bristol BS1 2NB (0272-294546)
  *Cambridge:* Carlyle House, Carlyle Road, Cambridge CB4 3DN (0223-63312)
  *Cardiff:* 16 St David's House, Wood Street, Cardiff CF1 1ER (0222-396116)
  *Glasgow:* 21 Bothwell Street, Glasgow G2 6NR (041-248 6014)
  *Leeds:* 1 Park Row, City Square, Leeds LS1 5NR (0532-445151)
  *Liverpool:* Graeme House, Derby Square, Liverpool L2 7UJ (051-236 5756)
  *London:* Ebury Bridge House, 2–18 Ebury Bridge Road, London SW1W 8QD
    (01-730 8451)
  *Manchester:* 3rd Floor, Rooms 320–25 Royal Exchange Building, St Ann's
    Square, Manchester M2 7AH (061-832 5282)
  *Newcastle:* Centro House, 3 Cloth Market, Newcastle upon Tyne NE1 1EE
    (091-232 5353)
  *Nottingham:* Severns House, 20 Middle Pavement, Nottingham NG1 7DW
    (0602-481184)
  *Reading:* Abbey Hall, Abbey Square, Reading RG1 3BE (0734-591733)


*Other agencies:*
  Scottish Development Agency, Small Business Division, Rosebery House,
    Haymarket Terrace, Edinburgh EH12 5EZ (031-337 9595)
  Welsh Development Agency, Head Office, Treforest Industrial Estate, Pon-
    typridd, Mid-Glamorgan CF37 5UT (044-384 1666)
  The Local Enterprise Development Unit (LEDU), LEDU House, Upper
    Galwally, Belfast BT8 4TB (0232-691031)

Council for Small Industries in Rural Areas (CoSIRA) Headquarters, 141 Castle Street, Salisbury, Wiltshire SP1 3TP (0722-336255) Contact here to find the address of your nearest local office

Highlands and Islands Development Board, Bridge House, 27 Bank Street, Inverness, IV1 1QR (0463-234171)

*Experience of others:*
For Management Extension Programme, contact MSC: see above

*Trade associations:*
Association of Independent Businesses, Trowbray House, 108 Weston Street, London SE1 3QB (01-403 4066)

The National Federation of Self-employed and Small Businesses Ltd, 32 St Anne's Road, West Lytham, St Annes, Lancashire FY8 1NY (0253-720911)

The Small Business Bureau, 32 Smith Square, London SW1P 3HH (01–222 9000)

*The young:*
Headstart, the Industrial Society, Peter Runge House, 3 Carlton House Terrace, London SW1Y 5DG (01-839 4300)

Instant Muscle, Haymill Centre, 112 Burnham Lane, Burnham, Slough, SL1 6LZ (06286-63926)

Livewire, National Extension College, 18 Brooklands Avenue, Cambridge CB2 2HN (0223-316644)

Project Fullemploy, 102 Park Village East, London NW1 3SP (01-387 1222)

The Prince's Youth Business Trust, 8 Jockeyfields, London WC1R 4TJ (01-430 0521). For loans contact Victoria Chambers, 16–20 Strutton Ground, London SW1P 2HP (01-222 3341/2/3)

*Ethnic Minorities:*
Ethnic Minority Small Business Centre, The Queens College, Glasgow, 1 Park Drive, Glasgow G3 6LP (041-334 8141)

Ismaeli Business Information Centre, 1 Cromwell Gardens, London SW7 2SL (01-225 0363)

Project Fullemploy (see above)

*Women:*
Women in Enterprise, 26 Bond Street, Wakefield, Yorks WF1 2QP (0924-361789)

Women's Enterprise Development Agency, Aston Science Park, Love Lane, Aston Triangle, Birmingham B7 4BJ (021-359 0981)

*Enterprise Agencies:*
For address of umbrella organization, Business in the Community, see above.

*Directory of Enterprise Agencies*, £1.50 from Business in the Community.


## CHAPTER 4. YOUR BUSINESS IDENTITY

Records of limited companies are kept at Companies Registration Office:
   *England and Wales:* Companies Registration Office, Companies House, Crown Way, Maindy, Cardiff CF4 3UZ (0222-388588)
   *Scotland:* Companies Registration Office, 102 George Street, Edinburgh EH2 3DJ (031-225 5774)
   *Northern Ireland:* Department of Economic Development, 64 Chichester Street, Belfast BT1 4JX (0232-234488)

For guidance on forming a limited company:
   *England and Wales:* Companies Registration Office, Companies House, Crown Way, Maindy, Cardiff CF4 3UZ (0222-388588)
   *Scotland:* Companies Registration Office, 102 George Street, Edinburgh EH2 3DJ (031-225-5774)

*Tolley's Company Law* (Tolley Publishing Company, 2nd edition, 1987) covers legal requirements of limited companies in great detail.

*Tolley's Employment of Directors* by P. S. Cooke (Tolley Publishing Company, 1987) covers legal duties plus benefits of directors.


## CHAPTER 8. TOE-DIPPING

A useful book for those interested in permanent toe-dipping is: *Earning Money at Home* edited by Edith Rudinger (Consumers Association, 1987)


## CHAPTER 9. OFF-THE-PEG

A couple of books worth reading on buying a business are:
   *How to buy a business* by Peter Farrell (Kogan Page, 1983)
   *Successful Acquisition of Unquoted Companies* by Barrie Pearson (Gower, 1983)

For those interested in management buy-outs:
   *Management Buy-out: A Guide for the Prospective Entrepreneur* by Ian Webb (Gower, 1985 – a slightly academic treatment)
   *Management Buy-outs* by Lance Blackstone and David Franks (Economist Intelligence Unit, 1987)

## CHAPTER 10. FRANCHISES

More detail about franchises, including if you want to become a franchisor is in:
*The Guide to Franchising* by Martin Mendelsohn (Pergamon, 1984)
*Taking up a Franchise* by Godfrey Golzen and Colin Barrow (Kogan Page, 1987)
British Franchise Association, 75a Bell Street, Henley-on-Thames, Oxon RG9 2BD (0491–578049)

## CHAPTER 11. THE RIGHT NAME

There are two useful leaflets produced by the Department of Trade: *Disclosure of Business Ownership* and *Control of Business Names*. You can get these from Companies House, Crown Way, Cardiff CF4 3UZ (0222-388588)

## CHAPTER 12. BEATING THE PIRATES

The Patent Office, State House, 66–71 High Holborn, London WC1R 4TP (01-831 2525)
Chartered Institute of Patent Agents, Staple Inn Buildings, High Holborn, London WC1V 7PZ (01-405 9450)
Institute of Patentees and Inventors, Suite 505A, Triumph House, 189 Regent Street, London W1R 7WF (01-242 7812)

## CHAPTER 13. GETTING THE MESSAGE ACROSS

There are two good books for further reading about advertising.
*Advertising, What it Is and How to Do It* by Roderick White (McGraw–Hill, 1983)
*The Effective Use of Advertising Media* by Martyn Davies (Business Books, 1985)

## CHAPTER 14. SELLING

Try:
*All About Selling* by Alan Williams (McGraw–Hill, 1986) for more ideas about selling skills, and
*How to Win More Business by Phone* by Bernard Katz (Business Books, 1985) for more on telephone selling.
Advertising Standards Authority, Brook House, 2–16 Torrington Place, London WC1E 7HN (01-580 5555)
Newspaper Publishers' Association, 6 Bouverie Street, London EC4Y 8AY (01-583 8132)

## CHAPTER 15. HOW TO SET A PRICE

A very readable book on pricing is:
*Pricing for Results* by John Winkler (Heinemann, 1983)

## CHAPTER 16. CHOOSING YOUR WORKPLACE

*How to Choose Business Premises* by H. Green, B. Chalkley and P. Foley
(Kogan Page, 1986) covers this topic in some detail.

English Estates, St George's House, Kingsway, Team Valley, Gateshead,
Tyne and Wear NE11 0NA (091-487 8941)

Job Creation Ltd, 139A New Bond Street, London W1X 9FB (01-409 2229)

## CHAPTER 17. GETTING EQUIPPED

The Data Protection Registrar's Office, Springfield House, Water Lane,
Wilmslow, Cheshire SK9 5AX

National Computing Centre Ltd, Oxford Road, Manchester M1 7ED (061-228
6333)

*Tolley's Data Protection Kit* (Tolley Publishing Company) explains if you need to
be registered and how to do it.

## CHAPTER 18. PROFESSIONAL BACK-UP

Institute of Chartered Accountants in England & Wales, Chartered Accountants Hall, P.O. Box 433, Moorgate Place, London EC2P 2BJ (01-628 7060)

Institute of Chartered Accountants of Scotland, 27 Queen Street, Edinburgh
EH2 1LA (031-225 5673)

Association of Certified Accountants, 29 Lincoln's Inn Fields, London WC2A
3EE (01-242 6855)

Institute of Management Consultants, 5th Floor, 32–3 Hatton Garden, London
EC1N 8DL

Royal Institute of Chartered Surveyors, 12 Great George Street, Parliament
Square, London SW1P 3AD (01-222 7000)

Incorporated Society of Valuers and Auctioneers, 3 Cadogan Gate, London
SW1X 0AS (01-235 2282)

Further reading:
*The Creative Handbook*, Thomas Skinner Directories.

## CHAPTER 19. GETTING THE RIGHT STAFF

The section on characteristics is adapted from the National Institute of Industrial
Psychology's Seven Point Plan.

Federation of Employment Services, 10 Belgrave Square, London SW1X 8PH (01-235 6616)
*How to be Your Own Personnel Manager* by Peter Humphrey (IPM, 1981) includes sections on recruitment.

## CHAPTER 20. YOUR RIGHTS AND DUTIES AS AN EMPLOYER

ACAS Code of Practice on dismissals is obtainable from Advisory, Conciliation and Arbitration Service (ACAS, Clifton House, 83–117 Euston Road, London NW1 2RB (01-388 5100)

Four reference books from Tolley Publishing Company:
*Tolley's Employment Handbook* by Elizabeth Slade (4th edition, 1987)
*Tolley's Payroll Handbook* by Edmund Moynihan (1st edition, 1987)
*Tolley's Guide to Statutory Sick Pay* (2nd edition, 1986)
*Tolley's National Insurance Contributions 1987/8* by Neil D. Booth

## CHAPTER 21. INSURANCE

British Insurance Brokers Association, 14 Bevis Marks, London EC3A 7NT (01-623 9043)

## CHAPTER 23. RAISING THE MONEY

Local Investment Networking Company, 4 Snow Hill, London EC1A 2DL (01-236 3000)
Venture Capital Report, The Refuge Building, 20 Baldwin Street, Bristol BS1 1SE (0272-272250)
British Venture Capital Association, 24 Upper Brook Street, London W1Y 1PD (01-836 5702)

There are various books which list out the names of venture capital sources. These include:
*The Small Business Guide* by Colin Barrow (BBC, 1984)
*Money for Business* (Bank of England, 1985)
*Raising Finance* by Clive Woodcock (Kogan Page, 1985)

## CHAPTER 24. STAYING AFLOAT

Collection agencies known at time of going to press:
ATP International Ltd, Sutherland House, 70–78 Edgware Road, London NW9 7BT (01-202 8212)

British Mercantile Agencies Ltd, Sidcup House, 12–18 Station Road, Sidcup, Kent DA15 7EH (01-302 2522)

Commercial Credit Consultants Ltd, 8 Anson Street, Liverpool L3 5NY (051-708 7008)

Credit Protection Association Ltd, 350 King Street, London W6 0RX (01-741 4401)

Dun & Bradstreet Ltd, 26–32 Clifton Street, London EC2P 2LY (01-377 4377)

Infolink Ltd, Templar House, Temple Way, Bristol BS1 6JB (0272-277830)

Inter-Credit International Ltd, Inter-Credit House, 205–7 Crescent Road, New Barnet, Herts EN4 8SW (01-440 8532)

Interdebt (UK) Ltd, Idenden House, Medway Street, Maidstone, Kent ME14 1JT (0622-674071)

Jardine Credit Management Ltd, Lloyds House, 18 Lloyd Street, Manchester M2 5WL (061-831 7021)

Further reading includes:

*Management of Trade Credit* by Thomas Guyon Hutson & John Butterworth (Gower, 1984)

*Financial Management for the Small Business* by Colin Barrow (Kogan Page, 1984)

*How to Collect Money That is Owed to You* by Mel Lewis (McGraw–Hill, 1987)


## CHAPTER 26. NOT WAVING BUT DROWNING

Studies about the causes of businesses failing include:

*Corporate Collapse, the Causes and Symptoms* by John Argenti (McGraw–Hill, 1976)

Reading about coping with bankruptcy, try:

*What to Do If Someone Has Debt Problems* by John McQueen (Elliot Right Way Books, 1985)

Contact:

The Association for Bankrupts, 4 Johnson Close, Lancaster, for support after bankruptcy.


## CHAPTER 27. KEEPING THE RECORD STRAIGHT

Two ready-made systems are:

Finco Small Business Book-keeping System, Casdec Ltd, 11 Windermere Avenue, Garden Farm Estate, Chester-le-Street, Co. Durham DH2 3DU (091-388 2906). Cost approx £40, plus continuing cost of replacements.

Kalamazoo Business Systems, Mill Lane, Northfield, Birmingham B31 2RW (021-475 2191). Cost approx. £100, plus continuing cost of replacements.

## CHAPTER 28. TAX AND THE SOLE TRADER

*Lloyds Bank Tax Guide 1987/8* by Sara Williams and John Willman (Penguin, 1987) has another exposition of the tax treatment for the sole trader and gives more detail about capital gains tax.

As a reference book on capital gains tax see *Tolley's Capital Gains Tax 1987/8* (Tolley Publishing Company).

## CHAPTER 29. TAX AND THE PARTNERSHIP

As a reference book:
   *Tax and Financial Planning for Professional Partnerships* by N. A. Eastaway & B. Gilligan (Butterworths, 1986)

## CHAPTER 30. TAX AND THE LIMITED COMPANY

As reference books:
   *Tolley's Corporation Tax 1987/8* (Tolley Publishing Company)
   *Tax and Financial Planning for Family Businesses* by N. J. Ince and G. J. R. Bell (Butterworths, 1984)

## CHAPTER 32. VAT

As a reference book:
   *Tolley's Value Added Tax 1987/8* (Tolley Publishing Company)

# INDEX

*Bold figures indicate the main subject entry*

# Business advice?

The Lloyds Bank Small Business Guide is full of advice on setting up and running a business.

And at Lloyds Bank you will find a comprehensive range of banking services designed to meet the changing needs of businesses today.

So, whether you're looking for flexible finance, investment accounts, international trade services, or electronic systems to help you manage your business efficiently — talk over your plans with one of our managers.

Call your local Lloyds Bank branch — your first stop for business banking.